ISBN 978-0-282-25967-9
PIBN 10845792

1 MONTH OF
FREE
READING

at
www.ForgottenBooks.com

By purchasing this book you are eligible for one month membership to ForgottenBooks.com, giving you unlimited access to our entire collection of over 1,000,000 titles via our web site and mobile apps.

To claim your free month visit:
www.forgottenbooks.com/free845792

English
Français
Deutsche
Italiano
Español
Português

www.forgottenbooks.com

Mythology Photography **Fiction**
Fishing Christianity **Art** Cooking
Essays Buddhism Freemasonry
Medicine **Biology** Music **Ancient
Egypt** Evolution Carpentry Physics
Dance Geology **Mathematics** Fitness
Shakespeare **Folklore** Yoga Marketing
Confidence Immortality Biographies
Poetry **Psychology** Witchcraft
Electronics Chemistry History **Law**
Accounting **Philosophy** Anthropology
Alchemy Drama Quantum Mechanics
Atheism Sexual Health **Ancient History**
Entrepreneurship Languages Sport
Paleontology Needlework Islam
Metaphysics Investment Archaeology
Parenting Statistics Criminology
Motivational

THE TAMILS

EIGHTEEN HUNDRED YEARS AGO

BY

V. KANAKASABHAI

PUBLISHED BY

HIGGINBOTHAM & Co

MADRAS AND BANGALORE

1904

Trial 2000.

KANISHKA
KING OF THE KOSHANS (A.D. 78—106)
(from his coins).

PRINTED AT THE M. E. PRESS, MADRAS.

TO

THE HONOURABLE DEWAN BAHADUR

Sir S. SUBRAMANYA IYER, K.C.I.E.

Actg. Chief Justice of Madras

THIS BOOK

IS

RESPECTFULLY DEDICATED

AS A TOKEN OF

ESTEEM AND GRATITUDE

FOR

THE GREAT INTEREST HE HAS ALWAYS SHOWN IN
EVERY MOVEMENT INTENDED FOR THE
BENEFIT OR ENLIGHTENMENT OF
THE NATIVES OF INDIA

PREFACE.

A series of articles on the "Tamils Eighteen Hundred Years Ago" was contributed by me to the *Madras Review* between the years 1895 and 1901. On the appearance of the very first article, Sir S. SUBRAMANYA IYER wrote to me suggesting that I should bring out all the information available in Tamil literature regarding the ancient civilization of the Tamils. I believe I have carried out the suggestion faithfully, as far as my leisure would permit. Since the completion of the series, many of my friends advised me to collect and publish the whole in the form of a book. I have therefore re-arranged the matter, dividing it into chapters, and added an Index, which I hope will facilitate reference. With a view to confine myself strictly to the subject of the book as shown in the title, I have carefully avoided touching upon the history of the Tamils before A.D. 50 or after A.D. 150:

MADRAS,
16th January, 1904.

V. KANAKASABHAI.

ERRATA.

9 19, line 28, read *Sembai* for *Smbai*.

21, footnote, l. 5, read *Adiyarkku-nallar* for *Nallarkiniyar*.

30, footnote, l. 1, read *Ammuvanar* for *Ammuvana*.

45, l. 11, read *the* for *th*.

45, l. 30, read *Yakshas* for *Yekshas*.

77, l. 12, read *palace* for *place*.

78, l. 13, read *Auvvaiyar* for *Avvaiyar*.

106, l. 26, read *Ay-andiran* for *Ay-andiram*.

107, footnote, l. 4, read *Mathuraik-kanchi* for *Mathuraik-kavelu*.

108, l. 13, read *Auvvaiyar* for *Avvaiyar*.

114, l. 16, read *Ayar* for *Aiyar*.

133, footnote, l. 9, read *Chilapp-athikaram* for *Chiapp-athikaram*.

134, l. 28, read *Whisks* for *Wisks*.

153, ll. 13, 15, 30, 35, read *Mathari* for *Matkavi*.

165, l. 6, read *her* for *the*.

165, l. 15, read *spathe* for *spaltre*.

174, l. 32, read *Kesakambalan* for *Kesakambalam*.

192, l. 5, read *flit* for *fit*.

193, ll. 8, 10, 15, 17, 18, 24, read *Karikál* for *Kárikal*.

194, ll. 21, read *Undertaken by* for *Undert a kenby*.

200, footnote, l. 6, read *Auvvaiyar* for *Avvaiyar*.

CONTENTS.

CHAPTER I.

Introduction.

CONTENTS.

CHAPTER V.
The Cholas.

CHAPTER VI.
The Pandyas.

CHAPTER VII.
The Cheras.

CHAPTER VIII.
Princes and Chiefs.

CHAPTER IX.
Social Life.

CHAPTER X.

The Kural of Tiruvalluvar.

CHAPTER XI.

The Story of Chilapp-athikaram.

CHAPTER XII.

The Story of Mani-mekalai.

CHAPTER XIII.

Tamil Poems and Poets.

THE TAMILS:
EIGHTEEN HUNDRED YEARS AGO.

CHAPTER 1.

INTRODUCTION.

EIGHTEEN hundred years ago, the most powerful and civilised empire in the known world was that of Rome. Under Trajan, the last of the great Roman conquerors, it had risen to the zenith of its power, and embraced a great portion of Europe, and all those parts of Asia and Africa which lay around the Mediterranean Sea. In the east, the vast Empire of China had attained its greatest expansion under the kings of the illustrious Han dynasty and extended from the shores of the Pacific Ocean to the Caspian Sea, and from the Atlas mountains to the Himalayan range. Between these two Empires lay two kingdoms—Parthia and Gandhara. Pacorus, king of Parthia ruled over Parthia Proper, Media, Persia, Susiana and Babylonia. Kanishka, the leader of the Sakas, who had emigrated from the central table-land of Asia and overthrown the Bactrian empire, was king of Gandhara, and his dominion stretched from Bactria to the Central Himalayas, and from the River Oxus to the River Jumna. East of Gandhara and south of the Himalayan range was the ancient empire of Magadha then ruled by the Maha-karnas, who belonged to the great tribe of the Andhras. The small state of Malava, founded by a tribe akin to the Andhras, on the northern side of the Vyndhia hills, had thrown off the yoke of the Magadhas: and Parthian adventurers held sway in the regions near the mouths of the Indus and in Guzerat. In the Deccan, the basins of the Mahanadi, Godaveri and Kistna still formed part of the Magadha empire, the southern boundary of which approached Tamilakam, or the land of the Tamils, in the southern-most portion of the peninsula. Buddhism was paramount, and non-Aryan races were in power, almost everywhere throughout India. To the Aryan races it was a period of humiliation, and to Brahminism one of painful struggle for existence. When, in later years, Brahminism was again favored by royalty, it appears to have exerted all its energy, to erase every trace of the rival faith and foreign dominion. Accordingly we find that the Sanscrit literature of the first century of the Christian era is now a perfect blank. Curiously enough, a considerable portion of the Tamil literature of that very period has come down to us, almost intact, and reveals to us the condition of not only the Tamils, but also of other races who inhabited the rest of India in that remote age.

The vast field of ancient Tamil literature is like an unknown land into which no traveller hath yet set foot. Many of the ancient classical works in Tamil have but recently seen the light. Hitherto they were preserved in manuscript on palmyra leaves, and jealously hidden by those Pandits into whose hands they had fallen. The archaic language in which they were composed, and the alien religions they favoured, alike prevented their becoming popular with Tamil students. In fact some of them were forbidden in Tamil schools, and Saiva or Vaishnava pandits deemed it an unpardonable sin to teach them to their pupils. Most of these manuscripts lay neglected in the libraries of Saiva or Jain monasteries: and there they would have crumbled to dust but for the enterprise of a few scholars who have with considerable labour and research, rescued most of them from oblivion and published them in print[1]. Several valuable works however still remain in manuscript, accessible only to a few individuals.

It is the general opinion of Western scholars that there was

---

[1] Foremost among these scholars I should mention Rai Bahadur C. W. Thamotharam Pillai, B.A., B.L., who has published the whole of Tholkapiyam with the commentaries of Chenavaraiyar and Nachchinarkiniyar and the Kalithokai by Nallathanar: and Mr. Saminathier, Tamil Pandit, Kumbakonum College, who has published the Paththuppadu; Chilappathikaram, and Purananuru. I should not omit to mention also Mr. Shunmugam Pillai, Madras, who has very pluckily brought forward an Edition of the Manimekalai, although there is no commentary accompanying the text.

no Tamil literature before the ninth century A. D.[1] But the fact appears to be that all that was original and excellent in the literature of the Tamils was written before the ninth century, and what followed was, for the most part, but a base imitation or translation of Sanscrit works. From a careful study of ancient Tamil poems, I am led to think that some of the earliest works were undoubtedly composed more than two thousand years ago, and that the Tamil people acquired wealth and civilisation at this early period by their commercial intercourse with foreign nations such as the Arabs, Greeks, Romans and Javanese. With the advance of their material prosperity, there was a sudden stimulus to their literary activity. The Augustan period of Tamil literature was, I should say, in the first century of the Christian era; and the last College of poets was then held in Madura in the Court of the Tamil king Ugra (the Terrible) Pandya. The works of not less than fifty authors of this period have come down to us. These poets were of various castes, various religious persuasions and belonged to different parts of the Tamil country. Some were Nigranthas, some Buddhists, and some of the Brahminic faiths. There were kings, priests, merchants, doctors, farmers, and artizans among their number. Amidst the gloom and uncertainty in which the ancient history of the country is shrouded, the works of so many authors of one age throw a flood of welcome light.

The information afforded by these poems, regarding the religion and social customs of the Tamil people, would alone guide us to fix the probable date of this literature in the earliest centuries of the Christian Era. For, we find from them that there were Buddhists in the Tamil country, but they had set up no images of Buddha and had no priests; there were Nigranthas who called the Buddhists, heretics, but who had not commenced the worship of their Saints or Tirthankaras; there were temples dedicated to Siva, Vishnu and Subramanya, but there were also other shrines in which the worship of Indra and Baladêva was continued; there were Brahmins who wore the sacred thread and called themselves the "twice-born" but neither kings nor merchants sought this

---

[1] Dr. Burnell in his South Indian Paleography and Dr. Caldwell in his Introduction to the Comparative Grammar of Dravidian Languages, have expressed this opinion.

distinction; there were Tamils living in walled towns and cities, but in some parts of the country they still led the life of nomads and had no settled habitation.

An additional proof of the antiquity of the poems above men-tioned may be adduced from the fact that the chief towns and sea-ports and the foreign merchandise of the Tamil country, as de-scribed in these poems correspond exactly with those given in the works of Pliny, Ptolemy and in the Periplus Maris Erythræi. Pliny died in 79 A. D.; and had completed his Natural History two years previously. The unknown author of the Periplus was a native of Egypt, and wrote his book after the time of Augustus Cæsar, and before the kingdom of the Nabathœans was overthrown by the Romans. A more definite indication of his date is furnished by his mentioning Zoskales as the king reigning in his time over the Auxumitæ. This Zoskales is identified with Za-Hakale who must have been king of Abyssinia from 77 to 89 A. D. We may con-clude therefore that the Periplus was written a little after the death of Pliny, between the years 80-89 A. D.[1] Klaudios Ptolemaios, or as he is commonly called Ptolemy, flourished in Alexandria about the middle of the second century A. D., in the reign of Antoninus Pius, and died in A. D. 163.[2] These authors furnish much interesting information regarding the Tamil people and their foreign commerce. Ptolemy especially gives a long list of the names of the maritime and inland towns. Most of the sea-ports mentioned by him can be readily identified from allusions to them in Tamil poems; but it is not equally easy to trace the position of many of the towns removed from the coast, because Ptolemy had utterly misconceived the form of the Indian peninsula. In his map of India he represents the sea-coast, from near the modern city of Bombay to a point beyond Masulipatam, as a zig-zag line running from west to east, and thus effaced the whole of the peninsula. Into this distorted map he tried to fit in the moun-tains, rivers and cities described to him, both by those who travelled frequently from Egypt to India and by those who visited Egypt from India. The names of the tribes and their chief cities as given by him are, however, wonderfully accurate, and give us some idea of

[1] McCrindle's translation of the Periplus Maris Erythræi, page 5.
[2] McCrindle's translation of Ptolemy's Geography of India and Southern Asia, page 1. Dr. Bhandarkar's Early History of the Dekkan, page 20.

the earnestness and diligence with which he must have collected his information.

That Ugra Pândya and the last College or Sangha of poets, belonged to a very early period may be inferred from numerous allusions in later Tamil works, of which I shall mention only one here. In the commentary to Iraiyanar Akapporul,[1] the author Nilakandan of Muchiri gives a brief account of the history of Tamil literature and alludes therein to the last Sangha of poets at Madura, presided over by Ugra Pandya. Every one of the stanzas with which the author illustrates his commentary contains the praises of the Pandyan king Nedumâran *alias* Arikêsari, victor of the battle of Nelvêli, and the king is described therein as alive at the time and ruling the Pandya, Chera and Chola kingdoms, having defeated and driven off the invaders who had come from the north. From the Udayêndram grant of Nandivarman Pallavamalla[2] I find that the famous battle of Nelvêli was fought between the Pandyan king and Udayachandra of Kollâpuram (Kolbâpar) who was the general of the Pallava king, Pallava malla Nandivarman. This Pallava king was contemporary with the Western Chalukya king Vikramaditya II. who reigned from A. D. 733 to 747 according to inscriptions in the Chalukya country.[3] Nilakandan the commentator, who praises Neduncheliyan the victor of Nelvêli, should have flourished therefore in the earlier half of the eighth century. It appears from his commentary that the works of the Sangha poets were current during his time in the form of collections or anthologies, such as Akam, Narrinai, Kurunthokai and Pathirruppathu. He quotes also from the Chilappathikaram. The Akam is a collection of 401 different pieces composed on various occasions by more than 200 poets. The Kurunthokai is a similar collection from the works of 205 authors. The Narrinai contains 401 verses composed by not less than 200 poets. The Pathirruppathu consists of ten poems

---

[1] See Thamotharam Pillai's edition of Iraiyanar Akapporul. The commentator (Nilakandan) states that his interpretation of the rules of the Akapporul is that handed-down through several generations from Nakkirar, one of the poets of the last Sangha of Madura. He gives a list of the names of teachers through whom the commentary was transmitted, but it does not appear to be a complete list.

[2] Salem District Manual, Vol. II., p. 356.

[3] See Indian Antiquary, Vol. VIII., p. 23 and Dr. Hultzsch's South Indian Inscriptions, Vol. I., p. 145.

by ten different persons. I counted the names of more than 514 different poets in these collections taken together. The number of these authors is so large that we may safely assume that the oldest of them. might have lived six or seven centuries before the age of Nilakandan. This would allow an average of about 100 authors per century, which is by no means a small number. The Akam contains many verses which allude to Karikal Chôla and the Chera kings Athan and Chenkudduvan.[1] Ten stanzas of the Pathirruppathu composed by Paranar, one of the poets of the last Sangha, are in praise of Chenkudduva Chera.[2] It is beyond doubt therefore that Chenkudduva Chera lived long before the close of the eighth century.

More definite information regarding the date of the last Sangha is furnished by the allusions to historic personages which occur in the poems composed during the reigns of the Chola king Karikal, his son-in-law the Chera king Athan and the latter's son Chenkudduva Chera[3] alias Imaya Varman. The last mentioned Chera King had a younger brother Ilanko-Adikal, who became a monk of the Nigrantha Sect. He was the author of a long poem the Chilappathikâram[4] in which he relates that at a certain festival held by his brother Imaya Varman at the Chera capital, Gajabâhu, the king of Lanka attended with an unnamed King of Mâlava.[5] This allusion to a king of Ceylon enables us to fix the date of Imaya Varman. In the long lists of the kings of Ceylon preserved in Singhalese chronicles, the name Gajabâhu occurs only twice. Gajabâhu I. lived in the early part of the second century A. D. and Gajabâhu II. in the twelfth century.[6] If the latter was the king referred to in the Chilappathikaram, Karikal Chôla, the grandfather of Gajabâhu's contemporary, Imaya Varman should have lived in the eleventh or twelfth century A. D. But in many

[1] Akam-Stanzas 55, 124, 396. This work is not published in print as yet.

[2] Pathirruppattu, Stanzas 51 to 60. This poem also has not appeared in print.

[3] Chilappathikaram XXI—11 to 15 and XXIX—1 to 8.

[4] This poem with the commentary of Nallarkkiniyar was published by Mr. Saminathior in the year 1892. The author's name is not given, but he is generally known by the title Ilanko-Adikal which signifies "a Royal monk." In line 1 of the Pathikam or Preface to the poem, it is stated that he lived as a monk in the Kuna-Vayil-Koddam (the East Gate Temple).

[5] Chilappathikaram, page 81 and XXX—160.

[6] Mahawanso, Dipawanso, Rajavali and Rajaratnakari.

Tamil poems[1] and inscriptions on copper-plates[2] recording the grants of Chola kings who lived in the tenth and eleventh centuries, Karikal Chola. I.[3] is described as one of the earliest and most remote ancestors of the Chola kings then reigning. It is evident therefore that the Gajabâhu referred to in Chilappathikaram could not be Gajabâhu II., but must have been Gajabâhu I. who was king of Ceylon from about A. D. 113 to A. D. 125.

The Chilappathikaram also mentions the fact that Chenkudduva Chera paid a friendly visit to the King of Magadha on the banks of the Ganges. It gives the name of the Magadha King as *Nurruvar Kannar* or the "Hundred Karnas" and this expression was long a puzzle to me, until it struck me that it was a translation of the Sanskrit title "Satakarnin." Several kings of the Karna or Andhra dynasty bore the epithet Satakarnin, and coins and inscriptions of these kings have been found, in which the Pali form of the word "Satakani" occurs. Sanskrit scholars have however misread the name as Sâtakarnin, instead of Satakarnin. The Tamil rendering of the name into "Hundred Karnas" in a contemporary poem leaves no doubt of the fact that the name is correctly Satakarnin, made up of the words Sata (hundred) and Karna (ears), the epithet evidently meaning a king who employed one hundred spies, or had one hundred sources of information. The Vayu, Vishnu, Matsya and Bhagavata Puranas state that the Mauryas ruled the Magadha Empire for 137 years, and after them the Sungas 112 years, and after them the Kanvayanas 45 years : and that after them there were 30 kings of the Andhra dynasty who reigned 456 years: but none of the Puranas gives a complete list of the names of the Andhra kings. The Matsya, which appears to be the oldest of the Puranas furnishes the fullest list, which contains the names of only 29 kings and the number of years during which each of the kings

---

[1] Kalingattu-parani, Vikrama-Chôlan-Ula Kulôttunga-Chôlan-Ula and Raja Raja Chôlan-Ula.

[2] The copperplates relating to the Chudamani Vihara at Negapatam, now preserved in the town of Leyden in Holland. See Archæological Reports of Southern India, by Dr. Burges, Vol. IV., p. 204. The plates recording the grant of Udaiyendra Mangalam, during the reign of Vira Narayana Chôla. See Salem District Manual, p. 369.

[3] There were other Karikal Chôlas after him.

reigned. In the early history of the emperors of Magadha, the only date which may be safely relied upon is that of Chandragupta, the contemporary of Seleucus Nicator, who began his reign in B.C. 310, and concluded a treaty with him in B.C. 305. The year of accession of Chandragupta may be fixed at B.C. 312, two years earlier than that of Seleucus Nicator, and calculating from that year the reign of the first Satakarnin ought to have extended from A. D. 77 to A.D. 133 according to the Matsya Purana as shown below :

Ten Mauryas for 137 years, B.C. 312—175.

Ten Sungas for 112 years, B.C. 175—63.

Four Kanvayanas for 45 years, B.C. 63 to 18.

Thirty Andhras of whom the first six are :

Sisuka for 23 years, B.C. 18—A.D. 5.

Krishna for 18 years, A.D. 5—23.

Simalakarnin for 18 years, A.D. 23—41.

Purnotsunga for 18 years, A.D. 41—59.

Sirivaswami for 18 years, A.D. 59—77.

Satakarnin for 56 years, A.D. 77—133.

The reign of this Satakarnin covers the entire period of the reign of Gajabâhu, King of Ceylon, which lasted 12 years from A.D. 113 to 125 according to the Mahawanso. Satakarnin, Emperor of Magadha, who is alluded to in the Chilappathikaram as the contemporary of Chenkudduvachera and Gajabâhu, is therefore doubtless the first Satakarnin in the list of the Matsya Purana, who reigned from A.D. 77 to 133. The synchronism of the Puranas and the Mahawanso is perfect, at least from the reign of Chandragupta up to that of the first Satakarnin; and this coincidence is a strong proof of the general accuracy of the traditional history preserved in Puranic accounts and in the Mahawanso.

The Mahawanso was composed in the fifth century A. D. and the Dipavanso still earlier ; and both these historical works mention Gajabâhu I. It appears that during the reign of his father " crooked nosed " Tissa, a Chôla king had invaded Ceylon, and carried away several thousands of captives ; and that in retaliation Gajabâhu invaded the Chôla dominions soon after his accession to the throne in A. D. 113. The tradition is that the captives were carried away to work on the banks of the River Kaviri, which were then under construction.[1]   This is quite in accordance with later Tamil poems and inscriptions[2] which speak of Karikal Chôla as the king who commenced the construction of the high banks along both sides of the bed of the Kaviri.   The construction of the Kaviri banks which extended along its course to a distance of about 100 miles from its mouth, was an undertaking of such magnitude that it could not have been completed during the reign of Karikal.   The Chôla King, who invaded Ceylon in order to procure captives to work at the banks, might have been therefore Karikal or his immediate successor.   This tradition is further evidence of the fact that Chenkudduva Chera was contemporary with Gajabâhu I. who lived in the early part of the second century A. D. Chenkudduvan's grandfather Karikal Chôla should have therefore reigned in the latter half of the first century A. D., or in other words, about *eighteen hundred years ago*.   It will appear further on, from my account of Tamil literature, that the poets of the last Sangha at Madura— many of whom allude to the Chêra kings Athan and Chenkudduvan—should be assigned to the same period.

I shall in the following pages first describe the ancient geography of the land of the Tamils, then their foreign commerce, the different races that spoke Tamil, their political history, and conclude with a brief account of their social life, mode of warfare, literature, philosophy and religion.

---

1 Mr. Hugh Nevill of the Ceylon Civil Service and Editor of the " Taprobanian " informed me that many ballads and stories still current in Ceylon refer to this tradition. Upham's translation of the Râjavali, chapter 35, p. 228. Râjaratnâcari, p. 57. Turnour's Epitome of the History of Ceylon, p. 21.

2 The Kalingattu Parani and the Leyden Grant.

CHAPTER II.

GEOGRAPHY OF TAMILAKAM.

The whole of the country lying south of the central plateau of Asia was known as Jambudvipa or "The Land of the Rose Apple trees" which are said to abound in it. In Jambudvipa, the region south of the Vyndhyas was called Dakshinapatha or The Southern side[1]; and the extreme south of the peninsula, which was occupied by the Tamil people, was Tamilakam, or the abode of the Tamils.[2] The limits of Tamilakam were from Venkata Hill[3] in the North, to Cape Comorin in the South, and from the Bay of Bengal in the East, to the Arabian Sea in the West. _Malayalam had not formed into a separate dialect at this period_, and only one language, Tamil, was spoken from the Eastern to the Western Sea.

The people who lived north of Venkatam were called Vadukar.[4] Immediately north of Tamilakam, above the Ghats, was Erumainad[5] or the "Buffalo land" the equivalent of which name in Sanscrit was Mahisha Mandalam. West of Erumainad were Tulu Nad, Kudakam (Coorg) and Konkanam. Other races in India were the Kalingar, Pangalar, Kankar, Kattiyar and Northern Aryas.[6] The following Kingdoms and towns, outside Tamilakam are alluded to by Tamil poets :—The Kingdom of Magadha and the town of Kapilai which was the birthplace of Buddha[7]: the Kingdom of

---

[1] McCrindle's Periplus, page 124.
   Dr. Bhandarkar's Early History of the Dekkan, page 1.

[2] Chilappathikaram iii. 37. Manimekalai xvii 62. Ptolemy and the author of the Periplus call it Limirike, but as pointed out by Dr. Caldwell (Dravidian Grammar, Introduction, page 14), it is evidently Damirike. In the Indian segment of the Roman maps called from their discoverer, _the Pentinger Tables_, the portion of India to which this name is applied is called Damirike—McCrindle's Periplus, page 126.

[3] Chilappathikaram viii. 1 and 2, Venkata Hill is the modern Tirupathi about 100 miles North-west of Madras.

[4] Akam, 294.

[5] Ibid. 252.

[6] Chilappathikaram xxv. 156 to 158. The Pangalar appear to have been the people who inhabited Lower Bengal. The Kankar were those who occupied the banks of the Ganges higher up, evidently the Gangaridae mentioned by Ptolemy. The Kattiyar were doubtless the people who gave the name Kattiwar to Guserat.

[7] Manimekalai xxvi. 12 to 44.

Mâlava and its capital Avanti: the Kingdom of Vajra:[1] the sea-port Gangai on the banks of the Ganges, which was in the territory of the Kannar:[2] Vâranavâsi, the modern Benares: Thuvarai or Dwaraka in Guzerat, the capital of the deified hero Krishna.[3] Ceylon was known as Lanka-dvipa or Ratna-dvipa: the highest mountain in the island was Samanoli[4] (now called Adam's Peak); and on its summit was an impression of Buddha's foot, which was an object of pilgrimage to Buddhists far and near. Between Ceylon and India was the island Mani-pallavam, on which there was one of the sacred seats of Buddha, then held in great veneration by all Buddhists. It is said to have been at a distance of thirty yojanas south of Puhâr, the ancient sea-port at the mouth of the Kaviri.[5] A ship sailing from the coast of Madura to Châvakam (Java) touched at Manipallavam.[6] To the east of Ceylon were the islands inhabited by a race of Nagas called Nakkasâranar or "naked nomads," who were cannibals.[7] Beyond these islands was Châvakam a large kingdom the capital of which was Nâgapuram. The king of this country claimed to be a descendant of the God Indra, and what is most remarkable, the language spoken in Chavakam appears to have been Tamil! This Chavakam was most probably Sumatra or Java.[8]

---

[1] Chilappathikaram ii. 99 to 103.

[2] Ibid. xxiii. 138—141.

[3] Ibid. xvii.

[4] Manimekalai xxviii. 103.

[5] Manimekalai vi. 211 to 214.

[6] Ibid. xiv. 74 to 81. The Dipawanso and Mahawanso give a glowing but fabulous account of Buddha's first visit to this seat: but the Tamil Buddhist poem Manime-kalai, which was composed three centuries earlier, gives a very simple version of the story which is as follows:—"Two Naga kings contended for this seat, but neither was able to lift it off the ground; determined however not to give it up, with eyes all aflame and breathing fury, they led their great armies and fought a bloody battle. The great Teacher (Buddha) then appeared before them and said, "Cease your strife, this seat is mine": then he sat upon it and preached the Law. Manimekalai viii. 54 to 63.

[7] Manimekalai xvi. 15. Ptolemy mentions three groups of islands inhabited by cannibals. Yule has identified them with the Nicobars, Nekkavaram of Marco Polo, Lakavaram of Rashid-ud-din, McCrindle's Ptolemy, 236 to 239.

[8] Manimekalai xxiv. 164 to 170. Ptolemy calls the island Iabadois or Sabadois (the island of barley) and its capital Argyre (Silver town) McCrindle's Ptolemy, page 249.

Tamilakam was divided into thirteen Nadus or provinces, the names of which were :—Pândi, Thenpândi, Kuddam, Kudam, Karkâ, Vên, Pooli, Panri, Aruva, Aruva-vadatalai, Cheetham, Malâdu and Puna-nâdu.[1] Of these, Pandinadu, which corresponded nearly to the whole of the modern district of Madura, was considered the most important, being that tract where pure Tamil was then spoken. The chief town in this Nadu was Mathurai, the capital of the Pandyan kingdom. It appears to have been so called after the sacred city of Muttra on the banks of the Jumna, which was most probably the capital of the northern kingdom of the descendants of the Pândus, the heroes of the Mahâbârata. This is evident from the appellation Thakkana-Mathurai or Southern Madura[2] given to it by Tamil poets of this age. The Pandyan king called himself Panchavan[3] (the descendant of the five,) and Kaurian[4] (of the line of the Kurus), names which clearly indicate his origin from the Pandus, who were five brothers. The city of Madura retains to this day its ancient name, and thus bears living testimony to the fact that the descendants of the Pandus, who ruled in Muttra, had in early times established their power in the most Southern parts of the peninsula.[5] It was a fortified city. There were four gates to the fort, surmounted by high towers, and outside the massive walls which were built of rough-hewn stone was a deep moat, and surrounding the moat was a thick jungle of thorny trees. The roads leading to the gates were wide enough to permit several elephants to pass abreast, and on the walls on both sides of the entrance, there were all kinds of weapons and missiles concealed, ready to be discharged on an enemy. Yavana soldiers with drawn swords guarded the gates.[6] Over the gates and walls waved many a standard which had been taken in battle. The principal streets in the city were the royal street, the market street, the

[1] Nachchinarkiniyar gives a slightly different list of the Nadus. Instead of Ven and Puna-nadu he mentions Olinadu and Ponkar-nadu. Tholkapiyam Cholla. thikaram, Sutram 400.

[2] Manimekalai, xiii. 13.
[3] Puranânuru, Stanza 58, line 8.
[4] Chilappathikaram, xv. 2.
[5] McCrindle's Ptolemy, page 60.
[6] Chilappathikaram, xiv. 62-67.

courtezan's street and the streets where dwelt the goldsmiths, corn dealers, cloth merchants, jewellers, &c.[1] The temple of Siva known as Velliambalam or "the silver shrine" appears to have been the grandest building in the clty.[2] There were other temples dedicated to Vishnu, Baladêva, Subramanya and Chintadêvi,[3] and there were separate monasteries for the Buddhist, Brahminic and Nigrantha ascetics.[4]

Madura was doubtless the most famous and important town in Tamilakam at this period, being the capital city of the Pandyas, who were renowned as the most powerful of the Tamil kings, and munificent patrons of poets. What distinguished it however from other towns in the Tamil country were the high towers over the four gates of the fort. Hence it was familiarly known as Nân—mâdak—kûdal or the "Cluster of four towers." The name was sometimes shortened into Mâdak—kûdal, or Kûdal.[5] The site of this ancient Madura or Kudal was most probably Pala Madura (or old Madura,) now in ruins, which is situated at a distance of about six miles to the south-east of the modern town of Madura. The ruins are now on the northern bank of the Vaigai, whereas ancient Mâdura stood on its southern bank ; but it is quite possible that the river had changed its course since the destruction of the old city. That Madura was in danger of being destroyed by the Vaigai may be inferred from a poet's description of Pandya in the following words : "Lord of the fortified city, whose walls knew of no siege by any other enemy, but the waters of the Vaigai when it is swollen with floods."[6] Outside the fort of Madura resided those men who led a life of religious devotion and poor classes of people such as the Pânar and other lower castes.[7]

West of Madura was the hill Parankunru sacred to Subra-

---

[1] Ibid. xiv. 143 to 218.

[2] Ibid. Pathikam 40-41.

[3] Ibid. xiv. 7 to 11.

[4] Mathuraikanchi, lines 467-487.

[5] Nakkirar's Tiru-murukârrup-padai, line 71. Kalith-thokai, stanza 35, line 17. Stanza 92, lines 11 and 65. The tradition that the name Nan-madak-kudal owed its origin to the four temples Tiru-Alavây, Tiru-nallaru, Tiru-mudankai and Tiru-naduvur appears to be an invention of the Puranic age.

[6] Kalithbhokai, stanza 67, lines 3 to 5.

[7] Mathursîk-kanchi, 340-342.

manya[1] according to the poet Nakkirar. This hill is south-west
of modern Madura but directly west of the ruins now known as
old Madura ; east of the capital was another hill, where there was
a temple dedicated to Vishnu. On the latter hill were three
sacred springs, to bathe in which was believed to be an act of
great merit by the votaries of Vishnu.[2] On the way from Madura
to Uraiyur (now a suburb of Trichinopoly) were the Sirumalai hills
which were covered with groves of mango and jack trees, arecanut
and cocoanut palms, and where onion, saffron, raggy, millet, hill
rice, edible roots, plantain and sugarcane were cultivated extensively.[3]

Of the boundaries of Pandinadu, or of the exact extent
and position of the other twelve Nadus comprised in Tamilakam,
there is no record in ancient Tamil poems. The accounts given
by commentators are also conflicting.[4] In the absence of any
connected account of the ancient geography of the country by
Tamil authors, I have had to make my own researches with the
help of the information available in the Periplus and in the works
of Pliny and Ptolemy.

There were four *Nádus* or provinces bordering on the
Arabian Sea, in the following order, from North to South : Pooli,

[1] Thiru-murukattup-padai, 71-77.
[2] Chilappathikaram, xi. 91-103.
[3] Ibid., xi. 80-85.
[4] Gunaságara in his commentary to the Yápparunkalam of Amrithaságara,
eighth sutram of the third part Olipiyal, gives the limits of Chen-Tamil-nadu or the
province where pure Tamil was spoken " as north of the Vaigai river, south of the
Marutha river, east of Karuvur and west of Maruvur." This would include approx-
imately, the northern half of the modern district of Madura and the Tanjore and
Trichinopoly districts It would exclude Madura, the capital of the Pandya. The
commentator Chenávaraiyar and after him, Naobchinár-kkiniyar accepted this
definition of Chen-Tamil-nadu, and they mention the names of the surrounding
Nadus in the following order from the South-east to the North-east of Chen Tamil
Nadu :—Ponkar, Oli, Then-pandi, Kuddam, Kudam, Panri, Karka, Cheetham,
Pooli, Malayamanadu, Aruva and Aruva vada thalai. Gunaságara gave the same
list with this difference that instead of Ponkar and Oli, he had Ven and Punal-
Nádus. Sankara-namach-chivayar rejected with very good reason, this definition
of Chen Tamil Nadu, in his commentary to Pavananti's Nannul, Chollathikaram,
Peyariyal, sutrams 14 and 16. He was of opinion that Chen Tamil Nadu ought to
have included Pandi Nadu and excluded the Chola country or Punal Nadu.

Kudam, Kuddam and Ven.[1]   The names were appropriate to the natural peculiarity of each province. Pooli, or " the sandy tract " extended most probably from the banks of the modern Agalappula to the mouth of the Ponani river. The soil of this part of the country is remarkably sandy. Kudam, or " the western land " denoted apparently the region between the mouth of the Ponani river and the southernmost mouth of the Periyar near Ernakulam. This would have been the most western land to the first immigrants who came into Malabar by the Palghat pass. Kuddam, or " the land of lakes " comprised the territory around the modern towns of Kottayam and Quilon which is to this day known by the same name to the natives of the country. The river Páli or Pálái which flows through this province formed at its mouth several islands and lakes, and hence this tract was called Kuddam or the "land of lakes." South of Kuddam lay Ven which stretched up to very near Cape Comorin. The low hills and valleys in this region were covered with luxuriant forests of bamboo, and therefore it was aptly named Ven-nad or the "bamboo land." East of Kudam was Karká, or the " rocky region."

The five Nadus abovementioned formed the Chera Kingdom the capital of which was Vanchi or Karur.[2] It was situated on the banks of the Periyar, far from its mouth and near the foot of the Western Ghats. The site of the town is now a deserted village, known as Tiru-Karur, three miles from Khothai-mangalam, and 28 miles east by north of Cochin, where the remains of an old temple and other massive buildings are still visible.[3] The town was strongly fortified,[4] and on the battlements were mounted various engines to throw missiles on those who

---

[1] The names Pooli-Nadu and Kuda Nadu survived till the Mysorean conquest of Malabar, in the latter part of the eighteenth century, though slightly altered into Payanad, Polanad and Kutnad. Paynad comprised 9 amshams around the modern town of Quilnody, and Polanad 22 amshams surrounding Calicut. Kutnad consisted of 24 amshams in the modern Taluk of Ponani. Malabar Manual, Vol. I, pp. 647 to 666.

[2] Chilappathikaram xxv. 9-22. Adiyarkku-Nallar the commentator of the Chilappathikaram identified Karur with Tiruvanjai-kalam, a later capital of the Chera kingdom, near the mouth of the Periyar: but Ptolemy places it much higher up the river, and 1 believe the latter is correct.

[3] Journal of the Asiatic Society, Vol. II, p. 336. Sewell's Lists of Antiquities, Vol. I, p. 261.

[4] Manimekalai xxviii. 2 to 68.

attacked the fort. Over the gates in the walls, were towers plastered with white mortar and adorned with flags. Surrounding the
walls was a broad moat in which man-eating alligators of large
size abounded. The king's palace, a temple of Vishnu called
Adakamadam or the "golden shrine,"[1] a Buddhist Chaitya,[2]
and a Nigrantha monastery[3] which was outside the Eastern gate
of the fort, appear to have been the most conspicuous buildings
in the town. If Madura was noted for its many mansions and
towers, Vanchi, with its flower-gardens and tanks full of crystal
water, limpid streams and little islands, shady bowers and parks
with artificial hills and waterfalls, was charming to every visitor.
Outside the fort resided the soldiers of the Chera king. Ascetics
and philosophers also dwelt in the silent and shady groves, far
away from the din and bustle of the capital.

Near the mouth of the Periyar was Muchiri, an important
seaport. A poet describes it as follows:—" The thriving town of
Muchiri where the beautiful large ships of the Yavanas bringing
gold, come splashing the white foam on the waters of the Periyar,
which belongs to the Cherala, and return laden with pepper."[4]
" Fish is bartered for paddy which is brought in baskets to
the houses " says another poet : " sacks of pepper are brought
from the houses to the market ; the gold received from ships, in
exchange for articles sold, is brought to shore in barges, at
Muchiri, where the music of the surging sea never ceases, and
where Kudduvan (the Chera king) presents to visitors, the rare
products of the seas and mountains."[5]

Thondi was another flourishing seaport on the western
coast. It stood on the banks of the Mâkkali[6] or the "big salt
river" which is now known as Agalappulai. " It was bounded "
says a poet "by groves of cocoanut trees bearing heavy bunches
of fruits, a wide expanse of rice-fields, verdant hills, bright
sandy tracts and a salt river, whose glassy waters are covered

---

[1] Chilappathikaram xxvi. 62 and xxx. 51. The commentator states that
Adakamadam was Thiru-ananthapuram (the modern Trivandrum) or Haripuram:
but there is nothing in the text of the poem to warrant this conclusion.

[2] Manimekalai xxviii. 127.

[3] Chilappathikaram Pathikam, line 1.

[4] Erukkaddur Thayankannanar—Akam 148.

[5] Paranar,—Puram 343.

[6] Poykaiyar,—Puram 48.

with flowers of brilliant colours."[1] This description suits exactly the village now called Pallikara which is situated at a distance of five miles north of the modern town of Quilandy. The name Thondi is not now remembered by the inhabitants; but the richest landlord in the village, a hereditary nobleman, is styled Thondippunathil Nair or Thondyil Kuruppachan. About twelve miles up the Agalappulai, near Kuttiadi, is a village still called Thondippoil, a name, which, I believe, signifies, the way to Thondi. The Agalappulai must have been navigable up to Thondi or Pallikara in former days; but since the Kotta river diverted into another channel, the Agalappulai has shrunk in size and is no longer navigable.[2]

Ptolemy gives the following list of seaports and rivers on the west coast of Tamilakam :—

Tyndis a city, Bramagara, Kalaikkarias, Mouziris an emporium; mouth of the river Pseudostomos, Podoperoura, Semne, Koreoura, Bakarei, mouth of the river Baris. Then he mentions the country of the Aioi and the following seaports in it.

Melkynda, Elangkon (or Elangkor) a mart, Kottiara the metropolis, Bammala, Komaria a cape and town.[3]

Of the inland cities he gives the following list : Inland cities of Limurike, to the west of the Pseudostomos are these : Naroulla, Kouba, Paloura. Between the Pseudostomos and the Baris these cities : Pasage, Mastanour, Kourellour, Pounnata where is beryl, Aloe, Karoura, the royal seat of the Kerobothras, Arembour Bideris, Pantipolis, Adarima Koreour. Inland town of the Aioi. Morounda.[4]

Pliny and Ptolemy agree in fixing the northern limit of the Tamil country on the western coast somewhere above Tundis (Thondi). The Periplus gives a clearer indication of the boundary as it states that Limurike (Dimirike) or Tamilakam commenced immediately south of the Island Leuke or " the White." This Island which is north-west of the modern town of Bada-

---

[1] Kurunkoliyar-kilar, Puram 17.

[2] "It would seem as if the Kotta river had at one time found its way to the sea by this outlet (Agalappula) instead of by the channel now in use."—Malabar Manual, Vol. I, p. 12.

[3] McCrindle's Ptolemy, p. 48 f.

[4] Ibid., p. 180 f.

gara, about eight miles from the coast, is still known to the natives
as Thoovak-kal or Vellaikal "the white rock." Europeans have
called it " the sacrifice rock," because, when the Portuguese first
settled at Calicut, the Kottakkal cruizers surprised a Portuguese
vessel and sacrificed all their prisoners on that rock.[1] I am unable to identify Naura. It appears to have been a small village
on the banks of the Akalappula. Tundis is of course Thondi
which was near the site of the modern Pallikkara about five miles
north of Quilandy. Even to this day trading vessels from Arabia
regularly visit old Kollam or Pantalayini Kollam[2], a village about
three miles south of Thondi.

Between Tundis and Muziris, Ptolemy mentions two towns on
the sea coast, Bramagara and Kalaikarias, and three inland, Naroulla, Kouba and Paloura. Bramagara may be identified with Brahma-
kulam, Kalaikarais was most probably Chalacoory, and Paloura is
doubtless Pâlayur which is still a large and populous amshom near
Chowghat. Mouziris[3] may unhesitatingly be taken to represent
Muchiri which, according to Tamil poets, was situated near the

---

[1] Malabar Manual, Vol. I, p. 356.
[2] This is the Pandarani of Portuguese writers, the Flandrina of Friar Odoric, the Fandreeah of Rowlandson's Tahafat-ul-mujabidin and the Fandarina of Ibn Batuta, Malabar Manual, Vol. I, p. (72). " Tanur itself " says Yule " may be Tyndis ; it was an ancient city, the seat of a principality, and in the beginning of the 16th century had still much shipping and trade. Perhaps, however, a more probable site is a few miles further north Kadalundi, i. e., Kadaltundi, the raised ground by the sea standing on an inlet three or four miles south of Beypoor. It is now a port, but persons on the spot seem to think that it must formerly have been one and in communication with the backwater." He adds in a note supplied by Dr. Burnell " The composition of Kadal and Tundi makes Kadalundi by Tamil rules" McCriudle's Ptolemy, p. 50. With due deference to so great an authority as Dr. Burnell, I should however state that I am not aware of any rule of Tamil Grammar by which the words Kadal and Tundi can combine and form Kadalundi. The only objection to my identification of Tundis with Thondi near Pallikkara will be that it is nearly 800 stadia from Muziris or Kadungollur and not 500 stadia as stated in the Periplus ; but the calculation of distances by sea voyages at this early period when navigators had no mechanical contrivances whatever to register the speed of vessels, cannot be expected to be correct.
[3] Muchiri is the Muyiri of Muyiri-kodu, which, says Yule "appears in one of the most ancient of Malabar inscriptions as the residence of the king of Kodungolur or Kranganur, and is admitted to be practically identical with that now extinct city." It is to Kranganur he adds that all the Malabar traditions point as their oldest sea-port of renown : to the Christians it was the landing place of St. Thomas the Apostle—McCrindle's Ptolemy, p. 51.

mouth of the Periyar and was frequented by Yavana merchants. Pseudostomos signifies in Greek "false-mouth" and is a correct translation of the Tamil or Malayalam expression "Alimukam" by which the mouth of the Periyar below Kadungolur is known even now. It was so called, because during the monsoon the river frequently made a new opening for itself in the low sand banks, which obstructed its entrance to the sea. The proper name of the river was Periyar or Porunai. South of this river at a distance of 500 stadia or about 58 miles, Ptolemy mentions another river called Baris. Neither the river Baris, nor any of the towns mentioned as situated between Muziris and Cape Kumari or Comorin, has been satisfactorily identified by the scholars who have hitherto examined Ptolemy's account of ancient India. I experienced the same difficulty till one day, when travelling by boat from Alleppy to Kottayam, the boatmen informed me that I should land at Vaikkarai. This brought to my mind Ptolemy's Bakarei and on further enquiry, I was glad to learn that the landing place at Kottayam is known as Vaikkarai, and the hill, on which the Dewan Peishkar's Court-house is built, is called Vaikkarai-kunnu or the Vaikkarai-hill. I came to know also that the river which flowed through Kottayam is called Pálái or Páli, and this corresponded to the Baris which Ptolemy places next to Bakarei. I was satisfied therefore that the ancient seaport of Bakarei was identical with the village of Vaikkarai near Kottayam.[1] I was surprised to find that the towns on the sea coast between Muziris and Bakarei named by Ptolemy, viz., Podoperoura, Semne and Koreoura may be identified with Udiamperur, Smbai and Kothora which are situated on the eastern coast of the backwater. *This led me to the startling discovery that in Ptolemy's time the sea coast was along the eastern shore of the backwater, and that neither the backwater, which extends at present to over 40 miles from Changanachery to Pallipuram, nor the long strip of land which forms its western bank, and on which now stand the flourishing sea-ports of Cochin and Alleppy, was then in existence.*

Nelkunda, the town from which pepper was exported in barges to Bakarei, appears to be Nirkunram. It is mentioned by

1 Yule conjectured that Bakarei must have been between Kanetti and Kollam (Quilon) in Travancore. McCrindle's Ptolemy, p. 134.

various authors, under varying forms of the name. In Pliny it is Neacyndi. It is Nelkunda in the Periplus, Melkunda in Ptolemy: in the *Peutingerian Table* it is Nincylda, and in the Geographer of Ravenna, Nilcinna. The site of this town is six miles east of Kottayam, not far from Meenachil, where the best pepper is grown to this day.

South of Bakarei, Ptolemy places the country of the Aioi. This was the territory of the Ay[1] a family of chiefs of the Pothiya hills, who were great patrons of poets. The towns Elankon, Kottiara and Bammala may be identified with the modern Vilavankodu, Kottaru and Ponnanai. It will appear therefore, that even south of Bakarei or the modern Kottayam, the sea coast has receded six or seven miles since the time of Ptolemy. Of the inland cities named by Ptolemy I would suggest the following identifications:

Pounnata	...	The modern Poonjarru near Meenachil, where the descendant of a fugitive king is said to reside at present.
Aloe ...	...	Alwaye, a famous place of resort for its medicinal water.
Karoura, the royal seat of Kerobothros.	}	Karuvai or Vanchi, the ruins of which are at Tiru-karur, 28 miles east by north of Cochin.[2]
Videris	...	Pithara.
Adarima	...	Atharimalai.

The region Kottanara[3] from which pepper was exported

---

[1] Puram, stanzas 127 to 136.

[2] "Karoura" says Caldwell "is mentioned in Tamil traditions as the ancient capital of the Chera, Kera or Kerala kings, and is generally identified with Karur, an important town in the Coimbatore District, originally included in the Chera kingdom. It is situated on the left bank of the river Amarâvati, a tributary of the Kaviri, near a large fort now in ruins—" (Introd., pp. 96, 97). This identification rests merely upon the similarity of the names Karoura and Karur. Dr. Caldwoll would not have made this mistake, if he had been acquainted with the ancient Tamil poems which I have taken us my authorities.

[3] Dr. Buchanan identified Cottonara with Kadattanadu the name of a district in the Calicut country celebrated for its pepper. Dr. Burnell identified it with Kolattanâdu, the district about Tellicherry, which he says is the pepper district. McCrindle's Periplus, p. 132. But when we compare Cottonara with the names of the ancient divisions of the Tamil-land, the identity of Cottonara with Kuddanâdu will readily suggest itself.

was doubtless Kuddanadu, the limits of which I have already described.

·Cape Kumari (the modern Comorin) was a sacred bathing place. Brahmin pilgrims came from Vâraṅâsi (or Benares) to bathe in Kumari and absolve their sins.[1] Similarly the Brahmins of Southern India went round the Pothiya hill, which was famous as the residence of the Vedic sage Agastya, then bathed in the sea at Kumari, and travelled northward to the Ganges to bathe in the sacred waters of that river.[2] Pilgrims from the banks of the Ganges to Kumari, and from Tamilakam to Benares appear to have kept up communication between the Northern and Southern Aryas. At the period of which I now write, the people remembered that *in former days the land had extended further south, and that a mountain called Kumarikkodu, and a large tract of country watered by the river Pahruli had existed south of Cape Kumari.* During a violent irruption of the sea, the mountain Kumarikkodu and the whole of the country through which flowed the Pahruli had disappeared.[3] Similar irruptions of the sea, and the subsidence of land on the south-western coast of Ceylon in the second century B. C. are recorded in the Buddhist annals of that island.[4]

---

[1] Manimekalai, xiii. N. 3 to 7.

[2] Chilappathikaram, xv. N. 14 & 15, and xxvii : N. 68, 69 and 110.

[3] Kalith-tbokai-stanza 104 N. 1 to 4. Chilappathikaram, xx. N. 17 to 22. "The river Pahruli, and the mountain Kumari, surrounded by many hills, were submerged by the raging sea." The commentator Nallarkiniyar states that between the Pahruli and Kumari rivers there was a tract of land extending to 700 Kavathams : and that it was divided into 7 Thenga Nadus, 7 Mathurai Nadus, 7 Munpalai Nadus, 7 Pinpalai Nadus, 7 Kunra Nadus, 7 Kunakarai Nadus, and 7 Kurumporai Nadus, or 49 Nadus, in all. But he does not quote his authority for this statement.

[4] During the reign of Tissa, the sovereign of Calyani, the province was submerged by the overflow of the ocean. This was about B. C. 200. Mahavansa. L. C. Wijesinha Mudaliar's edition, Chap. xxii, p. 84. The event is thus recorded in the Rajavali. "In these days the sea was seven leagues from Kalyany; but on account of what had been done to the priest (who had been tortured by the king of Kalyany) the gods who were charged with the conservation of Ceylon became enraged, and caused the sea to deluge the land.........In this time of Tissa Baja, 100,000 large towns' 970 fisher's villages, and 400 villages inhabited by pearl fishers making together eleven-twelfths of the territory of Kalyany was swallowed up by the sea. Rajavali : Vol. II., pp. 180, 190. Sir J. E. Tennent disbelieved the traditions of the former extent of Ceylon and submersion of vast regions by the

22

Ptolemy mentions the following provinces, rivers and towns on the east coast :—Country of the Kareoi : In the Kolkhic Gulf, where there is the pearl fishery : Sôsikournai, Kolkhoi an emporium, mouth of the river Solen. Inland cities of the Koreoi: Mendêla, Selour, Tittoua, Mantittour. Land of Pandion. In the Orgalic Gulf, Cape Koty, called also Kalligikon : Argeirou a town, Salour a mart. Inland cities of the Pandionoi: Tainour, Peringkarei, Korindiour, Tangala or Taga, Modoura the royal city of Pandion, Akour. Country of the Batoi : Nikama the metropolis, Thelkheir, Koroula a town: Inland cities of the Batoi: Kalindoia, Bata, Talara. In Paralia specially so called : the country of the Tôringoi: mouth of river Khabêros, Khabêris an emporium, Sabouras an emporium. Inland cities of the Paralia of the Sôrêtai : Kaliour, Tennagora, Eikour, Orthoura the royal city of Sôrnagos, Berê, Abour, Karmara, Magour.

The Arouarnori (Arvarnoi) : Podoukê an emporium, Melangî an emporium, mouth of the river Tyna, Kottis, Manarpha (or Manaliarpha a mart)—The inland cities of the Arvarnoi are these:—Kerauge, Phrourion, Karigê, Poloour, Pikendaka, Iatour, Skopoloura, Ikarta, Malanga the royal city of Basaranagos, Kandipatna.

North of the territory of the Arovarnoi, Ptolemy places Maisolia the region watered by the river Maisolos or the Krishna. Between Cape Comorin and Taprobane or Ceylon, he mentions an island Nanigeris and in the Argaric Gulf, another island Kory.[1]

The eastern coast extending from Cape Cumari was inhabited by a tribe called Parathavar who subsisted by fishing. They were the Kareoi of Ptolemy. The correct form of the name in Tamil is Karaiyar or the "Coast men," which is to this day the ordinary designation of the Parathavar tribe amongst the Tamils. Korkai, the chief town in the country of the Parathavar was the seat of the pearl fishery and the population of the town consisted mostly of pearl divers and chank-cutters.[2] The pearl

sea, and remarked as follows:—"But evidence is wanting to corroborate the assertion of such an occurrence at least within the historic period, no record of it exists in the earliest writings of the Hindus, the Arabians or Persians." Tenant's Ceylon, Vol. I., pp. 6 and 7. The mention of a similar catastrophe at the southern extremity of India, about the same period, in Tamil works, may be taken as strong evidence of the occurrence.

[1] McCrindle's Ptolemy, p. 57, ff. and 183, ff.
[2] Maduraik-kanchi, ll. 134, 144.

North of the Pandyan kingdom lay the country of the Vedduvar or Vedar[1] (the Batoi of Ptolemy), which was also known as Panri-Nadu or "the land of pigs"—the capital of this province was Nâgai or Nâga-paddinam. Very little is known of this town from Tamil poems of this period. It appears therefore that there was not much of communication between the Vedar and the rest of the Tamil people.

Beyond Panri-Nadu was Punal-Nadu or the Chola kingdom. The name Punal-Nadu signifies the land of floods. This province, which comprised the region around the mouth of the river Kaviri, was so called as it was subject to floods caused by the periodical freshes in the Kaviri. No dam had been built across the river at this period and there is no mention of the branch Coleroon which appears to have been formed by the river, many centuries later, after the construction of a dam near Trichinopoly. The Chola capital was Uraiyoor on the southern bank of the Kaviri. The site of this capital is still known as Uraiyoor and is a suburb of the modern town of Trichinopoly. It was strongly fortified with a wall and ditch, and a jungle of thorny trees surrounding the ditch.[2] Here was an ancient shrine of the Nigranthas which contained an image of Argha, with a triple umbrella under the shade of an Asoka tree. A town of even greater importance than Uraiyoor was Kaviripaddinam, which stood at the mouth of the river Kaviri and was a great emporium of trade. We have a full description of this town in the poems Chilappathikaram and Paddinappalai.[3] It was also known as Pukâr or Kâkanthi. The latter name is said to have been given to Kavirippaddinam, because it was once ruled by a prince called Kakanthan. The name Kakandi occurs in the Bharaut Inscriptions, which were engraved in the first or second century B. C. One of the inscriptions records the gift of the nun Sorna from Kakandi."[4]

Kaviripaddinam (the Kamara of the Periplus and Khaberis of Ptolemy) or Pukâr was built on the northern bank of the

---

1 Chilappathikaram, xxiii. 75 and 118, 119. McCrindle states that Tangala is now represented by Dindigul an important and flourishing town lying at a distance of 32 miles north by west from Madura. McCrindle's Ptolemy, p. 184.

2 Chilappathikaram, x. 242, xi. 1 to 4 and Akam, 121.

3 Chilappathikaram, v., 7 to 63.

4 It is also mentioned in the Pattavali of the Kharataragachha. Indian Antiquary, vol. xi., p. 247 and vol. xxi., p. 285.

the Kaviri river, which was then a broad and deep stream into
which heavily laden ships entered from the sea without slacking
sail. The town was divided into two parts, one of which was
called Maruvur-Pâkkam and adjoined the sea coast, and the
other, which was situated to the west of it, was called Paddinap-
pâkkam. Between these two portions of the city was a large
area of open ground, planted with trees at regular intervals,
where the great market was held. The principal streets in Paddinap-pâkkam were the Royal Street, the Car Street and the
Bazaar Street. The merchants, Brahmins, farmers, doctors and
astrologers resided in separate streets. Surrounding the palace
were the houses of charioteers, horse and elephant riders and
soldiers who formed the body-guard of the king. Bards, minstrels and panegyrists, actors, musicians and buffoons, chank-
cutters and those skilled in making flower garlands and strings of
pearls, time-keepers whose duty it was to cry out the number of
each nâlikai or division of time, as it passed, and other servants of
the palace, also resided within the limits of Paddinap-pâkkam.
Near the beach in Maruvur-Pâkkam were raised platforms and
godowns and warehouses with windows shaped like the eyes of the
deer, where the goods landed from ships were stored.[1] Here
the goods were stamped with the tiger-stamp (the emblem of the
Chola kings) after payment of customs duty, and passed on to the
merchants' warehouses.[2] Close by were the settlements of the
Yavana merchants, where many attractive articles were always
exposed for sale. Here were also the quarters of foreign traders
who had come from beyond the seas, and who spoke various
tongues. Vendors of fragrant pastes and powders, of flowers and
incense, tailors who worked on silk, wool or cotton, traders in
sandal, aghil, coral, pearls, gold and precious stones, grain merchants, washermen, dealers in fish and salt, butchers, blacksmiths,
braziers, carpenters, coppersmiths, painters, sculptors, goldsmiths,
cobblers and toy-makers, had their habitation in Maruvur-
Pakkam.[3]

The palace of the Chola king in Kaviripaddinam is described
as a magnificent building. "Skilled artisans from Magadha,
mechanics from Marâdam, smiths from Avanti, carpenters from

---

[1] Chilapp-athikaram. [2] Paddinap-palal—ll. 134—136. [3] Chilapp-athikaram.

4

Yavana and the cleverest workmen in the Tamil land " had combined to make the building so grand and lovely that later generations believed it to be the work of no other than Mayan, the
architect of the gods. The throne hall was of dazzling splendour,
the walls being covered with plates of burnished gold. Its roof was
supported by pillars, the shafts of which were made of coral
and the capitals set with gems of brilliant colors. It was
elaborately carved and painted, and from the edges of the roof
hung strings of lustrous pearls.[1] Besides the throne hall, there
were various objects of interest in the palace, among which may
be mentioned, a beautiful canopy of pearls sent by the king of
Vajra, a hall of state furnished by the king of Magadha and an
ornamental gateway presented by the king of Avanti.[2] In the
park surrounding the palace were " wells worked by machinery,
artificial hills and waterfalls, flowery arbours, broad lakes and deep
tanks, labyrinths and shady alcoves with beds all built of crystal."[3]
The park was also well stocked with small game such as "short-
legged quails and long eared hares, leaping deer and mountain
goats."[4] There were splendid temples in the city dedicated to the
worship of the celestial tree Kalpaka, the celestial elephant Airâ-
vata, Vijrâyuta (the thunderbolt of Indra the king of the Gods),
Baladeva, Surya, Chandra, Siva, Subramanya, Sâthavâhana, Nigrantha, Kâma (god of love) and Yama (god of death). There were
seven Viharas reputed to have been built by Indra, the king of the
Gods, in which dwelt no less than 300 Buddhist monks. The temple
of Yama was outside the walls of the town, in the burial ground.[5]
Outside the town were also two lakes called Surya Kundam and
Chandra Kundam or "the lakes of the Sun and Moon" which were
held very sacred.[6] In the broad moat surrounding the fort " the
waters of which were covered with beautiful flowers, the chirping
of birds never ceased."[7] On the fort gates were painted the figure
of the tiger, which as stated already was the ensign of the
Cholas.[8]

All the articles prepared in Egypt for the markets of
Tamilakam, as well as all the produce of Tamilakam itself finally

[1] Chilapp-athikaram. Manimekhalai, xix. 107—109.   [2] Chilapp-athikaram.
[3] Manimekhalai, xix. 102—105.   [4] Ibid. xix. 96—97.   [5] Chilapp-athikaram.
[6] Paddinap-palai, l. 39.   [7] Manimekhalai, v. ll. 110—112.   [8] Paddinap-
palai, l. 40.

centred on the Chola coast. "Horses were brought from distant lands beyond the seas, pepper was brought in ships; gold and precious stones came from the northern mountains; sandal and aghil came from the mountains towards the west; pearls from the southern seas and coral from the eastern seas. The produce of the regions watered by the Ganges; all that is grown on the banks of the Kaviri; articles of food from Elam or Ceylon and the manufactures of Kalakam" (in Burmah) were brought to the markets of Kaviripaddinam.[1]

The Toringoi or Soretai who according to Ptolemy inhabited the country watered by the Kaviri were doubtless the Choliyar. Of the other towns mentioned by Ptolemy in this region "Orthoura the royal city of the Sornagos" is of course Uraiyoor or as it is more commonly written Uranthai, which I have alluded to above as the old capital of the Cholas; Karmara is either Kalumalam the ancient name of Shiyâli, the headquarters of a Taluq in the Tanjore District, or Kamalai the modern Tiruvaroor.[2]

North of Punal-Nadu was Aruvâ-Nadu and beyond the latter Aruvâyadathalai or North Aruva. The two provinces Aruva and North Aruva were together known as Mavilankai or the great Lanka. The country is said to have been so named because its natural products were similar to those of Lanka or Ceylon.[3] The capital of this province was Kachchi the modern Kanchipuram. It was fortified like all other chief towns in Tamilakam. There was a Buddhist Chaitya recently built by the Chola king.[4] A Vishnu temple is also mentioned.[5] The whole of this

---

[1] Ibid., ll. 185—191.

[2] Pinkalanthai and Thivakaram.

[3] Chiru-panarrup-padai, ll. 119—120. In Yule's map Melange is placed at Krishnapatam a little to the South of the North Pennar River, which he identifies with Ptolemy's Tyna. McCrindle's Ptolemy, p. 67. Cunningham who takes the Maisulos to be the Godavari, locates Malanga in the neighbourhood of Elur. Cunningham's Geog. of Anc. India, pp. 539-40.

[4] Manimekhalai, xxviii., ll. 175-176.

[5] Perum-panarrup-padai, l. 373. When Hiuen Tsiang visited Kanobipuram, five centuries later, the circumference of the town was about 30 lis or 5 miles. There were about one hundred monasteries, wherein resided nearly 10,000 Buddhist monks. There were also about 80 temples of gods, visited by monks who went about naked (nigranthas) Si-yu-ki. Book X.

country was inhabited by the Aruvalar, a nomadic tribe, who were also called Kurumbar. It was the Chola king Karikal the Great, of whom I shall speak fully later on, who first settled these wandering tribes and divided their country into twenty-four Koddams or districts and parcelled it out to families of the Vellâla tribe. The list of the twenty-four Koddams and seventy-nine Nadus is as follows :—[1]

Koddam.			*Nadu.*
Pulal ...	...	...	Nayaru, Akudi, Athoor, Elumur.
Puliyur	...	...	Kunnathur, Porur, Mankadu, Amarur, Koddur.
Eekkadu	...	...	Kakkalur, Kachi.
Manavur	...	...	Pashalai, Illathur, Konnur, Purichai, Perumur.
Chenkadu	...	...	Ponnalur, Athikaththur.
Payyur	...	...	Virpathi, Chevoor, Venkal.
Eyil ...	...	...	Thandakam, Makaral, Koneri.
Thamal	...	...	Karuveedu, Vakaraivallai.
Uttukkadu	...	...	Palayur, Thamalur, Kunnam, Neevaloor.
Kalathur	...	...	Kurumbara, Vallipuram, Pattur, Nadunadu.
Chembur	...	...	Peraiyur, Pattanam, Mukanthur.
Amur ...	...	...	Kumuli, Paluvur.
Eethoor	...	...	Aram-uranganadu.
Venkunram	...	...	Perunagar, Arasoor, Maruthadu, Nellur, Thellaru.
Palkunram	...	...	Pasur, Thachoor, Meyoor, Singamporuta-valanadu.
Ilankadu	...	...	Ponnoor, Thennathoor, Makunam.
Kaliyur	...	...	Kaliyur, Thiru-puli-vanam, Virpedu, Erikeelnadu, Pavoor.
Chirukarai	...	...	Ayntha-nadu.
Paduvur	...	...	Perunthimiri, Arkkadu, Chenkunram.
Kadikai	...	...	Perunkanchi, Paranchi, Melkalathur.

---

[1] I take this list from a document called the Thondai-mandala-paddayam. It gives the names of 24 Koddams and 77 Nadus, although in the same document it is said that the total number of Nadus was 79. The names of these Koddams and Nadus occur in the Chola inscriptions of the eleventh century A. D.

Chenthirukai	...	Polyur, Valakulam, Alathur, Arun-kulam.
Kunrapattiram	...	Mangalam, Venkalur, Ninnayam.
Venkadam ...	...	Kudakarai, Pottappi, Thondaiman.
Velur... ...	...	Olukarai, Nenmili, Mathur.

Many of the inland towns of the Aru-Varni mentioned by Ptolemy may be identified with the capitals of the Koddams above mentioned as shown below :

Karige[1]	...	...	Kadigai.
Poleur	...	...	Puliyur.
Pikendaka	...	...	Palkunram.
Iatour	...	...	Eethoor.
Ikarta	...	...	Eekkadu.
Kandipatna	...	...	Kunrapattiram.

Milanga the royal city of Basarnagos appears to have been no other than Kânchipuram the capital of Mâvilankai. Phrourion, another city of the Aruvarnoi, was most probably the same as Sopatma mentioned in the Periplus. Phrourion in Greek, signifies " a garrisoned fort." Sopatma is evidently Sopaddinam, which in Tamil means a fortified town. This was a sea-port and was commonly known to the Tamils as Eyil-paddinam,[2] which conveys the same meaning as Sopaddinam, *i.e.*, a fortified town. In these ports were high light-houses built of brick and mortar, which exhibited blazing lights, at night, to guide ships to the ports.[3] The northern limit of Tamilakam on the east coast was at Vêrkâdu now known as Palavêrkâdu (or Pulicat).[4] Beyond this was the country of the Vadukas who spoke a language called Vaduku. The king of Erumai-Nadu, or the modern Mysore, was also called the "chief of the Vadukas." It is evident therefore that in this early period, *the people north of Tirupaty and those who resided in Mysore spoke one and the same language Vaduku, and that Telugu and Canarese had not become separate dialects.* In

---

[1] McCriudle identified Karige with Kudapa, the chief town of the modern Cuddapah District. Pikendaka, he thought may have been Pennakonda in the Bellary District.

[2] Chira-pan-arrup-padai, ll. 152—153.

[3] Perum-pan-arrup-padai, ll. 346—350.

[4] Old stanza quoted by Nachchinark-iniyar in the commentary to Tholkappiyam, Porul-athikaram, Sutram 113. Nakkirar, Akam 252.

the interior below the ghats, Venkadam or the modern Tirupaty was the northern limit of the Tamil land. It is most remarkable that after the lapse of eighteen centuries, during which many a kingdom rose and fell, and the Tamils, Telugus, Mahrattas, Musalmans, French and English successively rose to political power, the language boundary has remained unaltered on the eastern coast. The same cannot be said of the boundary of the Tamil land on the western coast, for, it has advanced there from Badagara to Kasaragod, a distance of about sixty miles.

North-west of Punal-Nadu and west of Aruva-Nadu was Maladu or Malayaman Nadu. This was the territory of a chief known as Malayaman or the mountain chief. He was a feudatory of the Chola king. The capital of this province was Koval on the banks of the river Pennai.[1] This town is now called Thirukoilur and is situated in the Tirukoilur Taluk of the modern South Arcot District. Another large town in Maladu was Mullur or the thorntown.

West of Maladu was Seetha-Nadu or the cold region which evidently included the northern half of the modern Coimbatore District and the Southern portion of the Nilgiri District, where the climate is much cooler than in other parts of Tamilakam. Between Seetha-Nadu and Kuda-Nadu, which, as I have already described, extended along the Western coast was Kalkâ-Nadu or the "rocky province." This part of the country is remarkable for the rocks and hills with which it abounds. It included the North-western portion of the Travancore State, which is to this day known to the natives as Kakkanadu.

Of the sub-divisions of the several Nadus no complete record is available except for a portion of Mavilankai, which I have given above. Tamil poets allude, however, to Kundur Kûrram in the Chera kingdom, and Milalai Kûrram in that of the Chola, from which it will be seen that the Chera, Chola and Pandya dominions were also divided into kûrrams or districts.[2]

---

[1] Ammuvana, Aksm 35.

[2] Pura-nanuru, 24.

CHAPTER III.

FOREIGN TRADE.

From the earliest times, the products of Tamilakam appear to have attracted the merchants of distant lands. It was most probably from Tamilakam that, during the reign of Solomon (about B. C. 1000) "once in every three years, the ships of Tarshish came bringing gold and silver, ivory, apes and peacocks." The names of the last two objects *Kapim* and *Tukim* as found in the Hebrew Bible are the same as those still used in Tamil: *i.e.*, *Kavi* and *Thokai.* Subsequently the Arabs and Greeks appear to have kept up the trade with Tamilakam. The Greek names for rice (Oryza), ginger (Zingiber), and cinnamon (Karpion) are almost identical with their Tamil names, *Arisi, Inchiver* and *Karuva,* and clearly indicate that Greek merchants conveyed these articles and their names to Europe from the Tamil-land. The Egyptian Greeks under the Ptolemies carried on an extensive trade in Indian commodities and Alexandria became, at an early period, the chief emporium of this lucrative commerce. Ships of small size which cautiously sailed along the coast carried the merchandise to ports on the Red Sea, and thence it was taken by caravans, to the nearest point on the River Nile, and by boats down the river to Alexandria. "I found" says Strabo (19 A. D.) "that about one hundred and twenty ships sail from Myos-Hermos (a port on the Red Sea) to India." About this time, a Greek named Hippalos, acting on information received probably from Arab or Hindu merchants, boldly stood out to sea, from Cape Fartak in Arabia, and sailing with the south-west monsoon trade winds found a direct route to the pepper bearing country in Tamilakam. Thenceforward the trade with Tamilakam increased considerably. The Romans who conquered Egypt were not slow to take advantage of the profitable trade with Tamilakam.

Pliny describes as follows the navigation to India " as it had been recently discovered and was practised in his day."

" Afterwards it was found the safest course to proceed direct from the promontory of Syagrus in Arabia (Cape Fartak) to

Patale[1] with the west wind (Favonius) which they call there the Hippalos, a distance reckoned at 1,435 miles. In the next generation it was judged to be both a safer and nearer course to proceed from the same promontory direct to Sigerus, a port of India. And this mode of navigation was preserved for a long time, until merchants discovered a shorter route and the profits of India were thus brought nearer to hand. The voyage is now made every year with cohorts of archers on board the ships, on account of the pirates who infest those seas. It will be worth while to set forth their whole course from Egypt, accurate information concerning it being now for the first time available. The subject is one worthy of attention, there being no year in which India does not drain our Empire of at least 55,000,000 sesterces (£486,979) sending us in return wares which are sold for a hundred times their original value."

"They begin the navigation in the middle of summer before the rising of the Dog-star or immediately after its appearance, and arrive in about thirty days at Ocelis[2] in Arabia, or Cane[3] in the frankincense-bearing region. There is also a third port called Muza[4] which is frequented not by those sailing to India, but by the merchants, who trade in frankincense and other Arabian perfumes. In the interior is a city, the capital of the kingdom called Sapphar[5] and another called Sane. But for those whose course is directed to India it is most advantageous to start from Ocelis. From thence they sail with the wind called Hippalos in forty days to the first commercial station of India named Muziris, which is not much to be recommended on account of the neighbouring pirates who occupy a place called Nitrias: nor does it furnish any abundance of merchandise. Moreover the station of shipping is far from the land and cargoes have to be loaded and unloaded in barges. The ruler of the country at the time of which I

---

[1] Patala, at the head of the delta of the Indus, McCrindle's Ptolemy, p. 146.

[2] The modern Ghalla or Cella. McCrindle's Periplus, p. 84.

[3] It has been identified with the port now called Hisn Ghorab. McCrindle's Periplus, p. 87.

[4] This port, once the most celebrated and most frequented in Yemen is now the village Musa about 25 miles north from Mokha. McCrindle's Periplus, p. 78.

[5] The metropolis of the Arabs of Yemen. It is now Dhafar or Dauffer or Zaphar. McCrindle's Periplus, p. 80.

speak was Coelobothras. There is another more advantageous port which is named Barace in the territory of a nation called the Neacyndi. The king of that country was named Pandion, who resided far from the port in a city of the interior which is called Madura. But the region from which pepper is brought to Barace in barges hewn out of single trees is called Cottonara (Kuddanádu). None of these names of nations or ports or cities are found in any former writer, from which it is evident what changes take place in the state of things in these countries. They commence the return voyage from India at the beginning of the Egyptian month of Tybis, which answers to our December, or at all events within the sixth day of the Egyptian month Mechir, that is, within our Ides of January. Thus it comes to pass they return home within the year. They make the return voyage from India with the south-east wind (Vulturnus) and when they have entered the Red Sea, with the south-west or south wind." [1]

The author of the Periplus commences his account of the commerce and navigation of the Erythraean Sea with a description of the roadsteads on the Red Sea and of their exports and imports. Then he describes the seaports of the African Coast and on the Arabian and Persian Coasts. Passing the mouth of the Indus, he mentions the gulfs of Barake (Kach) and of Barugaza (Cambay) then Barugaza (Broach) near the mouth of the Nammadios (Nerbada). South of Barugaza the country is called Dakhinabades (Dakshinapatha). Among the local marts in this region is Kalliena, (the modern Kalyana near Bombay). After Kalliena, he mentions seven seaports, then the islands called Sesekreienai and the island of the Aigidioi and that of the Kaineitai, near what is called the Khersonesos, places in which are pirates, and after this the island of Leuke (or "the white"). Then he proceeds as follows :—

"Below the White Island (Thoovak-kal) commences the kingdom of Keprobotas (Cheraputra) styled Limurike (Tamilakam) the first mart of which is Naoora, then Tundis (Thondi) a large village close to the shore ; and next to these, Mooziris (Muchiri) a flourishing place frequented both by the native vessels

[1] Malabar Manual. Vol I., pp. 250-251. E. H. Bunbury's History of Ancient Geography, Vol. II., pp. 418-419. Pliny's Natural History, vi., 23.

from Åriake (Aryakam) and by the Greeks from Egypt. It lies
upon a river, but at a distance of 20 stadia:[1] and five hundred
from Tundis (Thondi) the intermediate space is equal whether you
measure by land from river to river or take the passage by sea.
(Naoora, Tundis and Mooziris) are succeeded by Nelkunda which
is in another province under the Government of Pandion. This
mart is again five hundred stadia from Mooziris by measurement
between the two rivers or by the road on shore or by the course of
the vessel along the coast.

" Nelkunda (Nirkunram) lies on a river at the distance of a
hundred and twenty stadia from the sea : but at the mouth of the
river there is a village called Bakare (Vaikkarai near Kottayam) and
here the vessels which come down from Nelkunda lie in an open
road to receive their cargoes, for the river is full of shoals or mud
banks and the channel between them is not deep. Both Nelkunda
and Bakare are subject to a king who resides in the interior.

" There is a great resort of shipping to this port for pepper
and betel : the merchants bring out a large quantity of spice
and their other imports are topazes, a small assortment of plain
cloth, stibium, coral, flint, glass, brass and lead, a small quantity of
wine as profitable as at Barugaza, cinnabar, fine cloth, arsenic and
wheat, not for sale but for the use of the crew.

" The principal article obtained here is pepper, which is the
staple of the country as growing in the interior ; it is brought
down to this port in preference to all others, and is of that species
called Cottonarikon (Kuddanâdan) ; great quantities of the best
pearl are likewise purchased here, ivory, silk in the web, spike-
nard from the Ganges, betel from the countries further to the east,
transparent stones of all sorts, diamonds, rubies and tortoise shell
from the golden Chersonese or from the islands off the coast of
Limurike.

" The best season for the voyage is to leave Egypt in the
month of July or Epiphi : and the voyage was originally performed in small vessels from Kane and Endaimon in Arabia which
followed the coast during the whole passage. But Hippalos was
the first navigator who discovered the direct course across the

---

[1] The Olympic stadium which was in general use throughout Greece
contained 600 Greek feet, which were equal to 625 Roman feet or 606¾ English
feet. An English mile is equal to about 8¾ stadia. McCrindle's Ptolemy, p. 4.

ocean by observing the position of the ports and the general appearance of the sea. For at the season when the annual winds peculiar to our climate settle in the north and blow, for a continuance upon our coast from the Mediterranean, in the Indian Ocean the wind is continually from the south-west. And this wind has in these seas obtained the name of Hippalos from the pilot who first took advantage of it to make his passage to the east.

"From the period of that discovery to the present time vessels bound to India take their departure either from Kane on the Arabian or Cape Aromata on the African side; and from these points they stretch out into the open sea at once, leaving all the windings of the gulfs and bays at a distance and make for their several destinations in the coast of India; those that are intended for Limurike waiting sometime before they sail, but those that are destined for Barugaza or Skythia seldom more than three days.

"Upon leaving Ela-bakara or the Ruddy mountain the country which succeeds is under the government of Pandion: it is called Paralia (Purali) and lies almost directly north and south; it reaches to Kolkhoi (Korkai) in the vicinity of the pearl-fishery and Pandion is sovereign of the whole.

"But the first port after leaving the Ruddy mountain is Balita and next to that is Komar (Kumari) which has a fort and a harbour. This place is frequented for the purpose of ablution by those who have dedicated themselves to a religious life and taken a vow of celibacy. Women as well as men are admitted into this institution; and the legend respecting it reports that a goddess in some former period practised the same ablutions once a month at the spot.

"From Komar the district extends to Kolkhi and the pearl fishery which is conducted by slaves or criminals condemned to the service; and the whole southern point of the Continent is part of Pandyan's dominion.

"The first place that succeeds after leaving Kolkhi is the bay Argalus connected with a district inland (of the same name). Here and here only the pearls obtained in the fishery at the island of Epidorus are (allowed to be) perforated and prepared for the market, and from the same island are procured the fine muslins sprinkled with pearls.

"Proceeding from Argalus the most conspicuous of all the marts and anchorages on the coast are Kamara, Padooka and Sopatma. To these the traders from Limurike and the other provinces north of Limurike resort; and in the marts are found the native vessels which make coasting voyages to Limurike, the Monoxala of the largest sort called Sangara, and others styled Colandiophonta, which are vessels of great bulk adapted to the voyages made to the Ganges and the Golden Chersonese.

"To these marts are brought all the articles prepared (in Egypt) for the market of Limurike: and almost all the species of which Egypt is continually drained by its trade with Limurike finally centres on this coast, as well as all the produce of Limurike itself.

"But after passing Limurike and the provinces next in succession the coast winds round to the east ; and as the vessel takes this direction in her course, the island now called Palaisimoondus, but formerly Taprobane, lies out in the open sea to the west. The northern part of the island is civilized, but the passage to it from the Continent is seldom performed in less than twenty days. The whole extent is so large that it reaches almost to the opposite coast of Azainia (in Africa) ; and here pearls, precious stones, fine muslins and tortoise shells are to be obtained.

"But (returning now to the coast above Kamara, Padooka and Sopatma) lies Masalia, a district which extends far inland. In this country a great quantity of the finest muslins are manufactured; and from Masalia the coast lies eastward across a bay to Desarene, where the ivory is procured of that species called Bosarc." [1]

The western merchants who visited the Tamil land, were known as Yavanas. The word Yavana is derived from the Greek *Iaones*, which is the name of the Greek nation in their own language. In the old Sanscrit epic poetry, the word Yavana is invariably used to denote the Greeks.[2] Similarly in ancient Tamil poems also the name Yavana appears to have been applied exclusively to the Greeks and Romans. The Poet Nakkirar

[1] The Periplus of the Erythræan Sea and Voyage of Nearchus, translated by William Vincent, D.D., p. 105 ff.
[2] Weber's History of Indian Literature, p. 220.

addresses the Pandyan Prince Nan-maran in the following words:
" O Mara, whose sword is ever victorious! Spend thou thy days in
peace and joy, drinking daily out of golden cups, presented by thy
handmaids, the cool and fragrant wine brought by the Yavanas in·
their góod ships."[1]   The Yavanas alluded to by these poets
were undoubtedly the Egyptian Greeks, because as stated in the
Periplus, it was Greek merchants from Egypt who brought wine,
brass, lead, glass, etc., for sale to Muchiri (Muziris) and Vaikkarai
(Bakare) and who purchased from these ports pepper, betel, ivory,
pearls and fine muslins.   The Greeks sailed from Egypt in the
month of July and arrived at Muchiri in about forty days.   They
stayed on the Malabar coast for about three months and commenced their return voyage from Muchiri in December or January.
During their sojourn in Malabar, they would have naturally
imparted much of their civilization to the Tamils.   As the Indian`
seas were infested by pirates, the Greek merchants brought with
them cohorts of archers on board their ships.   Egypt being at
this period subject to Rome, the archers who accompanied the
Greek merchants must have been Roman soldiers.   The superior
arms and discipline of the Roman soldiers could not have failed to
inspire in the Tamils a desire to become better acquainted with
the Romans and to share their civilization.   The Pandyan King
was the first to realise the benefits of an alliance with the Romans.
He sent two embassies to Augustus Cæsar, desiring to become his·
friend and ally.   One of these reached Augustus when he was at
Terracona in the cighteenth year after the death of Julius Cæsar
(B. C. 26) and another six years afterwards (B. C. 20) when that
Prince was at Samos.   Roman soldiers were enlisted in the service of the Pandyas and other Tamil Kings.   During the reign of
the Pandya Aryap-padai-kadantha-Nedunj-cheliyan, Roman sol·
diers were employed to guard the gates of the fort of Madura.[2]
A poet of this period describes a Tamil King's tent on a battle
field as follows:—" In a tent with double walls of canvas firmly

---

[1] Puram, 56. The old commentator of the Puranáнúrа interprets the
words *Yavanar nan kalam thantha* to mean " brought by Yavanas in bottles." The
Hon. P. Coomara Swamy of Colombo, has pointed out that the word *kalam* may
mean bottles or ships. Journal of the Royal Asiatic Society, Ceylon Branch, Vol.
XIII, No. 45.

[2] Chilapp-athikaram, XIV. 11. 66-67.

held by iron chains, guarded by powerful Yavanas whose stern looks strike terror into every beholder, and whose long and loose coats are fastened at the waist by means of belts; while dumb Mlêchas clad in complete armour, who could express themselves only by gestures, kept close watch throughout the night in the outer chamber, constantly moving round the inner apartment which was lighted by a handsome lamp."[1] It is evident from this description that Yavana and other Mlêchas or foreigners, were employed as bodyguards by ancient Tamil Kings. Yavana vases and Yavana lamps with the figure of a swan on the top of each,[2] or lamps in the shape of a female statue in a standing posture, holding with both hands the receptacle for oil and wick, appear to have been in common use in the Tamil country.[3] There was a colony of Yavana merchants at Kavirip-paddinam which was the great emporium of trade on the Eastern Coast.[4] The Roman trade with the Tamil land and other parts of India was carried on, on such a large scale that, as stated by Pliny, there was no year in which India did not drain the Roman Empire of at least fifty-five millions of sesterces (£986,979) sending in return wares which were sold for a hundred times their original value.[5] That Roman gold poured largely into the Tamil country at this period, is attested by the numerous Roman coins; dating from the reign of Augustus to that of Zeno (B. C. 27 to A. D. 491) which have been found buried in different parts of the Tamil land. According to the Peutingerian Tables, which are believed to have been constructed about 226 A. D.; the Romans even at that date are said to have had a force of two cohòrts (840 to 1,200 men) at Muchiri to protect their trade, and they had also erected a temple to Augustus at the same place.[6]

Of the trade with eastern nations no detailed accounts are available ; but there are many allusions in ancient Tamil poems to voyages undertaken by merchants and others to Nâgapuram in Châvakam (Sumatra or Java), Kâlakam in Burma and seaports in Ceylon and Bengal.

[1] Mullaip-pâddu, 11. 59-66.   [2] Perum-pânârrup-padai, 11. 316-317.
[3] Nedu-nal-vâdai, 1. 101.   [4] Chilapp-athikaram, V. 1. 10.   [5] Ante : p. 32.
[6] Malabar Manual, Vol. I., p. 199.

CHAPTER IV.

TAMIL RACES AND TRIBES.

The oldest of the tribes who dwelt in Tamilakam were the Villavar and Mínavar. The Villavar or bowmen (from the Dravidian word *vil* meaning a bow) inhabited hilly tracts and jungles, and lived by the chase: and the Mínavar or fishermen (from the Dravidian *meen*, a fish) subsisted by fishing and resided in the valleys and plains, or on the sea-coast. The two tribes were evidently a primitive race which was spread over the whole of India, as they are still found in large numbers in Rajputana and Guzarat, where they are known as Bhils and Meenas, and in the Canarese country, where they are called Billavar.

These semi-barbarous tribes were conquered by the Nagas, who were a very numerous and civilised race, and who at one time or other ruled a great portion of India, Ceylon and Burma. They are mentioned in the Ramayana, and the Naga capital, which probably lay in the heart of the Dekkan is described in that epic as follows :—

> Near Bhogavati stands the place
> Where dwell the hosts of the serpent race,
> A broad-wayed city walled and barred
> Which watchful legions keep and guard.
> The fiercest of the serpent youth
> Each awful for his venomed tooth ;
> And throned in his imperial hall
> Is Vasuki who rules them all.
> Explore the serpent city well,
> Search town and tower and citadel,
> Scan each field and wood that lies
> Around it with your watchful eyes.[1]

From the Mahabharata we learn that there were Naga kingdoms between the Jumna and the Ganges about the 13th century B. C. When the kings of the Lunar race of Aryas wanted to found a second capital near the spot where Delhi stands at present, they had to dislodge the Nagas who occupied it. Arjuna, the

---

[1] Griffith's Ramayana IV. 205.
Indian Antiquary Vol. VIII. p. 5.

hero of the poem, in his banishment, is said to have married first
Ulipi, the daughter of a Naga king, then Chitrangadai, daughter of
Chitravahana, the Naga king of Manipura. Parikshit, the grandson of Arjuna was killed by Thakshaka, a Naga king, and hence
Janamejaya, the son of Parikshit had to wage a long and bloody
war with the Nagas and killed thousands of them. They appear
again in history in the 6th century B. C. when a Naga dynasty
ruled Magadha ; and it was during the reign of Ajatasatru, the
6th king of this race, that Gautama Buddha preached his new faith
which soon found favour with the Nagas.[1] The Ceylonese
historical works all begin with an account of the Nagas. It appears from these works that in the 6th century B. C. there were
powerful Naga kingdoms on the western coast of the island which
was called Nagadwipa or Naga island on that account. The Naga
capital was at Kalyani. The niece of the king of Kalyani was
married to a Naga king of the Kanawaddamano mountain, which
was evidently Kandamadanam, a hill near the modern Ramesvaram
on the Indian coast, opposite to Kalyani. In the ancient sculptures at Amaravati and elsewhere which were executed more than
eighteen hundred years ago, the human figures, which are represented with serpent hoods spread wide at the back of them, are
Nagas.[*] Some fragments of the sculptures which were removed from the ruins at Amaravati may now be seen at the
Government Museum, Madras. In these sculptures the Naga
kings are distinguished by the hood of a five or seven-headed serpent at their back, Naga princesses by a three-headed serpent, and
ordinary Nagas by a single-headed serpent. The artists who executed these sculptures with considerable labour and care seem to
have imagined that the Nagas partook of the nature of serpents,
and that their bodies were partly human and partly serpentine.
The ancient Tamil poets appear to have shared this belief, for, they
speak of the Nagas who were contemporary with them, as human
beings, while at the same time they describe the ancient Nagas
as serpents living underground. In describing the antiquity and
wealth of Kaviripaddinam, the Chola capital, the author of the
Chilappathikaram states that it was as ancient and famous as the

[1] Fergusson's Tree and Serpent Worship, p. 60.
[*] Archæological Survey of Southern India, Vol. I. The Buddhist stupas of
Amaravati and Jaggayapeta.

Metropolis of the Nagas and the Naga-nadu.[1] It appears therefore that within the recollection of the Tamil people who lived
eighteen hundred years ago, there was no kingdom older than that
of the Nagas. Kaviripaddinam itself is said to have been an
ancient seat of the Nagas who had " curved red lips, large bright
teeth, a voice like thunder, who delighted in doing mischief and
were always armed with the noose."[2] Another poet describes
the contest of two Naga kings for the sacred-seat of Buddha as
follows :—" In the nether regions, two kings who ruled the Naga
country contended for the seat, but neither was able to lift it off the
ground ; loath to give it up, with eyes all aflame and breathing
fury, they led their great armies and fought a bloody battle. The
great teacher (Buddha) then appeared before them and said ' cease
your strife, this seat is mine'; then he sat upon it and preached the
law."[3] The same poet states that the island of Manippallavam
where the sacred seat was placed, was situated at a distance of 30
yojanas south of Kaviripaddinam.[4] He refers also to a town in
Gandhara in Northern India, which in consequence of an earthquake " sank a distance of 400 yojanas to Naga-nadu."[5] From
these allusions it is evident that the Tamil poets of this period had
a very hazy idea of the ancient Nagas and their country. They
believed, in fact, that the Nagas inhabited Pâthâla or the lower
world, far below the surface of the earth. Of contemporary Naga
tribes and kingdoms they give a more satisfactory account. The
first meeting of the Chola king Killi-Valavan and a Naga princess
is thus described :—[6] ." One pleasant summer day when Killi
who wears the long crown studded with sparkling gems, sought the
shade of a green wood, he found a lovely damsel all alone in a bower
which was fragrant with sweet-scented flowers. Wondering who

---

[1] Chilappadikaram. i. 19 & 20   Arumpatha-urai-uchiriyar, and Adiyarkku-
Nallar the two commentators to the Chilappathikaram, who were evidently not
aware that there were kingdoms ruled by Nagas at this early period, interpret the
expressions Naga-nagar and Naga-nad, in the text, to mean Swarga and Pathala or
the world of the gods, and the world of the serpents!

[2] Mani-mekalai. i. 21—23.

[3] Mani-mekalai— VIII. 54 to 61.

[4] Ibid—VI. 211—213.

[5] Ibid—IX. 12—22.

[6] Mani-mekalai—XXIV. 30—61.

she was, the monarch stood a while entranced, and the God of Love armed with the conquering bow, swiftly shot his flowery darts deep into the king's heart. His eyes were charmed with her beauty : with ravished ears, he heard her musical voice : the perfumes of her person confounded his senses, and he who had commanded legions, now became her devoted slave. Full one month he spent with her in that grove in rapturous enjoyment· She told not who she was, nor whence she came, but at the end of that month, she disappeared as suddenly as she had met him at first. Yearning to meet her again, he who had smote many a rival king, now went in search of her, smitten by her matchless charms. He met a saint who could penetrate the caverns of the earth, or soar into the aërial regions, or dive into the deep ocean ; and having made the usual reverence, prayed to the saint to find out the hiding place of her who was dear to him as his own life. ' I know the princess' said the saint ' though I have not seen her myself, I have heard of her, listen thou O l monarch. There is a king, whose lance is ever victorious in war, and who rules Naganadu. His name is Valai-vanan and his wife is Vâsa-Mailai : their beloved daughter is the beauteous princess Peeli-Valai. At her birth a seer had foretold that a prince of the solar race would espouse her. Her son will come to you, but thou shalt meet her no more." That the Chola king Killi-Valavan married, though for a time only, the daughter of a neighbouring Naga king appears to be a historical fact. But Cheethalai-Chaththanar, the author of the poem Mani-mekalai, who was a contemporary of Killi-Valavan has, with a poet's license, given a romantic account of the marriage, probably because he considered it degrading to a Tamil king to marry a Naga princess.

There were several tribes of the Nagas, such as the Maravar, Eyinar, Oliyar, Oviyar, Aruvâlur and Parathavar. Of these, the Maravar appear to have been the most powerful and warlike tribe, and most hostile to the Tamils. " Of strong limbs and hardy frames " says a poet " and fierce looking as tigers, wearing long and curled locks of hair, the blood thirsty Maravar, armed with the bow bound with leather, ever ready to injure others, shoot their arrows at poor and helpless travellers, from whom they can rob nothing, only to feast their eyes on the quivering limbs of their victims."[1] They were so numerous especially on the East Coast, between the Kaviri and Vaigai rivers, where they are still to be found in large numbers, that they successfully resisted the armies of the Tamil Kings. "The wrathful and furious Maravar" says the Poet quoted above "whose curled beards resemble the twisted horns of the stag, the loud twang of whose powerful bowstrings, and the stirring sound of whose double headed drums, compel even Kings at the head of large armies to turn their back and fly."[2] Their prowess in battle was so much valued by the Tamil Kings that they were enlisted largely in the Tamil armies. A Marava chieftain named Nalai-kilavan Nagan served the Pandya as a Minister and Commander in his army.[3] Another Marava, Piddank-korran, chieftain of a mountain called Kuthirai-mali, was in the service of the Chera King.[4]

The Eyinar or Vedar were the most lawless of the Naga tribes. Cattle lifting and pillage and murder appear to have been the sole business of their life. They worshipped the dread goddess Kâli, and slaughtered buffaloes at her shrine, to secure her favor in their plundering raids.[5] Before starting on their expeditions they usually consulted omens in the chirping and flight of birds.[6] Their descendants are now known by the appropriate title of kallar or "thieves." Dhirataran Murti-Eyinar the great chief of Viramangalam referred to in the plates of Jatila-varman, a Pandyan King of the twelfth century A.D. appears to have belonged to this tribe.[7]

The Oliyar were another tribe of the Nagas who, it is said, were conquered by Karikâl-Chola.[8] We find them in power as late as the eleventh century A.D. from an inscription at Mâmallai-puram.[9] This inscription is dated in the 9th year of the reign of the Chola King Koppara-Kêsari-Varmman alias Udiayâr-Srî-Râjendna Dêva who defeated Ahawa-Malla, the western Chalukya King (1040—1069 A.D.) at the battle of Koppa. It is the copy of a deed by which a piece of land was granted to the Varâha-Swâmi

---

[1] Kalith-thokai, IV—1 to 5. [2] Ibid, XV—1 to 7. [3] Vada-nedun-tha. thbhanar-Puram Stanza 179. [4] Karuvur Kanthap-pillai Chaththanar-Puram St. 168. [5] Chilapp-athikaram—XII. [6] Ibid, XII—120 to 128. [7] Indian Antiquary Vol. XXII, p. 57. [8] Paddinap-palai—line 274. [9] Madras Journal of Literature and Science, Vol. XIII, part II, article IV.

temple at Mâmallai-pûram, and which was signed by the following Nagas, amongst other high officers of the Chola-King:—

> Olinagan Madaiyan Alagiya Chola
> Amurnaddu Muvendâ Velan
> Olinagan Chandra Sekaran
> Olinagan Narayanan
> Indupuravan Sanga-Nagan
> Uchan-Kilavan Muguli Nagan.

It appears from this deed that there were, besides the Olinagas, other tribes of the same race, such as Sanga Nagas and Muguli Nagas, in the eleventh century A. D.

Aruvalar was a local name of the Naga tribes who inhabited Aruva-Nadu and Aruva-Vadatbalai. The Oviyar were a family of the Aruvalar tribe who ruled at Eyil-Paddinam, and were Kings of Mâvilankai about the middle of the second century A. D. when there was a temporary decline of the power of the Cholas and of other Tamil Kings. They are described by a Tamil poet as "Chivalrous and intrepid warriors, fierce as tigers on the battle field."[1] The Oviyar were most probably the Basore Nagas alluded to by Ptolemy as Kings of Melangae.[2] It appears from Ptolemy that at Uraiyur, the Chola capital also, the Cholas were displaced by the Sôre Nagas who were evidently the descendants of Chola and Naga families who had intermarried.[3] About this period the Nagas appear to have risen to power even in Ceylon, judging from the names of the following Kings of the country as given in the Mahâwanso[4]:—

		A. D.
Mahalamana or Mallaga Naga...	...	125
Kuhana or Chanda Naga	...	173
Kudanama or Kuda Naga	...	183
Kuda Sirina or Sri Naga	...	184

The Parathavar were a Naga tribe who occupied the sea coast and maintained themselves by fishing or by sea faring. They dived for pearls or for conch shells, and knew the charm to keep off sharks from that part of the sea, where they dived. They were most powerful in the country around Korkai in Then-pandi-

---

[1] Chiru-pânârrup-padai. ll. 121-122.   [2] McCrindles' Ptolemy, p. 185.
[3] Ibid, p. 184.   [4] Mahawanso, List of Kings.

nad; "well fed on fish and flesh and armed with bows, their hordes terrified their enemies by their dashing valour."[1]

The Nagas, were skilled in many arts and especially in weaving. The Nagas of the Kalinga country were so famous in the art of weaving that the word kalingam in Tamil has come to signify a cloth. At the period which I describe, the Nagas inhabiting the Eastern Coast in the Pandyan territory were great weavers, and exported a large quantity of cloths and muslins. The fine muslins manufactured by the Nagas were highly prized by the Tamils and fetched fabulous prices in foreign countries.[2] Tamil poets allude to a famous chieftain Ay who offered to t h image of Siva, one of these priceless muslins which had been presented to him by Nila-Naga.[3]

It was from the Nagas that the Aryas first learnt the art of writing; and hence Sanscrit characters are to this day known as Deva-nâgari.

While the fair skinned Aryas who had entered India through the Kabul valley, were settled in the Punjab, a horde of the yellow races who inhabited the central table land of Asia, appear to have passed southward through the numerous passes between Thibet and Nepal, and occupied the Gangetic Valley. Sanscrit writers name these yellow races *Yakshas*: Pali chroniclers called them *Yakkos*: and Chinese historians speak of them as the *Yuh-chi*. These yellow races being natives of the higher regions of the earth, considered themselves to be superior to the inhabitants of the plains, and assumed the name of *Daivaputras* or "the sons of Gods." They were intellectually and morally a superior race of people, and eventually spread over the whole of Bengal, and emigrated thence by sea to Southern India and Ceylon.

When the Ramayana was composed the Yekshas had reached the southernmost parts of India, and they are alluded to in that poem as inhabiting the sea-coast facing Ceylon.

---

[1] Mathuraik-kanchi, ll. 140 to 144.

[2] "To Kolkhoi succeeds another coast lying along a gulf having a district in the interior bearing the name of Argalon. In this single place are obtained the pearls collected near the island of Epiodôras. From it are exported the muslins called *ebargareitides*."

McCrindles, Periplus Maris Erythraei, p. 140.

[3] Chiru-panarrup-padai, ll. 96—99.

" Then will you see Kaveris' stream
Whose pleasant waters glance and gleam
And to the lovely banks entice
The sportive *maids of paradise.*
      *   *   *

Thence hasting on your way behold
The Pandyas gates of pearl and gold,
Then with your task maturely planned
On ocean's shore your feet will stand.
Where, by Agastya's high decree
Mahendra, planted in the sea
With tinted peaks against the tide
Rises in solitary pride,
And glorious in his golden glow
Spurns back the waves that beat below,
Fair mountain, bright with creeper's bloom
And every tint that trees assume
Where *yaksha*, god and *heavenly maid*
Meet wandering in the lovely shade."[1]

In the fifth century B. C., when Vijaya the leader of the first colony of Aryas, from Bengal, landed in Ceylon, he found the island in the possession of the Yakshas, and he first married Kuveni, a Yaksha Princess.

Most of these Mongolian tribes emigrated to Southern India from Tamalitti,[2] the great emporium of trade at the mouth of the Ganges, and this accounts for the name " Tamils " by which they were collectively known among the more ancient inhabitants of the Dekkan. The name Tamil appears to be therefore only an abbreviation of the word Tamalittis. The Tamraliptas are alluded to, along with the Kosalas and Odras, as inhabitants of Bengal and the adjoining Sea-coast in the Vayu and Vishnu Puranas.[3]

The oldest of the Mongolian tribes who invaded Southern India and conquered the Nagas appears to have been the Mârar, and the chief of this tribe was ever afterwards known as Palayan or " the ancient," being the most ancient, of the Tamil settlers in

---

[1]. Valmiki's Ramayana, translated by Griffiths. Book IV. Chap XLI.
[2] The Pali form of the Sanskrit Tamralipti. It is now known as Tamluk, and lies on a bay of the Rupnarayan River 12 miles above its junction with the Hughli mouth of the Ganges. McCrindle's Ptolemy: 170.
[3] Vishnu Purana. Book IV. Chap XXIV.

he Southern part of India.[1] The capital of Palayan Máran vas Mohoor, the exact site of which I am unable to ascertain: It vas somewhere close to the Pothiya Hill near Cape Comorin.[2] The Pandyan King claimed to be a Maran and "Minavar Kon" or the King of the Minavar. The name Máran appears to be dentical with the name Mránmar, borne by the tribe which conquered Burmah before the first century A. D. In the accounts of Burmah written in Pali, the country is known as Maramma-desa.[3]

The next tribe of Tamil invaders was the Thirayer or "Sea Kings." They were a great seafaring race, whose home appears to have been Lower Bengal and who travelled by sea to Burmah, Cochin China, Ceylon and Southern India. A King of this tribe named Thirayan who reigned at Kanchi, the modern Kanchi-puram, contemporary with Karikal-Chola, claimed to be a descendant of the god Vishnu, whose bed is on the ocean, according to Hindu Mythology.[4] It was on this account perhaps that the Chola Kings who belonged to this tribe, boasted of being descendants of the solar race. The oldest of the Chola Kings mentioned in the Tamil poems of the first century A. D. is Muchukunta. He is said to have saved Amaravati, the capital of Indra, when it was besieged by the Asuras, and that in gratitude for the service, Indra sent five giants who killed the Nagas of Kaviri-paddinam and enabled the Chola King to take possession of that town.[5]

---

[1] Mathuraik-kanchi, l. 509.

[2] Mamulanar-Akam, stanza 250.

[3] " Sir Arthur Phayre derives Mranma from Brahma (see page 2 of his *History of Burma*). The exact derivation and meaning of the designation by which the Burmans are known have not yet been settled. The term Mranma is not met with in Burmese history till the first Century A. D. In *Marco Polos'* travels, Burma is referred to as the Kingdom of Mien. The Burmans are known among the Chinese as the Mien, and among the Shans as the Man, the same appellation by which the Mongols are known among the Chinese. In the accounts of Burma written in Pali, the country is known as Marammadèsa. If Sir Arthur Phayre's derivation is correct, it is difficult to justify the action of the learned priests of the 14th and 15th Centuries, in making use of the barbarous appellation Maramma in lithic inscriptions as well as in literary works, while they had the familiar term Brahma for their national designation." Taw Sein Ko, in the Indian Antiquary, Vol. XXII., p. 8.

[4] Perum-panarrup-padai, ll. 29—37.

[5] Chilapp-athikáram, V. ll. 95 to 97 and VI. ll. 14 to 17, Mani-mekalai, I. ll. 19 to 24.

The Tamil conquerors named the town Champâ-pati, most probaby after Champânagar, an ancient capital of Bengal (the site of which is near the modern town of Bhagalpur) from which they had emigrated.

There seems to be no doubt that Muchukunta was the first Chola King who conquered the Nagas. The name of the Thirai-yar in Sanskrit was Sâgarakula. The ancient Kings of Thondai-nad belonged to the Sagarakula, but the later Pallavas styled themselves Bhâradvajas.[1] Families of the Thirayar tribe who lived in Thondai-Mandalam (the modern Chingleput and North Arcot Districts) were known by the following names, as late as the sixteenth century A. D. [2]:—

Pangala Thirayar—Thirayar of Bengal.

China Thirayar—Thirayar of China, this was most probably Cochin China.

Kadara Thirayar—Thirayar of Kadaram, that is, Burmah.

Singala Thirayar—Thirayar of Ceylon.

Pallava Thirayar—Thirayar of Pallavam.

Another tribe of the Tamils was the Vanavar or " Celestials. They were evidently natives of a mountainous region in the North of Bengal, and when they settled in Southern India, they chose for their residence hilly tracts, such as the Kolli-hills (in the Salem District) the Western Ghats, and the Nilgiris. The Chera Kings belonged to this tribe and called themselves Vanavar or Celestials. They claimed affinity with the Vanavar inhabiting the Himalayas,[3] and expressive of their origin they adopted the titles of Vanavarmman or Imaya-Varmman.[4] Besides the Chera Kings, other mountain chiefs such as Nannan, lord of Muthiram [5] and Alumbil-Vel [6] called themselves Vana-

---

[1] Epigraphia Indica, part I., p 2.

[2] Thondai-mandala-paddayam.

[3] Chilapp-athikâram XXV. ll. 1 to 2.

[4] Pathirrup-paththu : Stanzas 11 to 20 are in praise of Nedun-cheralathan alias Imaya-varmman, I. Stanzas 31 to 40 are addressed to Kalankaikkanni-Nar-Mudich-Cheral alias Vana-varmman I. Stanzas 48 to 50 refer to Chenk-kudduvan Imaya varmman II. Stanzas 51 to 60 allude to Nadu-Kôdpadu-Chêral-âthan alias Vana-varmman II.

[5] Malai-padu-kadâm, l. 164. The Commentator Nachchinârk-iniyar misreads the expression Vana-viral-vêl as Mana-viral-vêl.

[6] Mathuraik-kanchi, ll. 344-345.

Viral-Vel or Chiefs of the Vanavas. One of the Chera Kings called Chenkudduvan, who was contemporary with Gajabahu of Ceylon (113 to 105 A. D.) is said to have been on intimate terms of friendship with the Karnas, Emperors of Magadha, and with their assistance he attacked the Aryas near the Himalayas.[1] The Karnas, who belonged to the great Andhra tribe ruled Magadha during the first and second centuries of the Christian era. They were lords of the Three Kalingas, and their dominion extended from the modern Telugu country on the one side, to Arakan on the other side of the Bay of Bengal.[2]

Mr. Fergusson, the great writer on Architecture, having observed the striking similarity of the style of Architecture prevailing in South Canara and Malabar to that of Nepal, wrote as follows:—" The feature, however, which presents the greatest resemblance to the Northern styles is the reverse slope of the eaves above the verandah. I am not aware of its existence anywhere else South of Nepal, and it is so peculiar that it is much more likely to have been copied than reinvented. I cannot offer even a plausible conjecture, how or at what time, a connection existed between Nepal and Thibet and Canara, but I cannot doubt that such was the case." "In fact there are no two tribes in India, except the Nayars (of Malabar) and Newars (of Nepal) who have the same strange notions as to female chastity, and that

---

[1] Chilapp-atbikaram XXVI. ll. 148-149 aud ll. 176—178.

[2] "Soodruka is known in the · native annals as Karna Dêva or Maha Karna. A plate has recently been dug up at Benares, on which is inscribed a grant of land made by their monarch who is styled the Lord of the three Kalingas. If this be not an oriental exaggeration, it would go to show that the great Karna of Magadha had extended his dominions as far as the coast of Telinga on the one side and of Arracan on the other side of the Bay, and to the sea coast of Bengal: for this is the locality of the three Kalingas as explained by historians. After a reign of eighteen years he was succeeded by his brother. Six monarchs in succession filled the throne after the founder, who all assumed the same patronymic, and were remembered as the seven Karnas : but we have nothing but this naked fact for our guidance, except the great veneration in which the name of Karna is traditionally held, not only in India, but throughout the Eastern Archipelago. This would almost justify the supposition that the Karnas, possessing the three divisions of the sea coast, had created a navy, and made their power felt in the islands of the East. In common speech, the natives are accustomed, when anxious to pay the highest compliment to a liberal man to compare him to Karna: and we incline to the belief that on such occasions they allude to the more modern Karna of Magadha, rather than to the antiquated hero of that name mentioned in the Mahabharat."

7

coupled with the architecture and other peculiarities, seems to point to a similarity of race, which is both curious and interesting: but how and when the connection took place I must leave it to others to determine. I do not think there is any thing in the likeness of the names, but I do place faith in the similarity of their architecture combined with that of their manners and customs " (Mr. Fergusson's History of Indian and Eastern Architecture, p. 270 and 305). The similarity of races, which Mr. Fergusson's professional instinct told him must be a fact, is fully borne out by the direct testimony of ancient Tamil poets. *The connection between Nepal and Malabar had broken off probably more than two thousand years ago. It is truly marvellous therefore that traces of this connection still linger in the language, the customs, and the style of Architecture of the latter country, after the lapse of twenty centuries!*

The three Tamil tribes Maranmar, Thirayar and Vanavar founded respectively the Tamil Kingdoms subsequently known as the Pandya, Chola and Chera Kingdoms.[1] From the edicts of the great Magadha Emperor Asoka, which were engraved in the latter half of the 3rd Century B.C., we learn that the three Tamil kingdoms were in existence in his time and were not subject to his authority.[2]

The latest of the immigrants into the Tamil country were the Kosar. It is said that they attacked Mohoor the Capital of Palayan-Maran and as they were repulsed there, the "Vamba-Moriyar" or the illegitimate Mauriyas came to their assistance, and drove in

"These Andhra kings appear to have maintained towards the close of their dynasty a constant intercourse with China: and we find the Chinese Government on one occasion sending an army to assist in putting down a rebellion in India."—Marshman's History of India, p. 63. Dr Bhandarkar's Early History of the Dekkan, p. 25.

[1] The Puranic authors have however tried to conceal this fact by asserting that the Pandya, Chola and Chera were descendants of an Aryan king. "The *Harivamsa* and *Agni Purana* make Pandya, Chola, Kerala and Kola great grandsons of Dushyanta of the line of Puru, and founders of the regal dynasties named after them. The descendants of Dushyanta however as specified in the *Vishnu Purana* do not include these personages, and their insertion seems to have been the work of the more recent authorities. The *Harivamsa* with no little inconsistency places the Pandyas and Cholas amongst the Kshatriya tribes degraded by Sagara. The *Padma Purana* has a similar addition to the list of those tribes in the Ramayana." Prof. H. H. Wilson's Historical Sketch of the Pandyan Kingdom. Journal of the Royal Asiatic Society. Vol. III. Art IX., p. 199.

[2] Indian Antiquary. Vol. XX., p. 242.

their handsome chariots on the Pothiya hill.[1] It appears therefore that the immigration of the Kosar took place in the 3rd or
2nd Century B.C., when the illegitimate Mauriyas were on the
Magadha throne. The Kosar are said to have come from four
different towns and they spoke four different dialects.[2] They
were a very warlike people and were remarkable for their regard
for truth.[3] In the first Century A. D., they were the Masters of
the Konga country (the Modern Coimbatore District)[4] while in
the Pandyan country they were the most honored of the subjects
of the Pandya, inferior in rank only to Palayan-Maran.[5] They
invaded Then-Pandi and the Chola territory also, but were repulsed
by the Kings Thithiyan[6] and Killi.[7]

The Kosar appear to be no other than the Koshans, a branch
of whom conquered Bactria in the second Century B.C. and the
north-western portion of India, in the first Century B.C. They
were the leaders of the four tribes of the Yuh-chi, i.e., the Asioi,
Pasianoi, Tocharoi and Sakarauloi :[8] and their great god was
Siva, as may be seen from the coins of Kanishka.[9]

As the Tamil immigrants came into Southern India at distant
intervals of time and in separate tribes, and were fewer in number
than the aboriginal Nagas and Dravidians, they had to adopt the
ancient Dravidian language, and in course of time, they modified
and refined it into the language now known as Tamil. The peculiar letter Rzha (ழ) found in the Tamil alphabet which does not
occur in the other Dravidian or Sanskrit languages, was doubtless
brought in by the Tamil immigrants. This letter, I understand,
occurs only in some of the Thibetian languages. It indicates most
clearly that the primitive home of the Tamil immigrants must have
been in the Thibetian plateau. That they were not of Aryan descent

---

[1] Mamûlanar-Akam, 250.
[2] Mathuraik-Kanchi, ll. 508-509.
[3] Old stanza quoted by Nachchinarkiniyar in his commentary to the
Tholkapiyam Porul-athikaram, Mr. Thamotharam Pillai's edition, p. 329.
[4] Chilapp-athikaram Urai-peru-kaddurai.
[5] Mathuraik-kanchi, ll. 772-774.
[6] Paranar-Akam, 195.
[7] Nakkirar-Akam, 204.
[8] Strabo XI. viii. 2.
[9] Catalogue of coins of Greek and Scythic kings of Bactria and India, by R. S.
Poole, p. xl.

is proved not only by the continued antagonism they displayed towards the Aryans, but also by ancient Sanscrit works in which the Dravidas are spoken of as an alien people.[1] That the Tamils had attained a high degree of civilization before the advent of the Aryans is established indisputably by the fact that the pure Tamil language is so copious and exact that it can do well without borrowing Sanscrit words. In fact, in the ancient Tamil classical works, the terms relating to Music, Grammar, Astronomy and even abstract Philosophy are of pure Tamil origin; and they indicate most clearly that those sciences were cultivated by the Tamils long before the arrival of the Brahmins or other Aryan immigrants. The Tamils obtained a knowledge of these sciences most probably from China, through Bengal or Burma, with both of which countries they had direct and constant intercourse. The Tamil language, unlike other Dravidian dialects, abounds in words with nasal letters such as nga, nja and nna: and this peculiarity is remarkable in ancient Tamil works, and in modern Malayalam. This is further evidence of the affinity of the Tamils and the Burmese and Chinese, the latter of whom call themselves "Celestials" like the ancient Cheras who were known as Vanavar or "Celestials"—

The modern Malayalam preserves, I believe, that form of language which was spoken by the early Tamil immigrants, some time after they had settled in Southern India. They had then learnt to use Dravidian words, but were not familiar with the personal signs of verbs. In this condition, the Malayalam of to-day resembles the Mongolian, the Manchu, and other primitive tongues of High Asia.

The early Tamil poets believed in the tradition that Agastya lead the first colony of the Aryas to the Pothya hills near Cape Comorin. How much of historical truth there is in this tradition it is difficult to determine; but the tradition seems to rest entirely on the Ramayana, in which epic, Agastya is represented as inviting Rama to overcome Ravana, the King of Ceylon. In the same poem

---

[1] Haughton's translation of Manava Dharma Sastra.

Chap. X. V. 43. The following races of Kshatriyas by their omission of holy rites and by seeing no Brahmans have gradually sunk among men to the lowest of the four classes.

Chap. X. V. 44. Paundracas, Odras, and Dravidas: Cambojas, Yavans and Sakas: Paradas, Pablavas, Chinas, Kiratas, Doradas and Chasas.

Panchavati which was situated on the banks of the Godaveri near the modern Nasik is said to have been two yojanas from the hermitage of Agastya.[1] It follows therefore that during the time of Valmiki, Agastya's hermitage was believed to be near the modern Nasik. Danda-karanya, the modern Mahratta country, is described as a forest infested by wild tribes who disturbed the religious rites of the Brahmins, while the country South of the river Kaviri is designated Janasthan, or a region inhabited by civilized people. In the passage describing the despatch of monkey soldiers in search of Sita, they are directed to go to the countries of the Andhras, the Pandyas, the Cholas and the Keralas in the South, and are told that they will there see the gate of the city of the Pandyas adorned with gold and jewels.[2] These descriptions in the Ramayana go to show that during Valmiki's time, the Aryas had some knowledge of the Tamil people and considered them as a civilized nation, and that they knew the Pandyan capital to be a very wealthy city. Another Sanscrit author, Katyayana who wrote his aphorisms called Varthikas, to explain and supplement the grammatical Sutras of Panini, and who is popularly known to have lived during the time of the Nandas in the first half of the fourth Century B. C., alludes to the Pandyas and Cholas and says that one sprung from an individual of the tribes of the Pandus, or the Kings of their country, should be called a Pandya."[3]

It is beyond doubt therefore that long before the fourth Century B. C. the Pandyan Kingdom in the South of India had come into existence. But of the founder of the Southern Pandyan Kingdom nothing definite is known. According to the Mahabharata current in South India, Arjuna is said to have married Chitrangada, the daughter of Malayadhvaja, King of Pandya. But as the section containing this account is not to be found in copies of the poem which are current in Northern India, it is doubtless an interpolation.[4] From other accounts however it

[1] Ramayana III. 13, 13. Bombay Edition.
[2] Ramayana.
[3] Vàrtika on Panini. IV. 1—168.
[4] "The traditions of the South however make Malaya Dhvaja, a more important character and consider him as the father of Chitrángadá, the wife of Arjuna. This opinion is grounded on a section of the Sabha Parvan of the Mahábbarat, where Sahádeva, whilst performing his military career in the Dekkan is

appears that the founder of the Southern Pandyan Kingdom was a princess. Megasthenes who resided as an ambassador of Seleukus in the Court of Chandra-gupta at Pataliputra, has the following account of the origin of the Pandyas: "Herakles begat a daughter in India whom he called Pandaia. To her he assigned that portion of India which lies to southward and extends to the sea, while he distributed the people subject to her rule into three hundred and sixty-five villages, giving orders that one village should each day bring to the treasury the royal tribute, so that the Queen might always have the assistance of the men whose turn it was to pay the tribute, in coercing those who for the time being were defaulters in their payments."[1] Pliny gives a similar account, " next come the Pandœ the only race in India ruled by women. They say that Hercules having but one daughter, who was on that account all the more beloved, endowed her with a noble kingdom. Her descendants rule over 300 cities and command an army of 150,000 foot and 500 elephants."[2] Ancient Tamil poems seem to support this tradition because they refer to a woman as the founder of the Pandyan Dynasty.[3] She appears to have been subsequently worshipped as a goddess in Madura. In the Chilappathikaram she is spoken of as Mathurapathi or "Queen of Madura" and she is described as dressed half in the attire of a warrior and half in that of a prin-

---

described as having an interview with her father Malaya Dhvaja, king of Pandya. This section is however perhaps peculiar to the copies of the Mahábhárat current in the peninsula, as it has no place in a fine copy in the Devanagiri character in my possession. In the first chapter too, it is there said that the father of Chitrángada is Chitraváhana, king of Manipur, to which Arjuna comes on leaving Kalinga. The Telugu translation of the Adi-Parvan agrees in the names of the parties but places Manipur South of the Kaveri. How far therefore it is safe to identify Malayadhvaja with Chitraváhana and Manipur with Madura, must depend upon the verification of the authenticity of different copies of the Mahábhárat. The result of a careful collection of seven copies at Benares, examined by Captain Fell, at my request, may be regarded as fatal to the identification, not one of them containing the section in question or the name of Malaya Dhvaja. The Bhágavat calls the bride of Arjuna, Ulipi, the daughter of the serpent king of Manipura. Prof. H. H. Wilson: *Journal of the Royal Asiatic Society*, Vol. III. Article IX. p. 199.

[1] McCrindle's Ancient India, p. 158.

[2] Pliny's Hist. Nat. VI. 21. McCrindle's Ancient India, p. 147.

[3] Chilapp-athikaram, XXIII. ll. 11 to 18.

cess.[1] The Manimekalai also alludes to her as Mathurâpathi.[2]
Taking together the tradition as reported by Megasthenes
and Pliny and the allusions in ancient Tamil works, it appears
that a princess who belonged to the race of the Pandus, then
reigning at Mathura on the banks of the Jumna, led a colony and
founded Dakshina-Mathura on the banks of the Vaigai. Like
Dido, who fled from Phœnicia and founded Carthage, it is most
probable that the princess was driven by some domestic affliction
to settle in a distant land. The later traditionary accounts speak
of this princess as a woman born with three breasts. It is quite
possible that owing to this personal deformity she was obliged to
seek a husband in a foreign country. She appears to have
married a king of the Marar tribe, which was already settled in
the Tamil country, and hence her descendants assumed the titles
of Pandyan and Maran.

The few Aryas who accompanied the Pandyan princess appear
to have merged in the Tamil people by inter-marriages with them.
The Pandyan Kings of the first and second century A. D. considered
themselves as Tamils, and not Aryas, although they claimed
descent from the Pandus. Not only the Pandyas, but also the
Cholas and Cheras of this period considered themselves as rivals
to the Aryas. Reference is made to frequent collisions between
the Tamil Kings and the Aryas, in which the latter were defeated.
One of the Pandyan Kings had the title Ariyappadai-Kadanta-
Nedunj Cheliyan, which meant that he had defeated an Aryan
army.[3] A Chola King is said to have routed the Aryas in a
battle at Vallam (near the modern Tanjore.)[4] The Chera
king Chenkudduvan defeated the Aryas on the northern bank of the
Ganges, with the assistance of the Karnas, princes of Magadha.[5]
Although the Aryas did not settle in the Tamil country by
force of arms, many Brahmin families appear to have come in, as
peaceful settlers. There was a large colony of them around the
Pothya hill, where they believed, the Vedic sage Agastya had
resided. They did not mix freely with the natives of the soil

[1] Ibid. XXIII, ll. 5 to 10.
[2] Manimekalai, XXVI. 13.
[3] Chilapp-athikaram. XXIII. p. 449 of Mr. Saminathier's edition.
[4] Akam. 335.
[5] Chilapp-athikaram XXVI. ll. 147 to 154 and ll. 176 to 178.

but lived apart in gramums or villages, and in large towns, they
resided together in separate streets. At Madura, Thaukal[1] and
Vayanankodu[2] in the Pandyan Kingdom, at Vanji, Poraiyur,[3]
Erakam[4] and Mankadu[5] in the Chera country and at
Kavirippaddinam, Mulloor,[6] Avinankudi[7] and Chenkanam[8]
in the territory of the Chola King, they resided in large numbers.
They claimed to be of several gotras or clans, all of which traced
their descent from two patriarchs reputed to be the sons of no less a
personage than Brahma the creator himself.[9] Brahmans of the
ancient family of Kapiyas are specially alluded to as residing in the
Chera dominions.[10] The Brahmins as a rule never allowed dogs
or fowls to enter their houses. They reared cows for the sake of
their milk, parrots to amuse their women and children, and
mangoose to kill the serpents which might intrude into their
houses or gardens.[11] Their chief employment was to keep up the
triple sacred fires in their homes, to perform yogas or sacrifices and
to chant Vedic hymns. To the other castes they posed as " heaven
compellers." They engaged as teachers occasionally. Some of
them were Tamil poets. Frequently they started on pilgrimage,
when they went round the Pothia Hill, bathed in the sea at Cape
Comorin and at the mouth of the Kaviri, and travelled to the
banks of the Ganges. On these occasions, they wore leathern
sandals to protect their feet; and carried an umbrella to save
themselves from sun and rain, a water-pot suspended by a string
and three staves tied together. It is interesting to note that
elephant drivers spoke to the animals in Ariyam. The Dravidians
used to catch wild elephants in pitfalls dug in the woods : but the
Aryas introduced the ingenious method of decoying wild elephants,

---

[1] Chilapp-athikaram XXIII. 11. 74-75.
[2] Mani-mekalai, XIII, 1. 15.
[3] Chilapp-athikaram.
[4] Tiru-murukattup-padai, 11. 177-189.
[5] Chilapp-athikaram XI. 1. 53.
[6] Chiru-panarrup-padai, 11. 187-188.
[7] Tiru-murukattup-padai, 1. 176.
[8] Chilapp-athikaram, XI. 1. II.
[9] Tiru-murukattup-padai, 1. 178. The Commentator Nachchinark-iniyar
misinterprets the meaning, which is plain—see Mani-mekhalai, XIII.
93 to 97.
[10] Chilapp-athikaram, XXX. 83.
[11] Perum-panarrup-padai, 11. 294-300.

by tame female elephants. As astrologers they had rivals amongst the Dravidians. The Brahmins were called in Tamil Pârppâr or "Seers" and the Dravidian astrologers were called Arivar or "Sages."[1] These sages like the Brahmins pretended to read the future by consulting the positions of the heavenly bodies and fixed auspicious times for celebrating marriages or other important domestic and public ceremonies.

The Ayar or the cowherd race was distinct from the other races abovementioned. Their name Ayar is derived from the Dravidian word Â meaning a cow. They were known as the Abhiras in Puranic history. In northern India they are still called Ahirs. In the Tamil land they were also called the Pothuvar or Commons (from the Dravidian word Pothu meaning common) apparently because they professed friendship to the Nagas and Tamils alike. Originally they appear to have had their own petty Kings, in the Chola country, but Karikal-Chola is said to have exterminated their line of kings.[2] The Ayar in the Pandyan dominion had a tradition that they came into the Tamil land, along with the founder of the Pandyan family.[3] They worshipped ordinarily the Yakshas.[4] Their favorite deity was however their national hero Krishna whose liaisons with shepherd girls and feats celebrated in the Mahabarata formed the theme of their festive songs. The shepherd lads and lasses who resided in Madura are represented as personating in their dances Krishna and his brother Bala-Rama, Asothai the mother of Krishna and his wife Pinnay.[5] They were familiar with all the legends regarding the boyish freaks of Krishna, who stole the butter churned by the shepherdesses, and concealed their clothes, while they bathed and sported in the Jumna. They had a peculiar custom among them of selecting husbands for their girls from the victors of a bull-fight.[6] A large area of ground is enclosed with palisades and strong fences. Into the enclosure are brought ferocious bulls

---

[1] Tholkâppiyam. Porul-athikaram, Sutras 193, 509-510.
   Kalith-thokai, stanza 39, l. 44.
[2] Paddinap-pâlai, l. 281.
[3] Kalith-thokai, stanza 104, ll. 4 to 6.
[4] Chilapp-athikaram, XV. l. 116.
[5] Ibid, XVII.
[6] Kalith-thokai, stanzas 101, and ll.

with sharpened horns. On a spacious loft, overlooking the enclosure, stand the shepherd girls whom they intend to give away in marriage. The shepherd youths prepared for the fight, first pray to their gods whose images are placed under old banian or peepul trees or at watering places. Then they deck themselves with. garlands made of the bright red flowers of the *kánthal* and the purple flowers of the *káya*. At a signal given by the beating of drums, the youths leap into the enclosure and try to seize the bulls, which, frightened by the noise of the drums, are now ready to charge any one who approaches them. Each youth approaches a bull which he chooses to capture. But the bulls rush furiously with tails raised, heads bent down and horns levelled at their assailants. Some of the youths face the bulls boldly and seize their horns. Some jump aside and take hold of their tails. The more wary young men skilfully avoid the horns and clasping the neck cling to the animals till they force them to fall on the ground. Many a luckless youth is now thrown down. Some escape without a scratch, while others are trampled upon or gored by the bulls. Some though wounded and bleeding again spring on the bulls. A few who succeed in capturing the animals are declared the victors of that day's fight. The elders then announce that the bull fight is over. The wounded are carried out of the enclosure and attended to immediately; while the victors and the brides-elect repair to an adjoining grove, and there forming into groups, dance joyously before preparing for their marriage.

The Jews appear to have visited the Western Coast in the early centuries of the Christian Era. They have a tradition that a large number of their nation came and settled in Malabar soon after the destruction of their temple at Jerusalem, which event took place in A. D. 68. There is no allusion however to the Jews in ancient Tamil literature. But the fact that they were settled in the Western Coast during the second century is established beyond a doubt by the ancient deeds engraved in copper, still in possession of the Jews and Syrian Christians of Malabar.[1] These deeds are written in ancient Tamil and in the archaic character known as Vaddeluttu or " round letters." They

[1] Deeds No. 1, 2 and 3 translations of which are given in Logan's Malabar Manual, Vol. II, pp. 115 to 123.

have excited much interest, not only because of their antiquity, but because of the curious fact that by them the ancient Chera Kings conferred on the Jewish Colonies, certain privileges which those Colonies still possess to some extent. They have been more than once translated, and there has been much diversity of opinion regarding the dates assigned to them. The earliest of the deeds is dated in the 36th year opposite to the 2nd year, during the reign of Sri-Bhaskara Ravi-Varman. The expression "36 year opposite to the 2nd year" has been variously interpreted. One scholar understood the 2nd year, to refer to the Cycle of Parasu Rama, another took the 36th year to refer to the 60 years Cycle of Brihaspati."[1] Neither of these Cycles are however applicable to all the deeds whose dates are given in double years. From the researches made by the Portuguese Missionary Beschi, who resided in Madura for forty years, it appears that the Cycle then used in Southern India was the Grahapparivirthi Cycle[2] of

[1] "The words irandam-andaikk-edirmuppatt-aram-andu were translated by Mr Whish "the thirty-sixth year of the second cycle (of Parasurama)"= 139 B. C.; and by Sir Walter Elliot ' the thirty-sixth year opposed to or in contradistinction to the second which would be the third cycle (of Parasurama)=861 A.D. Dr. Burnell suggested that the first andu might refer to the year of the reign, and the second to that of the King's age, while Dr. Caldwell took the second andu for the year of the reign, and the first for the year of the 60 year cycle of Brihaspati." Dr. Hultzsch in the Indian Antiquary, Vol. XX, p 288. Dr. Hultzsch was of opinion that the first year indicated the date of the King's appointment as Yuvaraja or heir apparent: and the second the year of his reign.

[2] "Grahapparivirthi cycle of ninety years. The Southern inhabitants of the peninsula of India use a cycle of ninety years, which is little known, according to Warren in the Karnatak. This cycle was analysed by the Portugese missionary Beschi, while resident for 40 years in Madura. The native astronomers there say it is constructed of the sum of the products in days of 15 revolutions of Mars, 22 of Mercury, 11 of Jupiter, 5 of Venus, 29 of Saturn and one of the sun. "The epoch of this cycle occurs on the expiration of the 3078th year of the Kaliyug in 24 B. C. The years follow the solar or sidereal reckoning. The concurrent cycle and year for any European year may readily be found by adding 24 and dividing by 90: thus 1830 A. D. $=\frac{1830+24}{90}=$ 20 cycles and 54 years."—Prinsep's Indian Antiquities by Thomas, Vol. II, p 156.

The Grahapparivirthi cycle is applicable to every deed or inscription in the Tamil country, whose date is given in double years. The inscription of the Kerala King Rama (Malabar Manual, Vol. II. p. 122) found at Tiruvannur, near Calicut, is dated in the fourth year opposed to the fourth year. The corresponding date in the Christian Era is 4 × 90 + 4—24 or A. D. 340. The Tiruppuvanam grant of

90 years. The Epoch of this Cycle occurs on the expiration of the 3078th year of the Kaliyuga, in 24 B. C. The years follow the ordinary Solar or Siderial reckoning. The concurrent Christian year for any year reckoned by the Cycle may readily be found by multiplying the number of the Cycle by 90 and adding the year and subtracting 24. Thus the 36th year of the 2nd Cycle is equal to 2×90+36—24 or 192 A. D. The deed of the Chera King Bhaskara-Ravi-Varman, which is dated in a year equivalent to 192 A. D., appears to be therefore the oldest of the copper plate inscriptions preserved in Southern India, and as such, it deserves to be carefully studied. To those students of history who place more faith in inscriptions than in ancient literature, this deed affords the most satisfactory evidence of the civilization of the Tamils in the second century A. D. The language of the deed being very old and obscure Tamil, and some of the terms used being obsolete, it is difficult to render it correctly into English, but I give below a translation of it conveying the meaning of the deed as close to the original as I can render it.

"Health and prosperity!

The grant vouchsafed by the King of Kings His Majesty Sri-Bhaskara-Iravi-Varmmar, during his reign—may it last for many hundred thousand years! [1]—in the 36th year against the 2nd year (Cycle), when he tarried at Muyirik-Kodu.

We have given to Joseph Rabban the principality of Anju-vannam, the (right to levy) tribute in money and in kind,[2] the revenue of Anjuvannam, the light by day, the spreading cloth,

Kulasekharadeva is dated in the 12th year opposite to the thirteenth year, which is equivalent to 13 × 90 + 12—24 or A. D. 1158. Kulasekharadeva was contemporary with Parakrama Bahu I of Ceylon (A. D. 1146-1179). Mahawanso — Chapter 76.77.

[1] The words, pala-nurayirattandu-chenkkol-nadatti-ala-ninra, mean literally "wielding the sceptre for many hundred thousand years":—but in the deed they should I think be interpreted as conveying a blessing.

[2] The words pidiyalum payanattalum have been translated by Dr. Gundert as "going with elephants and other conveyances." Madras Journal Lit. so, XIII part 1, p. 137. But the correct meaning appears to be "in money and in kind." Pidi means "ready cash" as well as a "female elephant"—Payanam or Pasanam means "a share."—The word Iduvadi is translated by Dr. Gundert as "the gateway with arches." But it is not used in this sense in any ancient work. The correct meaning appears to be "sandals" or "shoes."

the palanquin, the umbrella, the *Vaduca* drum, the trumpet, the sandals for the feet, ornamental arches, awnings and presents carried on poles balanced on the shoulders, along with the 72 privileges of a nobleman.

We have exempted him from paying the land tax and water rate ; and we have enacted with this copper deed that when the other inhabitants pay taxes to the Palace he shall not have to pay, when they receive (presents) he shall also receive.

Given to Joseph Rabban Lord of Anjuvannam and to his posterity, sons and daughters and nephews and sons-in-law as a heriditary grant.   Prosperity !

    Thus do I know Gôvardhana Mârtbândan,
        Lord of Vênâdu.
    Thus do I know Kotai Sri-Kandan,
        Lord of Vênavali.
    Thus do I know Mâna Vêpala Mâna Viyan,
        Lord of Erâla-Nâdu.
    Thus do I know Rayâran Châttan,
        Lord of Valluvanâdu.
    Thus do I know Kothai-Ravi,
        Lord of Nedum-Purayur.
    Thus do I know Mûrkhan Chattan,
        Commander of the Eastern Army.
    Kandan of Great Thalacheri Kilway,
        the Mountain Splitter.
    The writing of Kelappa."

From this deed we learn that about the close of the 2nd century, the Tamil Settlements on the Malabar Coast extended beyond Thalaicheri (modern Tellicherry) in the north, and up to the foot of the ghauts in the east.   The Chera Kingdom was divided into six or more provinces, the rulers of which aspired to the dignity of kings, and the Chera Monarch assumed the title of King of Kings or Emperor.   The chieftains of the Provinces formed a sort of council to the King, and it was with their assent that any grant was made, or privileges conferred under royal sanction.   It appears that a land tax and water cess were levied by the king throughout his dominions except in those parts where the landholders had been specially exempted.   Tribute from local Chiefs to the Lord of each province was paid in money or in kind.   It is curious to note that foreigners could use sandals or umbrellas or ride in palanquins, only with the permission of the King. Noblemen prided themselves on special privileges such as the cloth spread on the ground for them to walk upon, ornamental arches and awnings to be erected on the roads on which they travel, and the flourish of trumpets and drums to announce their arrival and departure. There were no less than seventy-two rights claimed by great landholders, but the nature of these rights does not appear from the deed.

Another deed issued during the reign of the same King Bhâskara-Iravi-Varmman records an endowment made to the Vishnu temple at Tirunelli (in the Wynad) by Porai Kilan or the Lord of Porayûr Nadu.[1] The endowment was placed under the control of the "five hundred" of Poraiyûr. The five hundred were doubtless an assembly of the heads of 500 families of the Nadu. It appears therefore that in this ancient period, although the Kings had apparently unlimited power over the lives and properties of their subjects, *much of the local administration remained in the hands of the people themselves.*[2]

---

[1] An excellent facsimile and translation of this deed have been published by Dr. Hultzsch.—Indian Antiquary. Vol. XX. p. 285.

[2] "The six hundred were the supervisors and protectors of the Nad"—Malabar Manual, Vol. I. p. 267. Another deed mentions the 600 of Ramavala Nadu.—Malabar Manual Vol. II. p. 122. These village republics continued in existence till the English annexed Malabar. "The Nad or country was a congeries of *taras* or village republics, and the Kuttam or assembly of the Nad or country was a representative body of immense power which, when necessity existed, set at naught the authority of the Raja, and punished his ministers when they did "unwarrantable acts." These are the very words used by the Honorable Company's representative at Calicut when asked to explain the origin of certain civil commotions which had taken place there in 1746. His report deserves to be quoted in full, for it gives a vivid insight into the state of things as it then existed. "These Nayars," he wrote "being heads of the Calicut people, resemble the parliament, and do not obey the King's dictates in all things, but chastise his ministers when they do unwarrantable acts." Malabar Manual. Vol. I, p. 89.

CHOLA GENEALOGY.

A CHOLA KING.

(Name not mentioned)

Ver - pahradakkaip-peru-virar-Killi (killed in battle with Kudak-kô-nedunj Chêral Athan)

Uruvap-pahrêr-ilanj-chêd chenni (married the daughter of Alunthûr-Vêl)

Karikâl-Chola (A.D. 50-95) *alias* Tiru - mâ - valavan (married the daughter of Nânkûr-Vêl; and died at Kurâp-palli).

Chêral Athan = *alias* Vâna-Varmman.

Sonai daughter

Mâvalattân

Nedunk-Killi (who died at Kâri-âru.)

Chenk - kudduvan *alias* Imaya-varm-man.

Ilanko-adikal (author of Chilappathi kâram.)

Ched-chenni-Nalank-Killi (A. D. 95-105).

Killi-valavan (A.D. 105—120) (married Sithâ-thaka, a descendant of Maha-bali: also Peeli-valai, daughter of the Nâga King Valai-vanan)

Peru-nar-Killi (A.D. 120-150) (performed the Râja-sûya Yâga.)

CHAPTER V.

THE CHOLAS.

Of the personal history of the Kings who ruled the Chera, Chola, and Pandiya dominions, only fragmentary notices appear in the ancient poems which have survived to this day. The same King is sometimes mentioned in these poems under different titles; and different Kings of one dynasty appear to have borne the same name. To collect these detached notices and weave a connected history out of them is not an easy task: and as I attempt this for the first time, it is quite possible that further researches may show that some of my statements are not correct. I shall confine myself in the following account to the history of the Tamil Kings, whose reigns cover the period from A. D. 50 to A. D. 150. I take this opportunity to translate many of the relics of ancient Tamil poetry, of historical interest, which will give the reader a more correct and vivid idea of the customs, manners and beliefs of the people, than what any description of them in my own words can possibly convey.

As mentioned by me already, the allusion in the Chilappathi-karam to the fact that Chenkudduva Chera *alias* Imaya Varmman was contemporary with Gajabahu of Ceylon and the Karnas of Magadha, forms an important landmark in the history of Tamil literature. It is stated in the same poem that Chenkudduvan was over 50 years of age when he invited Gajabahu to attend the consecration of a temple to Kannaki at his capital Vanji.[1] Gajabahu was King of Ceylon from A. D. 113 to A. D. 125. Supposing that Gajabahu visited the Chera capital in the last year of his reign, Chenkudduvan who was then 50 years of age should have been born about A. D. 75. His mother was the daughter of Karikal Chola. The date of birth of the latter should therefore be fixed at least 40 years, earlier than that of his grandson Chenkudduvan. It may be safely assumed that Karikal Chola was born about A.D. 35. It is said that Karikal ascended the throne when he was quite a youth and that he ruled the Chola Kingdom for an

---

[1] Chilapp-athikaram. XXVIII—129-130.

unusually long period. The period of his reign may therefore be fixed about A. D. 50 to A. D. 95.

Karikal was the son of the Chola Prince Uruvap-Pahrêr-Ilayon or Ilanj-chêd-chenni.[1] His father had died before he was born, and rival claimants seized the Chola throne, and conspired to cause his death by fire. He escaped however, but his feet were scorched and blackened, and henceforth he was known as Karikal or "Black foot."[2] His uncle Pidarth-Thalayan assisted him in regaining the throne of his ancestors.[3] Brought up in adversity, he had early learned lessons of wisdom, and proved to be one of the wisest and most powerful of the Kings of his period. Au anecdote of his youth is recorded which shows his ready wit and independence of mind. In those days the King was also the supreme judge in all Civil and Criminal cases. An intricate case had come up to Karikal for decision.[4] His aged ministers appeared anxious about the result The youthful king understood the meaning of their looks. He retired at once into his private apartments, and there, tied false grey hair on his head, and appeared back in Court, in the disguise of an old man. Resuming his seat on the throne he examined the parties so skilfully that from their own answers he was able to pronounce a correct judgment, which elicited the applause of his grey-headed ministers.

Karikal was a great warrior. In his first battle on the plain of Vennil, he defeated the combined armies of the Pandya and Chera. The Chera King Athan I. who commanded his own forces, was wounded on the back. As this was considered in those days an indelible mark of cowardice, the valiant Chera unable to bear the disgrace, sought a voluntary death. The bard Kalath-thalaiyar who was with the Chera army at the engagement, mourns over the defeat of his King, and describes the gloom of his sorrowing subjects, in the following verse.[5]

"The drum no longer thunders. The lute has forgotten its music. The large milk pans now lie empty. None tastes the

---

[1] Porunar-arrup-padi—130.
[2] Third stanza, at the end of Porunar-arrup-padi.
[3] Palamoli.
[4] Palamoli—21, Manimekhalai—IV. 106-107.
[5] Puram—65.

honey collected by the busy bees. No longer the farmers plough their fields. No more is there any festive gathering on village lawns. Like the sun who sets behind the hills, when the full moon rises in all its splendour, our valiant King wounded on the back by a rival Monarch, has laid aside his sword in disgrace (and seeks death by starvation) alas ! How sad and cheerless are these days.".

Another bard Vennil-Kuyathiyar who was with the Chola King, appears to have been also struck with the unlucky fate of the Chera and addressed Karikal as follows.[1] "Oh ! descendant of that warrior who sailing on the wide ocean compelled the winds to fill the sails of his ships. Oh ! Karikal Valava. Lord of mighty elephants ! Who hast displayed thy valour in this battle. Is not he, even nobler than thee, who ashamed of the wound on his back, starves, without food, to gain a glorious death ?"

Karikal defeated a confederacy of nine princes in another battle.[2] He rooted out the line of Shepherd Kings, and brought under his sway all the tribes of the Oli-Nagas and Aru-Valar.[3] He subdued the Kurumbar a nomadic tribe.[4] His kingdom extended beyond Kanchipuram, which town he enlarged and beautified. He is said to have been in terms of friendship with the Kings of Avanthi, Vajra and Magadha.[5] Later poets in their dreamy eulogies of this great King credit him with the feat of having carried his arms up to the golden Meru, and planted his tiger standard on the summit of that mountain, which is spoken of in Indian legends as the centre of the Earth.[6] The periodical freshes in the Kaviri river used to inundate a great portion of the Chola country; and so frequently did this happen, that it was known as the Punal-Nadu or the "land of floods." Karikal who had defeated his enemies and consolidated his empire, now turned his attention to the improvement of his dominions. He formed the grand plan of controlling the frequent floods which wrought much damage in Punal-Nadu. He commenced at once

[1] Ibid.—66.
[2] Akam—124—Paranar.
[3] Paddinap-palai ll. 274-275.
[4] Akam—140—Narkirar.
[5] Chilappa-athikaram-V. ll. 99-104.
[6] Kalingattup-parani.

to raise high banks along both sides of the Kaviri and constructed sluices and canals to distribute and regulate the water supply.[1] The irrigation of the countries watered by the Kaviri was improved to such an extent that it was a common saying that every grain sown there yielded a thousand-fold. Karikal's sagacious mind was not slow to discover that the position of his capital at Uraiyur, so far from the Sea Coast, was disadvantageous to commerce. He therefore fortified Kavirip-paddinam the grand emporium of trade at the mouth of the Kaviri, and made it his capital.[2] The impetus given to commerce and agriculture by his wise measures speedily bore fruit, and his country became so wealthy and prosperous that his grateful subjects ever afterwards called him " Karikal-Peruvalathan " or " Karikal the great Chola."

Karikal was also known by the name Perum-Thiru-Mavalavan.[3] Towards the close of his reign, the Pandiyan King Velli-ampalathu-Thunjia-Peru-Valuthi appears to have gone on a visit to Karikal. When the two monarchs were seated together, the poet Kari-Kannan of Kaviripaddinam addressed them as follows:—[4]

" Thou art the Lord of the Kaviri whose floods carry fertility (to many a land) ! This King is the lion of the warlike race of the Panchavas, who, not disheartened by the death of his elders, valiantly protects his good subjects, like the long shoots of the shady baniyan tree, which strike root in the ground and keep the tree alive although the parent trunk is withered ; and who though young has speedily scattered his enemies like the thunder bolt which smites whole broods of serpents. Thou art the warrior of Uranthai, where charity abides ! This King unlike other monarchs, whose realms can boast of only well watered fields and plentiful harvests, is Lord of the sandal trees of the hills, the pearls of the sea and the three thundering drums, and rules with mercy the city of Kudal, which is the seat of Tamil learning. Majestic like the two gods, one of whom, fair in complexion, bears the flag of the Palmyra (Baladeva) and the other of dark hue, whose weapon

---

[1] Chilapp-athikaram—X, ll. 108-111.
[2] Paddinap-palai, ll. 285-288.
[3] Ibid, l. 299—the second stanza at the end of Porunar-arrup-padai.
[4] Puram—Stanza 58.

is a wheel (Vishnu). You both are now terrible to your enemies. Is there anything more pleasant than the friendship of two great Kings like you. Pray, listen to my words. May you be famous for ever! Each of you is powerful enough to contend with the other. But if you do not break your friendship, you would not fail to conquer the whole of this sea girt earth. Therefore be good, be just to each other, and as your ancestors did, listen not to the evil counsels of those who wish to divide you. Let your friendship last for ever, as warm as it is this day. May your lances be victorious on every battle field! May the flags of the striped tiger and of the fish wave on the top of every mountain in your enemies' lands!"

His generous nature and munificence to the poets who visited his court are well depicted in the poem Porunar-árruppadai which was composed by Mudath-Thâmak-Kanniyâr, about the close of the King's reign.[1] The poem is written as if it is addressed by the author to another poet whom he advises to visit Karikâl, describing to him all the kindness with which Karikâl received the author. It is very interesting, as it brings out clearly the cordiality with which Tamil Kings treated poets in this ancient period. I give below a translation of the poem omitting such parts as are not interesting to the general reader :—[2]

"Oh! Minstrel! Ever ready to quit the town thou visitest as soon as the festival held in it is over! When thy amiable wife graceful as the peahen; her hair dark and glossy; her forehead bright as the crescent moon; her eyes gentle and melting under brows arched like the death dealing bow; her lips red like the petals of the Ilavam flower; her voice sweet as music; her teeth brilliant like rows of pearls; and ears heavy with jewels and hanging like the loops of scissors used in trimming the hair; her neck slightly bent with modesty; her slender fingers fair as the *Kanthal* which blooms on the tops of lofty mountains * *
* * when thy wife played on the lute with the fingers now softly touching, now deftly gliding over and anon rapidly striking its chords and sweetly sang a hymn, then didst thou devoutly sprinkle

---

[1] Porunar-arrup-padai.
[2] I have followed to a great extent the translation given by the Hon. P. Comaraswmy, J. R. A. S., Ceylon Branch, Vol. XIII., No. 45.

water and offer thy prayers to the gods of the forest, for a safe passage through the woods where wild elephants roam and where leafless trees afford little or no shade to the travellers weary and footsore. Blessed be thou chief of minstrels! Thy good luck has brought thee hither, and saved thee the trouble of wandering into inhospitable regions. May thy life be prosperous! Master of the seven strings of the lute! If thy desire be that thyself and thy family should get rid of poverty which has oppressed thee sorely hitherto, get up without delay.

"Like a hungry bird seeking a tree laden with ripe fruits, I went one early morning to the gates of a King's palace, and without waiting to ask the permission of the gate keepers I entered the palace. Though faint and weary with my journey, I felt at once relieved and filled with joy. I drew near to the Monarch and began a song, sounding a small drum which I carried in my hand. He addressed me at once as one who had long known me and spoke so kindly, that begging at his gate was, I felt, no disgrace. He caused me to be seated in his presence and looked at me so benignly that my frame thrilled with unspeakable pleasure.

"My patched clothes wet with sweat, in which nits and lice held sway he caused to be removed and clad me in fine flowered muslins. His smiling handmaids adorned with jewels poured out in golden cups intoxicating wine, and I drank until I forgot my sorrows and fatigue; and laid me down to rest a while. When I awoke I felt no inconvenience except what was caused by excess of drink. Indeed I felt so happy that I could not believe the change and thought I was in a dream. But I was soon satisfied that it was reality.

"Hearing my pupils singing his praises he sent for us, and as we drew near and saluted him in the mode usual on such occasions, he made us eat of the flesh of goat spitted and roasted, till we could eat no more. Then sweetmeats of various forms were set before us, and as we feasted, beautiful dancing girls with lutes in their hands sang and danced to us. Several days having passed in feasting and drinking he desired that we should eat of rice, and a feast of rice boiled in milk and other sweet preparations was spread before us, and we ate until we were full unto the throat. We spent our days in this manner till, like the ploughshare which hath often furrowed hard soil; our teeth became blunt and food and wine were no more welcome. Then, one day, said I gently, Oh! King who levieth tribute from all thy enemies, give me leave to go back to my native village. Looking at me as if he was displeased, he said, "art thou then departing from us so soon." He then presented to me elephants male and female, and their calves shambling in gait, and I received what I thought proper, and departed bidding farewell to poverty for ever.

"The generous donor was the son of Uravap-pahrêr-Ilayôn who wields the ever victorious spear, terrible in his anger, like Muruga, the God of war; who was born entitled to Kingship even from his mother's womb, who has compelled his enemies to serve him, and has spread distress in the countries of those Kings who did not seek his friendship—as the sun rising from the ocean increases in brightness and splendour, so from his youth, ever growing in strength and valour, he now, mighty as Yama, the God of death, bears on his shoulders the weight of a matchless empire. Like a young lion which in its first chase kills a mighty elephant, so in the first battle on the field of Vennil, he smote the Pandya and Chera Kings. He is the great King called Karikâl Vâlavan who wears the bright garland of atti flowers.

"If approaching the great King thou worship his feet, he would look on thee tenderly as a cow watching its new born calf. Before he listens to thy song, he will clothe thee with silk, and give thee to drink of wine in cups of gold. He will feast thee all the days of thy stay, and when thou departest he will tie golden lotus flowers on the knot of hair on thy head, and to thy wife he will present necklaces of gold and pearl. He will give thee a chariot whose top is made of ivory, drawn by four milk-white steeds with flowing manes coloured red; and many elephants and well watered villages he will give thee. If thou handest over to thy followers the presents thou hast received, and hasteneth thy departure, he will, reflecting that nothing in this world lasteth long, unwillingly part with thee, and graciously go forward seven paces with thee, and ask thee to mount thy chariot and then bid thee farewell.

"Such is the king who has long reigned over the Chola Kingdom: who even when young, dispensed justice to the satisfaction of the old: whose long and blameless reign full of love and

mercy to his subjects is renowned throughout the world. May he
live for ever !"

The foot of Karikâl, lord of the land of floods, where honey
bees form their hives on stalks of corn—which was raised to step
on the three worlds, has measured only this earth : for, alas ! it
was scorched by fire."

Verses addressed to him by the poets Uraiyur—Maruthuvan
Thâmotharanar and Konaddu—Erichchalur—Mâdalan—Mathurai
—Kumaran also are found in the collection of ancient poems known
as Pura-nânûrû.[1]

Karikâl Chola's daughter Nar-Sonai was married to the Chêra
King Athan II. and became the mother of Chenkudduva Chêra
and of Ilankô-adikal, the author of the Chilappathikâram.[2] The
poet Karunk-kulal-âthanar who was present at the death of Karikâl gives expression to his grief in the following stanza :—

" He who stormed his enemies' forts dauntlessly ; who feasted
his minstrels and their families and treated them to endless
draughts of toddy ; who guided by priests learned in their duties,
and attended by his noble and virtuous queens, performed sacrifices
according to Vedic rites, in sacred spots which were walled round,
and in the midst of which stood the tall sacrificial pillars which
were crowded by vultures : He, the great and wise king is alas ! no
more. Poor indeed is this world which has lost him. Like
the branches of the *vengai* tree, which stand bare, when their bright
foliage has been cut down by shepherds to feed their cattle in the
hot season, are his fair queens, who have cast off their jewels."[3]

Karikâl was succeeded by Chedchenni Nalank-killi about A. D.
95. He was an amiable and accomplished prince and was therefore called Nalankkilli, or " the good Killi." His predecessor
having left the kingdom in a most prosperous condition, Nalank-
killi had only to maintain it in peace and good order, but he was
anxious to invade neighbouring kingdoms and extend his own
dominion. The poet Kovur-Kilar addressed him as follows when
he was encamped with his army on one of his expeditions :—[4]

---

[1] Puram 60 and 197.
[2] Chilapp-athikaram XXX. 173 to 188.
[3] Puram 224.
[4] Puram 31.

"As true wealth and happiness follow in the wake of virtue, the umbrellas of thy two rivals (the Pandia and Chera) follow thine, which is resplendent like the full moon. Ambitious of fame thou wouldst stay nowhere but in thy camp. Thy elephants whose tusks are blunt with battering the walls of thy enemies' forts, chafe at being idle and are restless. Thy soldiers who wear the warriors' anklets are eager to march, though they have to cross wide forests to reach thy enemies' lands. Thy war steeds, starting from the eastern sea stay not till the waves of the western ocean wash their hoofs, and northern kings, trembling with the fear that thou mayest march against them, watch (their frontiers) with sleepless eyes."

His frequent absence from his capital appears to have weakened his authority over the younger members of the royal family; and Nedunkilli, a Chola prince, was induced to revolt against him. He took possession of the capital, Uraiyur; but the king, hearing of this rebellion, hastened to Uraiyur and laid siege to the fort. During the siege, a minstrel Ilanthathan, entered Uraiyur, and Nedunkilli suspecting him to be a spy, was about to seize and kill him, when, the poet, Kovur-kilar pleaded for the minstrel and saved his life. The stanza addressed by him to Nedunkilli on the occasion is as follows:—[1]

"They fly like birds and cross many a forest in search of patrons and sing their praises as best their tongue can speak them: pleased with what they get, they feast with all their train; eat without saving, give without stinting and pine only for honor:— the minstrel race who live on what others willingly give them. Do these ever think of doing evil to others? No! Exulting in their triumphs over rival bards, while their rivals' faces are cast down, they walk proudly, as they have for their patrons great kings of this earth like thyself."

From Uraiyur, the rebel prince fled to Avur, another fortified town in the Chola kingdom. Nalankilli pursued him thither and besieged Avur. The siege continued so long that the inhabitants were reduced to starvation. The miseries endured by the people and the army in Avur are described in the following stanza:—[2]

"The male elephants that have not been led along with

---

[1] Kovur-Kilar, Puram, 47.   [2] Ibid, Puram, 44.

their females to bathe in the lakes outside the fort, nor fed with balls of rice mixed with butter, chafe at the posts to which they are chained, and rolling on the ground trumpet loud as thunder. Children cry for want of milk, women tie their hair without flowers, people weep and wail for want of water to drink. To stay here any longer is, alas! Disastrous! Thou master of fleet steeds! If thou wouldst be just, open the gates and give up the fort to thy King, if bent on war, lead out thy soldiers and fight the enemy. Doing neither, to close the strong gates of the fort and to shut ourselves within these high walls is shameful indeed."

The poet rebuked Nedunkilli for not obeying the King and succeeded eventually in reconciling the rebel prince and the King. One of the stanzas uttered by him is as follows:—[1]

"He does not wear the white flowers of the Palmyra. He does not wear the garland of the dark Margosa. You wear a wreath of the Ar, and so does he who wages war with you. If one of you loses the battle, it is your royal race that loses. It is not possible that both of you can win. A war between you is ruinous to your ancient house. Alas! how cruel is this evil war which makes your enemies rejoice."

It was the custom in this period for each King and his generals to wear on the battle-field garlands of a particular kind of flower, to distinguish his party from that of his enemy. The Pandya wore the flowers of the Margosa, the Chera those of the Palmyra, and the Chola the flowers of the Ar. In the stanza translated above, the poet says, that it is not the Pandya or the Chera that fights with the Chola, but a prince of the Chola family, as both wore the garlands of the Ar.

Distracted by civil wars, the Chola Kingdom was not very prosperous during the reign of Nalankilli. He was wanting in some of the qualities necessary for a successful ruler. If he was good, he was also proud of the resources of his Kingdom and boastful as may be seen from the following stanza composed by himself:—[2]

"If gently approaching my feet, one prays for a favor, I shall grant him even my ancient Kingdom, nay, I shall risk my

[1] Ibid, Puram, 45.   [2] Puram, 73.

life for his sake. If slighting the strength of the mighty, any one is so senseless as to oppose my will, he, like the fool who stumbles on a sleeping tiger, cannot escape with his life. If I do not attack such men, and destroy them, as a huge elephant tramples under its feet a tender sprout of the bamboo, may I delight in the embraces of harlots with flowing hair, whom the good ever shun."

He is said to have captured seven fortified towns in the Pandyan Kingdom. There is no other record of his having added any territory to his dominions. He appears to have died after a short and troubled reign. The following stanza, in which the poet Muthukannan Chatban exorted him to be gracious to those who visit his court is interesting :—[1]

"Mark those born in the noblest families, faultless as the lotus flower, with a hundred petals, who have ruled this earth. Few of them are famous in song or story. But many have dropped unhonoured like the dry leaves of the lotus. The great, whose deeds are the theme of poets' songs, move on aerial chariots, we are told, in the other world. Oh! my sire, Ched-Chenni-Nalan-killi! that everything decays and grows by turns: that everything dies and is born again, even the ignorant in this world may learn from the Moon, which visible to all (waxeth and waneth by turns). Therefore be gracious to all who seek thy favour, whether they be strong or weak. May thy enemies be those ungracious wretches who never help others but live for themselves."

On the death of Nalank-killi, Killi-Valavan succeeded to the Chola throne. His right to succession was however disputed by other princes of the Chola family. No less than nine of the princes revolted and sought to divide the kingdom. But Killi-Valavan's cousin, Chenkudduva-Chera promptly came to his assistance, defeated the confederate princes at Nèrivàyil, and established Kalli-Valavan's authority.[2] Killi-Valavan then attacked Malayamàn, the chief of Malàdu. This chief had evidently assisted the Chola princes who rebelled against the king, and the latter therefore resolved to crush his power. He defeated and slew Malayamàn, and seized his sons, who were of tender age, and intended to throw them under the feet of elephants to be trampled

---

[1] Ibid, 27.
[2] Chilapp-athikaram XXVII. ll. 118 to 123.

to death. The poet Kovûr-kilar interceded on their behalf, and addressed the king as follows :—

" Thou art the descendant of him who saved the pigeon and others from distress. These young boys are the children of one whose tribe is famous for its patronage of the learned. Afraid of the ferocious elephant, they shed tears and are now gazing in fright at thy Royal Court. Having listened to my words, thou mayest do whatever thou thinkest proper." [1]

Killi-Valavan invaded the Pandyan territory and advanced up to Madura, but was defeated under the walls of that town by Pala-yan Maran, the Commander of the Pandyan army.[2] After the death of his cousin Chenkudduva Chera, the Chola King marched into the Kongu country which formed part of the Chera dominions. The resistance offered by the Chera forces was so weak, that the Chola King led his army to the gates of Vanji, the Chera capital, without any difficulty. The Chera King was afraid to venture out of the fort, and Killi-Valavan destroyed therefore the buildings, fields and gardens outside the walls of the town. I translate below some of the verses addressed to the King by the bards who accompanied his army :—

" Like a thunderbolt which scorches and burns up the trees on a mountain, underneath which lies concealed in a cave, a venomous five-headed serpent, thou descendant of Sembyan, who once generously saved a pigeon ! Lord of the victorious lance and gallant army l while he, the master of many elephants holds the fort, the walls of which are impregnable as if made of brass, in the deep and broad moats surrounding which are deadly crocodiles—thou destroyest all that is good outside the fort." [3]

" Thou descendant of him who to save a pigeon had himself weighed on a pair of scales made of ivory, no act of charity can increase thy fame. When we think of thy illustrious forefathers, one of whom stormed the wondrous castles which hung in air, no victory can add to thy prowess. As thy courts of law at Uraiyur ever decide impartially, no act of justice on thy part can enhance thy merits. Thou Valava, lord of the fleet war steeds, who wearest garlands of the Ar, whose powerful arms are as strong as iron in smiting thy enemies, how shall I sing of thy might, when thou dost

---

[1] Puram, 46.   [2] Akam, 345 Narkirar.   [3] Puram, 37.

besiege Vanji to conquer the Vánavan, lord of the handsome high chariot, who has set his flag of the bow on the lofty Imaya mountains which yield gold."[1]

" Whether thou killest or savest, thou knowest best what thou, shouldst do. But it is shameful that thou should, with (thine, army and) drums decked with garlands, wage war with a King who has (like a coward) shut himself up in his capital, while the sound of the felling of trees—with the long handled axe whose edge is sharpened by the blacksmith's file, on the sandy banks of the Porunai, where young girls wearing bracelets and sounding. ankle-rings used to play with *Kalarchi* nuts of golden colour—echoes in his place within the fortified walls."[2] ;

Killi-Valavan first married Peelivalai, the daughter of the Naga King, Valaivanan whose territory lay on the Western Coast of Ceylon.[3] Subsequently he took for his consort Sithathakai, the daughter of a King (probably of Mahishámandalam, or the modern Mysore) who claimed to be descended from Mahabali, the mythical King to conquer whom the god Vishnu is said to have been born as a Brahmin dwarf.[4] By Sithathakai, he had a son named Udaya-Kumara who grew up to be a handsome and promising youth but was murdered one night accidentally.[5] The King then appears to have sent for his other son born by the Naga Princess. She sent her son in a merchant vessel which sailed from Manippallavam to Kavirippaddinam. On the way, on a dark and stormy night, the passengers landed on an island and there they left the prince in the dark, and sailed again when the weather cleared. Finding afterwards that the prince was missing, they searched throughout the island and the neighbouring coasts, but without success. The sad news of the loss of the prince reached Killi-Valavan just about the time that the festival of Indra was to commence. The King neglected to perform the festival and went in search of his son. A sea wave rushed over Kavirippaddinam and destroyed the town. It was believed by the superstitious people of that age that Manimekhala or the goddess of the ocean sent the wave to punish the people for their having not performed the festival of Indra, the King of the gods.[6] Killi-Vallavan died

---

1 Ibid, 89. 2 Ibid, 36. 3 Mani-mekalai XXIV. l. 54 to 57.
4 Ibid, XIX. l. 51—55. 5 Ibid, XX. l. 107. 6 Ibid, XXV. l. 196.

shortly afterwards at a place called Kula-murram. One of the poets present at his death expressed his feelings as follows:—[1]

" The messenger of death, who took the life of Valavan, lord of the strong chariots and conquering legions, would not have escaped the King's wrath, if he had come like one commanding or ready to seize the King. No, he should have come begging for the life of the King with raised hands like a bard singing his praises."

Killi-Valavan was succeeded by another Killi who was known as Rajasuyam-Vedda-Peru-Nar-Killi. He performed a magnificent sacrifice and invited to the grand ceremony the neighbouring Kings, Ugrap-peru-Valuthi and the Chera King Ma-Ven-Ko or the Fair Prince. The poetess Avvaiyâr who was present at the ceremony addressed as follows the three Kings who were seated together:—[2]

" Ye Monarchs ! lords of the bannered chariots and white umbrellas, may you ever, as you have done to-day, shower into the outstretched hands of Brahmins golden flowers with water: drink of the sweet liquor which your servant maids glittering with jewels hand to you in golden cups, and bestow costly gifts on the poets who sing your praises. Only the good deeds that you do now will help you when you depart this life. You three seated together in royal state are now like the three sacred fires which the twice-born preserve day and night, with ceaseless vigilance. May you be blessed with health ! May you live for many many days as countless as the stars in the sky and the rain-drops in heavy showers l"

---

[1] Puram, 226.   [2] Ibid, 367.

80

PANDYA GENEALOGY.

NEDUNJ-CHELIYAN I
(A.D. 50—75)
(conquered an Aryan army : and died on his throne.)

|

Verri-vêr-Cheliyan
(A.D. 75—90.)

|

NEDUNJ-CHELIYAN II
(A.D. 90—128)
(victor at the battle of Alankanam : captured the Chera King
Yânaik-kad-chêy : died at Velli-ambalam.)

|

Ugrap-peru-valuti
(A.D. 128—140)
(captured the fortress Kânappêr : attended the Râjasûya sacrifice
performed by the Chola king Peru-nar-killi.)

|

Nan-mâran
(A.D. 140—150)
(died at Ilavantikaip-palli.)

CHAPTER VI..

The Pandyas.

Contemporary with Karikal Chola the Great was the Pandyan king Ariyap-padai-kadantha-Nedunj-Cheliyan "or the Nedunj-Cheliyan who had defeated an Aryan army." [1] Some one of the Aryan kings of the Dekkan appears to have invaded the Tamil country during his reign, and the Pandyan king drove back the invaders, inflicting a signal defeat which earned from him the title of "Conqueror of the Aryan army." No particulars whatever of this decisive engagement are to be found in the ancient Tamil works now extant. His memory is however preserved to posterity by his romantic death which is related in the epic poem Chilapp-athikâram. [2] It is said that he had ordered his palace guards to behead Kovilan, a merchant of Kavirippaddinam, on the suspicion that he had stolen one of the queen's anklets. But the merchant's wife Kannaki proved to the satisfaction of the king that the jewel was not the queen's. Kannaki also spoke to the king of those Chola monarchs of her native country, one of whom had cut off his own flesh to satisfy an eagle, and had saved a dove, and of another king who had killed his own son for having rode in his chariot over a calf and caused its death. The Pandyan king stung with shame and remorse swooned and fell from his throne and never recovered his life. His queen ascended the funeral pyre. One of the verses composed by this king in which he extols the benefits of learning and exhorts his subjects to educate their children is preserved in the anthology called Pura-nanuru. [3] It is as follows :—

"Help your teacher in his need, pay him amply, follow him faithfully, and acquire learning. Amongst her own children, a mother loves not the son who is illiterate. Of the members of the same family, the eldest is not always honored, but it is the wisest of them whose counsel even a king would seek. Of the

---

[1] Chilapp-athikâram, Maduraik-kandam—1 : 14.
[2] Ibid., canto xx.
[3] Puram—183.

four castes of men, if one of the lowest is learned, a man of even the highest caste would resort to him."

On hearing of the sudden death of Nedunj-Cheliyan, the Pandyan prince Verri-vĕr-Cheliyan who was then Viceroy of Kotkai hastened to Madura and ascended the throne.[1] He appears to have died after a short reign and was succeeded by his son Nedunj-Cheliyan II who was then a boy of tender age. Soon after his accession, his kingdom was invaded by the Chola army which advanced up to Madura. Palayan-Mâran the commander of the Pandyan army was however able to gain a brilliant victory, and the invaders were forced to retreat into their country. The youthful Pandya was present at the engagement. When he heard of the invasion he is said to have vowed to drive the invaders out of his kingdom. The stanza uttered on this ocaasion by the youthful king, who dabbled in verse like most of the Tamil kings of this period, is as follows :—[2]

" My rival kings proud of their well armed soldiers, chariots and steeds and huge elephants which have legs like pillars and wear big bells which ever resound, have laughed at those who praised my kingdom, and scorning me as quite a youth, have too boldly marched against me, speaking words of menace and contempt. If I do not defeat them in a pitched battle and capture them with their war drums, let my subjects curse me as a cruel monarch, who too weak to save them has left them to the mercy of the enemy. May the poets honored by the whole world, chief among whom is the learned and wise Maruthan of Mankudy, quit me and my kingdom as unworthy of their song. May I become so utterly destitute that I may have nothing to give to the poor or to those who look to me for support."

The bard Idaik-kunrûr-kilar who was with the Pandyan army during the battle describes the appearance of the young Pandya in the following verses :—[3]

"Having bathed in the cool waters of the lake outside the gate of his ancient city, and wearing on his head a wreath of the bright leaves of the margosa, the gallant Cheliyan has come to

---

[1] Chilapp-athikaram— xxvii. II. 127-135.
[2] Puram—72.
[3] Ibid.—79-77.

the battlefield riding on an elephant with drums resounding before him. Countless are the warriors arrayed against him. Alas! how few will survive this short day's fight."

"On his feet which wore tinkling little bells, now shines the warrior's anklet. On his forehead which was covered with luxuriant locks, are now worn the bright leaves of the margosa twined with the twigs of the Ulinjai. On his arms adorned with pretty bracelets is now seen the strong bow. Who is this youth that attired thus stands conspicuous on his high chariot? May he be blessed! Though a flower garland is on his chest, the necklace he wore as a boy has not been taken off. To-day his food was served without milk. Unmoved he saw column after column of the enemies' forces as it advanced to the attack. Them he neither admired nor scorned; and when his own soldiers grappled with the foes and slaughtered them till their cries seemed to echo in the skies, neither glad nor proud was he of the victory achieved by his army."

The Pandya was not satisfied with driving back the invaders but determined to carry the war into the Chola dominion. He collected a large army of skilled archers and lancers and led them into Milalai-kurram,[1] the southern province of the Chola kingdom, of which the ruler was Evvi, chief of an ancient clan of the Vellala tribe. He defeated Evvi and annexed Milalai-kûrram to his dominion. He annexed also Muttûrru-kûrram the easternmost province of the Chera kingdom. These exploits naturally excited the envy of all the neighbouring kings. A formidable league was formed by the Chola and Chera kings who united their forces with those of five other kings, viz., Thithiyan, king of Pothiyam, Elini or Athikamân, chief of Thakadûr; Erumaiyûran or the ruler of the Buffalo country (Mysore); Irunko Vcnmûn and Porunan.[2] They expected to crush the power of the Pandya; but the latter rose equal to the occasion. He watched their movements closely and without giving them time to take any concerted action, or to enter and lay waste his territory, he boldly attacked them at their rendezvous at Thalai-âlankânam. Though taken by surprise, the allies offered a stout resistance and the battle raged fiercely one whole

---

[1] Ibid., 24.   [2] Akam— 36.

day before the Pandya could drive them from the field. All the kings and chieftains in the Tamil land and the flower of their troops had been engaged in this battle, and hence the victory gained by the Pandyan king was considered the most brilliant feat of arms of this period. The joy of his subjects knew no bounds. The poets and minstrels who crowded in his court extolled him as the greatest warrior of the age.

The Pandya next conducted an expedition personally into the Chêra territory and succeeded in capturing the king Chêy who was surnamed Yanaik-kan or "the elephant eye" from the peculiar form of his eyes. The Chêra king managed however to escape from custody[1] and Nedunj-Cheliyan pursued him up to the shores of the Western sea, and defeated the Chêra army again in a battle near the town Muchiri.[2] Alumbil Vel, one of the fudatory chiefs of the Chêra was dispossessed of his lands.[3] The Pandya defeated also the chiefs of Kudda-nad and annexed the Nad to his kingdom. He captured the sea-port of Muthu-vellil from a tribe called "Tholuvar" and the famous emporium of Saliyur (in the Gulf of Manaar) from the Nagas.

Nedunj-Chelyan II ascended the throne a few years before the death of Karikal Chola. After his victory at Thalai-âlankânam, he appears to have been on terms of friendship with the great Chola, as may be seen from the stanza composed by the poet Karik-kannan of Kavirippaddinam, a translation of which has been already given in my account of Karikal[4] Nedunj Cheliyan died in the Siva temple at Madura which was called the "silver shrine," and he was therefore known in subsequent literature as Velli-amballathu-thunjchiya Peru Valuthi or "the great Valuthi who died in the silver shrine." The period of his reign was most probably from about A. D. 90 to A. D. 128.

The poet whom Nedunj-Cheliyan II honored most was Maruthanar of Mankudi who composed the Idyll "Maduraik-kanchi" in his praise. The poet gives an excellent character of his patron:—[5]

"Sincere art thou ever in thy friendship, though the gods themselves may tempt thee to be false offering thee paradise and ambrosia: thou wilt not obey another's command though the most

<hr>

[1] Puram—17. [2] Akam—57. [3] Maduraik-Kanchi—ll. 344-345.
[4] Ante—Vol. II. p. 328. [5] Maduraik-kanchi—ll. 190—205.

powerful kings of this earth attack thee : thou wilt not stoop to commit a wicked deed, though all the gold buried in the southern hills by Bana may be obtained thereby : thou delightest ever in doing good."

The object of the poem was to wean the king's mind from worldly ambition and to awaken in him a desire for the salvation of his soul. The concluding lines of the poem, in which the author reminds the king of his pious ancestors and prays that he may emulate their example are as follow :—[1]

"Illustrious like Muthu-kudumi who performed many sacrifices, and like Nilan-tharu-thiruvin Nediyon whose praises were sung by eminent poets versed in the ancient lore of the land, thou art praised for thy prowess and thy virtues by many a sage; having conquered what was difficult to conquer and extended thy dominions, having learned all that the wisest know and established thy fame, thou art resplendent like the morning sun in the midst of the ocean, and like the full moon in the midst of stars, surrounded by princes of thy royal house, served by the Kosar renowned in war, chief amongst whom is the great Maran of everlasting fame, and honored by the five corporations and a host of vassal princes. Drink thou daily of the fragrant wine which thy handmaids wearing brilliant jewels present to thee in cups of gold : and live thou nobly thy full span of life.!"

The king's love of his soldiers and solicitude for the wounded in camp are well described in the poem Nedu-nal-Vâdai written by Nar-kirar.[2] "In the midnight, though a chill north wind is blowing, the king leaves his pavilion with a few attendants who hold flaming torches, a noble steed saddled and adorned with little bells is led behind him : a white umbrella decked with strings of pearls is held over him to keep off the drizzling rain : with his left hand he holds up his flowing robes, while his right hand rests on the shoulder of a stalwart youth who carries the king's sword slung on his arm : and the king graciously enquires after each wounded soldier as one of the generals goes before him holding a lance wreathed with garlands of the margosa and points out one by one the heroes wounded in the previous day's fight."

After Nedunj Cheliyan II succeeded the Pandyan king Ugra-

---

[1] Ibid., ll. 759-782.   [2] Nedu-nal-vâdai, ll. 172-188.

peru-valuthi whose name is well known to all the students of
Tamil literature as that of the king in whose court Kural, the immortal work of Tiru-Valluvar was published in the presence of 48
poets. This king had the title of Kanapper-thantha-Ugrapperu-
valuthi which meant that he conquered and annexed the fortified
town of Kanapper which was then considered an impregnable fort.
An ode addressed to the monarch praising his capture of the fort is
as follows :—[1]

"Hail monarch of fame eternal ! Victorious king ! Whom
bards have praised for thy prowess in capturing the great fortress
of Kanapper whose high walls seem to reach the sky, whose battlements gleam like the stars, the ditch surrounding which fort is as
deep and fathomless as the sea, the thorny jungle beyond which
is so dense that no ray of sunshine ever enters it ; for the loss of
which fort Venkai-marpan mourns daily as it is now hard to
regain as the water poured on red-hot iron. May thy foes perish
and be forgotten. May thy lance be victorious for ever !"

Nothing further is known of this king, and it appears most
probable that his reign did not extend to more than a few years.
He was succeeded by the prince Nan-Maran or the "Good
Pandya." Two of the stanzas addressed to this king by the
poets of his court are as follow :—[2]

"O Mara ! who wearest the garlands of flowers ! like the
matchless eye which shines in the forehead, adorned with the
crescent, of that god, whose throat is black and who gave victory
to the mighty immortals by destroying the three castles of
the Asuras, using a mountain for his bow, a snake for
the bow-string and a matchless arrow, thou art supreme amongst
kings. Although a monarch's power may seem to depend upon
his ferocious battle elephants, fleet warsteeds, tall bannered
chariots, and fearless soldiers, it has its real foundation on justice.
Therefore be not partial to thy subjects nor deal unjustly with
strangers ; be valiant as the fierce sun, benevolent as the mild
moon and gracious as the clouds which shower rain so that
there may be no poverty in thy land. Long mayst thou live for
many years as countless as the sands which strong winds heap up

---

[1] Puram—21.   [2] Ibid., 55 and 56.

in hillocks in the beautiful harbour of Chenthil, sacred to the god Muruga, where the foam-crested waves of the sea ceaselessly break upon the shore."

"In fierce wrath thou art like the god of death. In resistless strength thou art like Baladeva. In fame thou art like Vishnu who smites those who do not praise him. In carrying out whatever thou wishest thou art like Muruga. What is there that thou canst not achieve? Therefore give alms freely to those who seek thy charity. Spend thy days joyously drinking daily of cool and fragrant wine brought by Yavanas in their good ships which thy handmaids who wear shining bracelets on their arms, present to thee in handsome cups of gold. Thou Mara, who wieldest the conquering sabre ! like the sun whose fiery rays dispell darkness and like the moon whose mild beams brighten the evening, live for ever, and be eminent amongst the kings of this earth !"

This king died at a place called Ilavanthikaip-palli and hence he was called by subsequent writers Ilavanthikaip-palli-thunjchiya-Nan-Marau or " the good Mara who died at Ilavanthikaip-palli."

CHERA GENEALOGY.

ATHAN I.

(A. D. 40—55).

(Wounded on the back at the battle of Vennil, and starved himself to death).

ATHAN II = SONAI.

(A. D. 55—90). | (Daughter of Karikal Chola).
(*Alias* Vâna-Varmman or Chelvak-kadunk-ko.

Venmâl = Chenk-kudduvan *alias* Imaya-varmman.
(A. D. 90—125).
(Captured V i y a l u r : attacked Mohoor : and conducted an expedition by sea to the banks of the Ganges.)

Ilanko-adikal (author of the Tamil epic poem Chilapp-athikâram).

Yânaik-kad-chey
(A. D. 125—135).

(Captured by the Pandya Nedunj-Cheliyan II and subsequently escaped).

Perunj-cheral-Irumporai
(A. D. 135—150).

(Who killed Athikamân Elini and captured Thakadûr.)

CHAPTER VII.

The Cheras.

Of the Chera kings of this period Athan I. was the earliest sovereign, contemporary with Karikal-Chola. He was wounded on the back while fighting at the head of his army against Karikal at Vennil [1] as related by me already in the life of Karikal. The Chera king unable to bear the disgrace of having received a wound on the back while fighting, determined to put an end to his life by starvation. It is said that some of his favourite companions also voluntarily died with him unwilling to part from him even in death. [2]

His successor on the throne was Athan II., surnamed Chelvak-kadunk-ko-vâli-Athan. He gained the friendship of Karikal by marrying his daughter Sônai. [3] Being the son-in-law of the most powerful of the Tamil kings of this period, his reign appears to have been peaceful and prosperous. The poet Kapilar who was a Brahmin by birth enjoyed the special regard of this monarch. While in a pleasant mood the Chera king took hold of the hands of the poet and observed that they were remarkably soft. Kapilar who was an adroit flatterer complimented the king on the strength of his hands and gracefully acknowledged that the hands of the poets of his court cannot but be soft. The stanza sung by him on the occasion is as follows :—[4]

" Thou warrior king, whose broad shoulders cause pangs of love to fair ladies, and terror to thy foes ! to drive the fierce war elephant with a goad adorned with gold and to urge the animal to burst open the gates of thy enemies' forts which are secured with iron bars : to hold up the reins of thy noble steed and clear the deep moats, the banks of which have been levelled by the soldiers: to draw with all thy might the string of thy bow and discharge arrows taken from the quiver hung on thy back when riding in the chariots, to do all these acts of strength, thy arms are long and sinewy and thy hands are broad and powerful. But the hands of

---

[1] Ibid., 65. [2] Akam 55. [3] Chilapp-athikâram, xxix. [4] Param 14.

thy bards are soft as they have no other work but to eat of boiled rice, roasted flesh and spiced mixtures."

On another occasion the same poet composed in honor of the king an ode which is remarkable for boldness of conception and felicity of expression. The ode is addressed to the sun, and the poet draws a series of comparisons between the king and the sun, in all of which he shows that his patron is superior to the luminary. I cannot reproduce in a translation the elegance of expression of the original, but the meaning is as follows :—[1]

> " Bright orb that marchest proudly in the sky !
> Behind the hills thou hidest from our sight,
> And thou art seen by day and ne'er by night :
> Though soaring in the sky so wide and high,
> Alone thou darest not to show thy face,
> But comest guarded by a thousand rays !
> How canst thou vie with Cheral Athan bold,
> Who countless chiefs in fealty doth hold,
> Who knows no fear on the battle field
> And counts no cost the weak and poor to shield,
> Who scorns divided empire for his sway,
> And leads the legions that smite and slay ? "

Though this was in fact a pure conceit in words, the parallel drawn was so startling, that the king was doubtless highly flattered by this gem of poetry, and he rewarded the poet with a free gift of several villages.

Athan II. had two sons, the elder of whom was called Chenk-kudduvan and the younger was known as Ilankko-Adikal or the "royal monk." The latter prince composed the poem Chilapp-athikaram. He relates in this poem [2] that on a certain occasion when he and his brother were seated in the audience hall at the foot of the throne occupied by their father, a seer appeared before the king. He surveyed the features of the king and his two sons and foretold that the king would soon depart his life and that the younger son had every sign of becoming a sovereign. This remark of the seer annoyed Ilanko-adikal, who loved his elder brother dearly, so much that he resolved to renounce the world at once and embrace the life of a monk of the Nigrantha sect, so that all hopes of his succession to the throne may be cut off.

---

[1] Ibid., 8,   [2] Chilapp-athikaram, xxx. ll. 171 ff.

The king died at Chikkar-palli and was henceforth known as Chikkar-palli-thunjchiya chelvak-kadunk-ko-vâli-Athan or "Athan, the fierce king who died at Chikkar-palli."

Chenkudduvan *alias* Imayavarmman succeeded his father Athan II about A. D. 90. Soon after his accession to the throne he captured Viyalûr the capital of Irunko-vênmân king of a mountainous country where gold mines were worked.[1] Some years afterwards Nalank-killi the son of Karikal-Chola died, and the Chola crown passed to Killi-valavan, grandson of Karikal Chola and cousin of Chenkudduva Chera. Killivalavan's authority was not however acknowledged by other members of the Chola royal family. Nine of the Chola princes revolted. Hearing of this rebellion Chenk-kudduvan marched with a large army to the assistance of his cousin. He defeated the nine rebel princes at Neri-vâyil and established the power of his cousin.[2] Soon afterwards he attacked Mohoor, the capital of Palayan-Mâran in the southern part of the Pandyan kingdom. He undertook this expedition to Mohoor on behalf of a chieftain named Arukai who had been illtreated by Palayan-Máran.[3] Being in close friendship with the Karnas, kings of Magadha, he accompanied his widowed mother Sonai to the banks of the Ganges where the queen bathed in the sacred waters. Many years later Chenk-kudduvan again visited the Ganges under peculiar circumstances which are related as follows in the Chilapp-athikâram :—[4]

"Kothai, the lord of the "celestials," who wields the sharp sword, who overthrew the Kadambu which stood encircled by the sea, and who set the banner of the bow on the Imaya mountains to the astonishment of the "celestials," who inhabited that region, while seated one day in his silver palace with his queen Venmâl was pleased to command that arrangements be made to proceed on a short tour to visit the mountains covered with green woods on which the clouds ever rest and the music of whose water-falls never ceases. He set out from Vanji with a large retinue of the daughters of the "celestial race" desirous of sporting with them in the flowery groves, and encamped on a sand-hill on the banks of the Periyâr, where the river quits the

[1] Ibid., xxviii. ll. 115 ff. [2] Ibid., xxviii. ll. 118 ff. [3] Ibid., xxviii. ll. 124 ff.

[4] Ibid., cantos xxv to xxx.

mountains and descends to the low country spreading its waters around islets and groves and halls and temples. From there he viewed the lovely scenery and the rapid current of the river which bore cn its bosom many a bright and fragrant flower. The king and the ladies were delighted by the songs of the hill-tribes. Anon, there broke on their ears the distant shouts of the hunters who captured wild elephants in pitfalls or who tore the hives of honey-bees, the splash of cascades, the trumpeting of elephants and the clang of armour amongst the soldiers who accompanied the king. While the king and his company thus enjoyed the scene, the hill-men appeared bearing on their heads the white tusks of elephants, bundles of the fragrant aghil wood, tails of the yak, pots of honey, Blocks of sandal wood, lumps of red lead, arsenic and of the sulphuret of antimony; bunches of cardamom and pepper, the flour of the *Kúrai* root, the edible roots of the *Kavalai*, ripe cocoanuts and the sweet fruits of the mango and the jack; festoons of green leaves, garlic and sugarcane and flowery creepers, bunches of arecanuts and plantains, cubs of the lion and the yáli; the young of tigers and calves of elephants; the young of monkeys and the whelps of bears; the kids of mountain goats and of mountain deer;-the young of musk deer; the mongoose, long-tailed peacocks, civet cats, wild fowls and prattling parrots. Presenting these products of their hills they exclaimed :—

"May thou be victorious for ever! For seven births are we thy subjects. Under the shade of a *Venkai* tree in the forest, a fair girl who had lost one of her breasts lay alone and in agony and breathed her last. Whence she came or whose daughter she was, we know not. Long mayst thou live for many hundred thousand years!" Cháthan the master of sweet Tamil, who was in the king's company, charmed by the royal presence, related the story of the hapless maid to the king and queen. She was, he said, the wife of a merchant of Kavirippaddinam, who having lost all his wealth to a beautiful actress of that town, came to Madura accompanied only by his faithful wife; a pair of valuable anklets was all the property left in the hands of his wife. The husband wished to sell one of the anklets, and with the money realized by its sale, he intended to start afresh the life of a merchant. His ill-luck led him to the king's jeweller who having already stolen one of the queen's anklets reported to the king that the stolen jewel had been brought to him for sale by a stranger and pointed out the merchant to the royal guards who came to arrest him. The merchant, surprised by the sudden turn of affairs, was unable to explain to the guards how he came by the jewel; the guards suspecting him to be the thief beheaded him on the spot, and took the jewel to the palace. The sad news of the execution of the merchant reached his wife, who was then lodging in a shepherd's house. With tears streaming from her eyes, she ran to the spot where her husband lay a mangled corpse, and having heard from the people of the town that her husband was beheaded, because he had stolen one of the queen's anklets, the disconsolate widow demanded an audience of the king and appearing before him proved to his satisfaction that the anklet found in the possession of her husband was her own and not that of the Pandyan queen. The king stung with remorse swooned from his throne and never recovered his life; and the queen ascended the funeral pyre. The unhappy widow cut off one of her breasts and threw it in the streets of Madura praying that the wicked town be destroyed by fire; and accordingly the palace and a part of the town were burnt to ashes. She then quitted Madura and travelling westwards came into the Chera kingdom and there died. Chenkudduvan and his queen Venmal were much affected by this story. The queen observed that the chaste but unfortunate widow was worthy of being worshipped as a goddess. The king approved of this idea, and looked at the learned men of his court for their advice; and they said that an image may be carved out of a block of granite from the Pothiya hill and anointed in the waters of the Kaviri, or that the statue may be fashioned from a stone from the Himalayas and bathed in the sacred waters of the Ganges. The king exclaimed that to obtain a stone from Pothiyam and bathe it in the Kaviri river was unbecoming one of his martial race : and he decided therefore to obtain a stone from the Himalayas. His minister Villavan-Kothai addressed the king as follows :—·

" May thou be victorious for many years. Thy rival kings defeated in the battle-field of Kongu, abandoned their banners of the tiger and the fish, and the fame of thy victory has spread through the world. My eyes shall never forget thy victorious march against the combined armies of the Konkanas, Kalingas, Karunadas, Pankalas, Gangas, Kattiyas, and the northern Aryas, when thy queen-mother bathed in the sacred stream of the Ganges. If it is thy desire to march to the Himalayas to obtain stone for carving the image of a goddess, it is well that written messages be sent to the kings of the north intimating the fact." Then the prince of Alumbil spoke out as follows:—

"The envoys of foreign kings reside outside the gates of Vanji and through them those kings may learn the purpose of our march. It is enough to proclaim our journey by beat of drums in our capital."

The king and his party returned soon after to Vanji and under his command, the king's intention to proceed to the banks of the Ganges was proclaimed by beat of drums which were carried throughout the town on the royal elephant. When the king entered the audience hall and took his seat which was supported by figures of lions, the high-priest, the chief astrologer, the great ministers of state and the generals of his army who had assembled to receive him exclaimed " Long-live king of kings " and prayed for his orders regarding the expedition. Looking at the generals and gallant officers of his army the martial king responded:—

"Pilgrims from the Himalayas have informed us that the princes of the north had sneerd at the Tamil kings ; and we shall not therefore return from his expedition without defeating those kings and compelling them to carry on their heads stone from the Himalayas for fashioning the statue of a goddess."

The high-priest then addressed the king :—

"Appease thy wrath Imaya-varmma, it cannot be thee, of whom the northern kings spoke contemptuously. Is there any king in this country who can face thee in the battle-field except the Pandya and Chola ? Art thou not the refuge of every one who flies to thee for assistance ?"

Then the chief astrologer learned in the science, which treats of the twelve signs of the Zodiac and the position of the planets and stars and of the five parts of Astrology, stood up and said:—

"Mighty monarch, may victory ever attend thee! This is the auspicious time; if thou art pleased to start at once in the direction that thou wishest to proceed all thy rival kings shall bow at thy sacred feet."

Hearing this the king ordered at once that the royal sword and unbrella should be carried northwards. The warriors shouted joyously, the big drums thundered, the banners fluttered, and the five corporations, and the eight great assemblies, the priests and astrologers, the judges and ministers all exclaimed :— "Blessed be the king." The royal sword and umbrella adorned with garlands of flowers were carried on the chief elephant in royal state to a fort outside the town. The king then entered his audience hall and there feasted the generals and chiefs of his army. Next day, while the morning drum was sounding at his palace gate, the king started from his palace wearing on his crown wreaths of Vanji flowers and visited the temple of Vishnu, and having offered his prayers to the god, he mounted his elephant. He received from the priest the symbols of the sacred feet of Siva and placed them devoutly on his crown and on his shoulders; and amidst the blessings of the priests from the golden temple of Vishnu, he left Vanji, seated on his elephant, under the shade of a white umbrella, accompanied by his military officers and a mighty host of warriors on foot, on horses, on chariots and on elephants. He made his first halt at the foot of the Nilgiri hills. These hills do not appear to be the modern Nilgiris, but were most probably the rocky hills which project boldly forth to within sixteen or eighteen miles of the shore of the Bay of Bengal at Balasore in the Orissa district, which were known to the old navigators as the Nilgiri mountains. The journey from the Chera kingdom to Orissa appears to have been performed by sea, as stated at the end of the poem, where Chenk-kudduvan is praised as the king who with his army crossed the sea and reached the banks of the Ganges. When the Chera king was encamped at the foot of the Nilgiris, Sanjchaya, a general in the service of the Karnas, the rulers of the Magadha empire, arrived with one hundred dancing girls, two hundred and eight musicians, one hundred pole-dancers, one hundred chariots, ten thousand horse, twenty thousand waggons and one thousand body guards. The officer at the gate having announced the arrival of Sanjchaya and his company, the Chera king was pleased to command that Sanjchaya and his chief attendants be admitted to his audience. Accordingly Sanjchaya appeared before the king and bowing low addressed him as follows :—

"Long live thou ruler of this earth! The Satakarna who is thy intimate friend has sent thee the following message through me. If it is the desire of the king of the celestials to obtain stone from the lofty Himalaya mountains to fashion the image of a god, we shall help him to obtain the stone and anoint it in the sacred flood of the Ganges."

The Chera king replied to Sanjchaya :—

"Kanaka and Vijaya, sons of Balakumara having lost watch and ward over their tongues have reviled the Tamil kings, ignorant of their strength. This army is therefore on its march nursing its wrath. Inform this to Satakarna and let him collect a fleet of ships to carry my army across the great river Ganges."

Having despatched Sanjchayan he admitted to his presence the one thousand body guards and received from them a tribute of fragrant sandal wood and pearls. Breaking up his camp the king marched with his army to the banks of the Ganges and crossed over in a fleet of ships provided by the Karnas. On the northern bank the Karnas themselves welcomed the king. Taking leave of them the king proceeded further north to the country known as Uttarai where at a place called Kuyilaluvam he encountered the army led by the Aryan princes Kanaka and Vijaya and their allied kings, Uttara, Vichitra, Rudra, Bhairava, Chitra Singha, Dhanuttara and Sveta. The Chera king rejoiced at the sight of the noble army of the Aryan kings and boldly led his Tamil soldiers who marched forward to the beat of thundering drums, the booming of conch-shells and the stirring blasts of trumpets. The archers, lancers and swordsmen fought long and fiercely and the carnage was terrible. The battle-field was covered with heaps of the slain, soldiers, horses and elephants and at last the Tamils bore down everything before them, and

Kanaka, Vijaya, and several other princes fell captives into the hands of Chenk-kudduvan. He compelled Kanaka and Vijaya to change their royal garments for the garb of religious mendicants and sent them with his minister Villavan-Kothai and a military escort to the Himalayas. After the battle, the king returned to the southern banks of the Ganges, where the Karnas had constructed a magnificent palace in the midst of a lovely park for the use of the king and several mansions and buildings for his officers and army. Here the king distributed honors and rewards to those who had distinguished themselves in the battle, and to the sons of those who had fallen in battle. The king returned to Vanji after an absence of thirty-two months. His queen and the subjects received him with great rejoicings. From the banks of the Ganges he had sent the Aryan princes Kanaka and Vijaya in charge of his body-guard to be exhibited at the courts of the Pandya and Chola kings. After visiting Kavirip-paddinam and Madura, Nilan the commander of the body-guard returned to Vanji and informed the king that the Chola and Pandya kings condemned the cruel treatment accorded to the unfortunate Aryan princes. The Chera king was annoyed with the remarks made by the Tamil kings. The Brahmin Madalan who was then present, addressed the king as follows :—

"King of kings, may thou be ever victorious l Thou hast conquered Viyalur where wild elephants slumber in the shade of the pepper vine. Thou hast defeated nine Chola princes in a pitched battle at Neri-väyil and won a grand victory at Idumbil and now crossing the wide ocean thou hast defeated the Aryan princes who attacked thee on the banks of the Ganges. Master of the victorious army! wise monarch! may thou be appeased; may thou live as many years as there are grains of sand on the banks of the river Porunai. Pray, listen to my words, and scorn them not Although thou art now fifty years of age thou hast spent all thy life in war and has not performed any religious sacrifice. Thou knowest well that our life is not everlasting. For, of the ancient heroes of thy race not one is alive. He who conquered the Kadambu in the middle of the sea, he who set the emblem of the bow on the Imaya mountains, he who enabled the Brahmin poet who composed verses in his praise, to attain heaven by per-

forming sacrifices, he who controlled the god of death, he who
ruled the land of the Yavana and who entered the mountains
which yield gold, the hero who led a gallant army and stormed
the fortress of Akappa, he who bathed in the waters of the river
Ayirai and in the two seas, he who established the worship of
the four Bhûtas in his capital Vanji and performed sacrifices:
all these kings are dead and gone. Thou knowest also that
wealth and power are not lasting, for, hast thou not seen the
defeat and disgrace of the Aryan princes who scorned the
Tamils? Need I say that youth is also fleeting for thy hair
is turning grey?"

Dwelling on the Brahminic belief in the transmigration of
souls he advised the king to perform a magnificent sacrifice called
Rajasuya so that his soul may be blessed in its future births.
The king acted on this advice, and preparations were immediately
ordered for the performance of Rajasûya on a grand scale and for
the consecration of a temple to Kannaki. The kings of Kongu
and Maluva and Gajabahu of Lanka attended these ceremonies.

Chenk-kudduvan was succeeded by Chèy who was surnamed
Yânaik-kan or "the elephant eye." He was a very warlike prince
and constantly moved about the frontiers of his dominions
harassing the neighbouring kings. It was perhaps on account of
these incursions that the Pandyan king Nedunj-Cheliyan II
invaded the Chera territory, and by skilful manœuvres succeeded
in taking the Chera a prisoner.[1] The latter however escaped
soon afterwards and regained his power. The Chola king Râja-
sûyam-vedda-peru-nat-killi was also at war with Yanaik-kad-
Chey: and Thèr-van-malayan chief of Malâdu is said to have
assisted the Chola in this war.[2] Kurunk-koliyûr-kilar, a poet
of his court, praises the king for having once saved the town of
Vilankil from his enemies. One of the stanzas composed by
the poet is as follows:—[3]

"Thou king of the lofty Kolli hills, valiant Chèy, whose
eyes are like those of the elephant! whose encampment is so
extensive that it needs no sentries, and where the shouts of the
soldiers who dance wildly in their drunken revels ever sound like

[1] Puram 17.   [2] Ibid., 125.   [3] Ibid., 22.

the noise of the sea waves lashing the shore : who feedest thy dependents out of the tribute paid to thee by vassal kings : may thy boundless wealth be everlasting! The poets that sing of thee need not praise others any more, for thou art so liberal that they are never in want. Having heard that the kingdom ruled by thee is like a paradise on earth, I came and my eyes are gladdened. Ever active thou leadest thy armies into foreign lands eager to conquer and to earn a deathless fame!"

The poet Kudal-kilar who was present at the death of this king states that his death was portended by the fall of a brilliant meteor seven days previous to the occurrence. The following verse uttered by him on the occasion is specially interesting as it shows that the Tamils studied Astronomy independently of the Brahmins and that Tamil names were in common use for the lunar asterisms and the signs of the solar Zodiac :—[1]

"On the day of Kuddam (Karttika) when the Sun was in the sign of Adu (Mesha) at midnight when the asterisms from the first star of Mudap-panai (Anuradha) to the last star of Kulam (Punarvasu) were visible in the sky, and while the asterism which is in the zenith during the first half of the month of Pankuni (Phalguna) was declining from the zenith, the eighth asterism before it was setting, and the eighth asterism after it was rising, a brilliant meteor which illumined the whole sky fell towards the north-east, showering fiery sparks against the wind. Seeing this falling star myself and other minstrels prayed fervently that the monarch of the fertile country which abounds in water-falls may be saved from death, and with a heavy heart we awaited the result of this dreadful omen. On the seventh morning the fatal day arrived and the king who was like the dark-coloured god Vishnu and who was clever in capturing his enemies and lavish in dispensing charity, has gone to the world of the immortals. His huge elephant lies down dejected stretching its trunk on the ground. His big drums roll on the floor uncared for. His white parasol lies without its handle. His fleet steeds stand pensive in their stable. Alas! having joined the company of celestial women, has he now forgotten his beloved queens ?"

---

[1] Ibid., 229.

Yanaik-kad-Chey was succeeded by Perunj-Cheral-Irumporai. The poet Mochu-kiranar appears to have been a favourite of this king. One day the poet, finding a couch furnished with cushions and covered with fresh flowers in a part of the palace, laid himself down on it and fell sound asleep. The king who happened to pass by that spot seeing that the poet was tired and perspiring, fanned him with his own hands. The poet awoke and was startled to find that the king was fanning him. Learning then that the couch was intended as a stand for the war-drum, he uttered the following stanza :—[1]

"I laid myself down to sleep on this couch which is covered with flowers soft as the froth on fresh oil, not knowing that it was intended for the royal war-drum, which is beautiful to behold with its black barrel adorned with the long feathers of the peacock and strings of beads wound with golden flowers of the ulinj-chai. Thou should have cut me in two with thy sword for my insolence. But thou hast kept thy sword in its sheath and as if this action was not enough to spread thy fame throughout the Tamil land, thou hast with thy strong arms fanned me to cool my sleepy brows. Is it because thou knowest that the blissful abodes in the next world are open only to those, the fame of whose good deeds filled this world, that thou mighty monarch hast acted thus?"

One of his feudatory chiefs named Elini having revolted he had to proceed with a large army and besiege Thakadûr the fort of the rebel chief. Elini was the descendant of an ancient line of chiefs who called themselves Athikaman. Their capital Thakadûr is believed to be the modern Dharmapuri in the Salem District. Elini repaired and strengthened the fortifications of the town and was determined to gain his independence or die in the attempt. But the Chera king completely invested the town and cut off all means of communication and supplies from outside. The thorny jungle which surrounded the town was cleared by the Chera soldiers, the moat was filled up and the gates burst open by elephants. The Chera army then rushed into the fort, and in the meleé that ensued, Elini and his lieutenants performed prodigies of valour, but were over-powered by numbers and fell fighting to

[1] Puram 60.

the last. The bards Arichil-kilar and Pon-mudiyar were present in the camp of the Chera king during the siege: and a few of their verses which have been preserved to this day contain vivid accounts of some of the incidents of the assault on the fort. When the Chera forces approached Thakadûr Elini and his general Perum-pakkan led out their army to engage them outside the fort. Perum-pakkan stood in front of his army awaiting the assault. The bards Arichil-kilar and Pon-mudiyar addressed the Chera kings as follows, when they saw Perum-pakkan laughing defiantly at them :—[1]

"The youthful warrior decked with garlands, who rejoicing in his strength stands facing our army, mounted on a handsome glittering chariot, drawn by high spirited horses; if he attacks us in his rage, he would overthrow even majestic rutting elephants. Eager for the assault, he shakes his lance which seems to emit flashes of lightning, and laughs at his foes."

"The dauntless young warrior who wears the dark beard, holds the reins of his steeds and looks first at his own swelling shoulders, then at the array of battle elephants behind him, then at the rows of chariots behind the elephants, then at his own steeds, then at the coming arrows, then at his lance, then at his armlets and laughs at us."

In the first day's engagement Elini's troops were driven into the fort. On the second day, the thorny jungle which sorrounded the fort was cleared; and the following stanza was uttered by the bards, when the Chera king asked them what they thought of the progress of the siege.[2]

"Yesterday (Elinis) steeds fled like stags, the elephants fainted and fell like rocks, and his valiant soldiers were routed by showers of hissing arrows. Thou victorious king who bearest on thy body fresh wounds received in battle ! to-day the heads of the slain with arrows sticking to them, kicked by our elephants, lie by the roadside like young palmyra fruits cut open; and our dark-eyed youths, who know no fatigue, have cleared the jungle, shouting at the enemies' men and killing them wherever they appeared. To-morrow we shall march, to the beat of drums, and storm the fort."

---

[1] Thakadur-yathirai.   [2] Ibid.

CHAPTER VIII.

PRINCES AND CHIEFS.

The Chera, Chola and Pandya having been the only crowned heads among the Tamils for many centuries, they were collectively known as " the three kings."   There were however several princes and chiefs ruling over extensive provinces in the Tamil land, who were more or less subject to one of the three kings. Some of them attempted at times to throw off their allegiance and set up as independent kings, but they were speedily subdued. First amongst the feudatory princes I should mention the Thirayan whose capital was at Kânchipuram.   This prince belonged to the tribe of Thirayan or " Sea kings," from whom the Cholas also derived their decent.   During the infancy of Karikâl Chola, the Great, the Thirayan of Kânchi usurped the Chola kingdom and ruled over it for a long period.   From the poem Perumpân-ârru composed in honor of the Thirayan, it appears that the king bore the titles of Pal-vér Thirayan and Thondaimân and was a warrior of great renown.[1]   Had the Thirayan removed at once the seat of his authority to Uraiyûr the ancient capital of the Cholas, he might have continued in possession of the Chola kingdom and bequeathed it to his descendants.   But he remained at Kânchi and Karikâl who escaped from prison, found little or no difficulty in regaining the throne of his ancestors.

Other chiefs feudatory to the Chola were the rulers of Venkadam, Malâdu and Milalai-kuram.   Of the chiefs of Venkadam, Pulli was contemporary with the poet Mâmûlar [2] and Athanungan with the poet Kallil-âth-thirayanar.[3]   These chiefs were constantly at war with the Vadugar, who inhabited the country immediately north of Tamilakam.

Malayamân was the hereditary title of the chiefs of Malâdu. The principal town in his province was Koval the modern Tirukoilur on the banks of the river Pennai.[4]   An extensive and fertile mountain plateau called Mullûr-malai formed part of his territory.   Here Malayamân-Kâri granted lands to many Brah-

---

[1] Perum-pân-arru.   [2] Akam 204-310-358.   [3] Puram 175-389.   [4] Akam 35.

min settlers, and such a large number of them were attracted to the spot that ancient Tamil poets spoke of the place as "the famous Mullûr crowded by Aryas."[1] Kapilar the Brahmin poet addressed Kári as follows praising his munificence to Brahmins and minstrels:

"The sea cannot over-run it. No enemy can assail it, Kári, who wearest the warrior's anklet! thy land is the property of the Brahmins who preserve the sacred fires. The presents bestowed by neighbouring monarchs on thee, as the great vassal of one of the three kings, thou givest away to the minstrels who sing the praises of thy clan. Nothing deemest thou as thy own save the person of thy spouse who is as chaste as the Northern Star, and yet art thou supremely happy."[2]

Another bard solicited his patronage in the following verse :—

"Thou descendant of that dauntless hero who wrested the plates of gold which had adorned the foreheads of his enemies' elephants, and out of those plates made lotus flowers and tied them to the heads of his minstrels: Warrior chief of the mountain Mullûr! on which the waterfalls descend with deafening sound through dense woods : that thou and thy warlike clan may prosper for ever, the learned Brahmin (Kapilar), than whom there is no wiser man on earth, has sung so well and made thy name immortal, that nothing is left to other minstrels to praise: even as no other ship can sail across the Western Ocean over which travel those vessels which bring gold to the shores of the Vánavan (Chera) we attempt in vain to sing of thee (as Kapilar has done) : thou lord of the valley of the Pennai who hast routed rival kings who came with elephants and with thundering drums to fight with thee! driven by want and drawn by thy fame, we seek thy charity."[3]

Kàri waged war with Ori, the chieftain of the Kolli hills, and having killed him in battle restored the Kolli hills to the rightful sovereign, the Chera.[4] Elated by success in his wars with neighbouring chiefs, Kári aspired to be an independent king and assumed the diadem. He was hence known as Tiru-mudik-kàri or "the crowned Kári." Not long after this event, the Chola monarch who

---

1 Ariyar thovanriya pêr ichai Mullûr.   3 Puram 122.
3 Param 126.   4 Akam 205.

was incensed at the presumption of his feudatory chief, invaded Maládu with a large army, and defeated Kári in a sanguinary engagement in which he was slain. The Chola intended to kill the sons of Kári and put an end to the family of the Malayamán, but their lives were saved by the intercession of the bard Kóvár-kilár.[1] Kári's son Kannan whose life was spared in this manner lived to perform a signal service to the Chola king. For, some years afterwards, the Chola, hard pressed by his enemies, had to flee from his capital and seek an asylum in the inaccessible heights of the Mullûr mountain, in the territory of his vassel Kannan. The latter who inherited all the valour of his father, revived the drooping spirits of the royal party, and rallying his forces succeeded in driving off his enemies and re-established the authority of the Chola. The grateful monarch made Kannan his prime minister and conferred on him the high title of Choliya-Enáthi.[2]

Má-vel-Evvi, the great Vellála chief of Milalai-kurram belonged to a powerful clan, which was considered ancient even eighteen hundred years ago.[3] His territory lay on the southern bank of the river Káviri ; and consisted almost entirely of fertile fields in which rice and sugar-cane were extensively cultivated. " The gates of his mansion were never closed and he never sat to his meals except with a large company" says a poet who partook of his hospitality.[4] He died of the wounds received in battle, while fighting bravely at the head of his troops, against Akuthai, one of the generals of the Pandyan king Nedunj-Cheliyan victor of Alankánam who had invaded his territory [5]

Vêl Pâri, a relative of Evvi, was the ruler of a petty principality called Parambu : but as a patron of poets he has left a name which will live in the memory of the Tamils as long as they speak the Tamil language. After the fall of Evvi, Pâri took possession of the high mountain of Parambu, and the lands surrounding it, and acted as an independent prince acknowledging the authority of none of " the three kings." He was a bold and gay adventurer, simple-hearted and generous, and passionately fond of poetry. Every wandering minstrel was welcomed in his mansion. The sons of song were nowhere petted and feasted as they were in Pari's palace. They found in him a union of all those virtues

[1] Puram 46.   [2] Puram 174.   [3] Puram 202.   [4] Puram 234.   [5] Ibid., 233.

which they loved to praise in their rhapsodies, reckless courage, lavish liberality and a gaiety which no reverse could check. He soon became their idol and his fame spread throughout Tamila kam. The bards recounted in glowing language, in the courts of the Chera, Chola and Pandya the princely hospitality with which they were entertained by Pâri. This excited the jealousy of the three kings and they sent their forces to besiege Parambu. The defiles of the mountain passes, with which Pari's followers were familiar, were strictly guarded by them, and Pari, by his personal bravery maintained for some days an unequal contest with the large and well-equipped army that surrounded him. At length the enemies forced their way up the mountain and attacked Pari who was killed in the encounter.[1] The poet Kapilar who was the boon companion of Pari, uttered the following stanzas when Parambu was besieged by the armies of the three kings:—

"It is hard to conquer Parambu though the three kings invest it with their allied armies. Three hundred in number are the villages in the fertile Parambu-Nâd: and all the three hundred are now the property of bards. Myself and Pari remain: and here is our hill if ye come to us singing as minstrels do."[2]

"Is it easy to seize the Parambu of which Pari is the lord? Though the three kings who possess thundering drums, blockade the hill, it will yield four products for which no ploughing is required: first, the thin-leaved bamboos supply rice; second, the jack trees furnish sweet fruits, third, the stout Valli creepers yield edible roots; and fourth, honey drips on the hill, when monkeys leap on the hives; spacious as the sky is the summit of the hill, and numerous as the stars are the springs therein. If you post a chariot on every farm and an elephant to every tree around the hill you cannot storm it with your soldiers, nor cut your way with swords. I know by what stratagem the hill can be captured. If striking the tuneful chords of a small lute, ye come singing and dancing followed by your songstresses, he would grant ye all his lands and his mountain."[3]

Of the brave kinsmen of Pâri, every one had fallen in his defence; and only his two daughters were left to lament his untimely death. The troops of minstrels who had lived on his

---

[1] *Ibid.*, 105-120.   [2] *Ibid.*, 110.   [3] *Ibid.*, 109.

charity were loud in their expression of grief for their departed chief, and their tears mingled with those of the two orphan girls who were now friendless. Kapilar the favourite bard of Pâri took charge of his daughters and while leaving Parambu addressed the mountain as follows :—

"We loved thee once! When the toddy jars were ever open, and sheep were slaughtered, and rice cooked with flesh was served as much as we wanted. Now Pâri, having died, forlorn and helpless with tears streaming from our eyes, we bid thee farewell ; noble Parambu! And we depart in search of proper husbands for Pâri's daughters, whose tresses are fragrant and whose arms are adorned with bracelets." Kapilar took the girls first to Vichchick-kô and then to Irunko-vêl who were two petty chieftains in Tamilakam ; and both the chiefs having declined to wed them he gave them away in marriage to Brahmins.[1]

Nannan, lord of Chenkanmâ in the valley of the Cheyyâr, was another famous chief in the Chola kingdom. The poem Malai-padukadâm was composed in his honor by Perunk-kausikanâr. It appears from this poem that there was a temple dedicated to Siva, under the name of Kari-undik-kadavul, on the top of the mountain Naviram in his territory.[2]

Ay, Porunan and Palayan-Mâran were the principal chieftains who owed allegiance to the Pandyan king. Of these, Mâ-vêl-ây belonged to the tribe of Vellâlas and was lord of the Pothiya hill and the land surrounding it. The chief town in his province was Aykudi.[3] Ay-andiram who was one of the rulers of Aykudi is said to have once defeated the Kongas and driven them to the Western Sea.[4] Thithiyan, a successor of Ay-andiran joined the confederacy of princes against the Pândya Nedunj-cheliyan and was defeated by him in the battle of Alan-kânam.[5] Porunan was the family name of the princes of Nânjil-nâd which was situated west of the Pothiya hill.[6] His territory is still known as Nânjil-nâd and forms a portion of the modern state of Travancore.

Palayan-Mâran, prince of Mohoor, was the head of the ancient tribe of Marar who were settled near the Pothya hill and who

[1] Ibid , 117.
[2] Malai-padu-kadâm,
[3] Puram, 127-132.
[4] Ibid., 130.
[5] Akam, 36.
[6] Puram, 137-140,

were the original stock from which the Pandyan kings were
descended. During the reign of the Pandyan, Nedunj-cheliyan I,
Palayan-Mâran was next to the king, the highest dignitary in the
state.[1] When the Chola king Killi-Valavan besieged Madura
with a large army, Palayan Maran attacked him with a powerful
force consisting of warriors mounted on fleet steeds and fierce
elephants and utterly routed the Chola army.[2] The Chera king
Chenk-kudduvan is said to have once invaded the territory belonging to Palayan Maran in order to chastise him for an insult
offered to one of the princes feudatory to the Chera.[3]

The chiefs of Alumbil, Kuthirai-malai, Pali and Thakadoor
were subordinate to the Chera king. Alumbil Vel was lord of
Alumbil, a town situated most probably in Kuddanad. The
Pandya Nedunj-cheliya I, who invaded the dominion of the Chera
attacked and defeated Alumbil Vel and annexed all his territory to
the Pandyan kingdom.[4] After the death of that redoubtable monarch, Alumbil Vel appears to have recovered his territory and we
find him to be one of the leading noblemen in the court of the
Chera Chenkkudduvan.[5] Piddan-Korran, lord of the mountain
Kuthirai-malai was the commander-in-chief of the Chera army.[6]
Venman was the title of the princes of Pali, a fortified town in the
gold mining district, which comprised the whole of the country now
known as Coorg, North Wynaad and north-east Malabar.[7] Two
other towns in the province were Arayam and Viyalur.[8] Nannan-
Venmân, a prince of Pali acquired notoriety as a murderer, having
condemned to death a girl whom her relations offered to save with
a ransom of nine times her weight in gold![9] A prince of this
line was defeated by the Chera king Kalankaik-kanni-nâr-mudich-
cheral in the battle of Perunthurai.[10]

Athiyaman, chief of the tribe of Malavar, was the ruler of
Thakadoor the modern Dharmapuri in the district of Salem.[11]
His ancestors introduced the cultivation of sugar-cane into
Southern India.[12] Nedumân-anchi was the head of the Athyamân

---

1 Mathuraik-kânchi.
2 Akam, 345.
3 Chilapp-athikâram, xxvii., 124, 126.
4 Mathuraik-kâvolu.
5 Chilapp-athikâram.
6 Puram, 172. 7 Akam, 257-396.
8 Akam, 97, Puram, 202, 203.
9 Pen kolai purinta Nannan.
10 Akam, 198. 11 Puram, 230.
12 Puram, 99.

clan during the reign of the Chera king Perunj-cheral-Irum-porai. He invaded Maladu and sacked Kovalur the capital of Malayaman.[1] The bard Paranar praised his achievements on that occasion. Being an ambitious and warlike chief he wished to extend his territory, and although the Chera king was willing to bestow on him all the land which lay around Kuthirai-malai, within sight from the top of that high mountain, the chief asked for more. This led to war and the Chera king had to march with his army to Thakadoor to subdue the refractory chief. During the siege of Thakadoor, Neduman-anchi was mortally wounded and died soon afterwards. I have described the siege already in the account of the Chera king Perunj-cheral-Irumporai. [2] The poetess Avvaiyar who was a great favourite in the court of the Athiyaman describes in the following verse the terror with which neighbouring chiefs beheld him and his fierce soldiers :—

" Those who see thy brigades of war elephants marching with their tusks blunted by battering thy enemies' forts, renew the strong bars with which the gates of their fort are bolted; those who see thy troops of horse whose hoofs are covered with the blood of their foes whom they had trampled to death, block the entrances to their fort with stout thorny trees : those who see thy sharp lances which pierce the hardest shields, repair and strengthen their shields ; those who see thy fierce soldiers who bear on their body many a scar caused by sword cuts, waste not the arrows from their quivers : and thou, not deterred by the poisonous smoke of the seeds of the *Iyyavi*, which thy enemies burn at their fort-gates to keep off your army, seize and kill them like the god of death. Alas ! Who can save the fertile lands of thy enemies whose fields are covered with waving corn?" [3]

[1] *Ibid.*   [2] Thakadur Yaththirai.   [3] Puram, 98.

the physicians attended to all matters affecting the health of the king and his subjects: the astrologers fixed auspicious times for public ceremonies and predicted important events: the ministers attended to the collection and expenditure of the revenue and the administration of justice.[1] Separate places were assigned in the capital town, for each of these assemblies, for their meetings and transaction of busi ness.[2] On important occasions they attended the king's levee in the throne hall or joined the royal procession. It will be very interesting to know more of the constitution of the "Five Great Assemblies;" but no further information is available in the ancient poems which are now extant. The power of Government was entirely vested in the king and in the "Five Great Assemblies." It is most remarkable that this system of Government was followed in the three kingdoms of the Pandya, Chola and Chera, although they were independent of each other. There is reason to believe therefore that they followed this system of Government which obtained in the country from which the founders of the "three kingdoms" had originally migrated, namely, the Magadha Empire.

The person of the king was surrounded with much pomp and dignity. He was served by a numerous company of attendants. They are frequently mentioned as "the eight groups of attendants" which were as follow :—[3]

Perfumers, garland-makers, betel-bearers, arecanut-servers, armourers, dressing valets, torch or light-bearers and body-guards.

The king wore a long crown of a conical shape made of gold and set with precious stones. Armlets of gold on his arms, an anklet of gold on the right leg, and a necklace of pearls or precious stones were the other principal ornaments usually worn by him. A superb umbrella adorned with strings of pearls was held over him while he was seated on his throne, or wherever he went outside his palace. He generally rode on an elephant or on horseback or on a chariot drawn by horses. Big drums resounded at his palace gate, early at dawn and at sunset. Time criers were employed

---

[1] Chilapp-athikÂram, arum-patha urai on line 157, canto v.
[2] Mathuraik-kânchi.
[3] See foot-note (1) p. 169.

CHAPTER IX.

Social Life.

From the foregoing brief history of the three kings and their subordinate chiefs it will be seen that they were frequently at war with each other and that their subjects lived in the midst of wars and wars' alarms. It may well be asked therefore how it was possible for the arts of peace to flourish under such conditions. The answer is simple. It was only the men, trained to the profession of arms, who engaged in war, while the rest of the people resided within walled towns, and followed unmolested their different callings. The poorer classes who lived in villages remote from the capital towns were exposed to frequent attacks from the neighbouring chiefs and suffered terrible hardships. Their cattle were carried away, their houses were burnt down and they were driven out of the village or slaughtered if they offered the least resistance. The large population of the great cities such as Madura, Karur and Kavirippaddinam enjoyed however almost perfect immunity from the horrors of war. The inhabitants of most of the important towns, which were strongly fortified, were likewise secure from the evils attending an occupation by a hostile army. It was in these fortified towns that trade and manufactures were carried on to the mutual advantage of the artisans and the public. Caravans of merchants travelled from town to town escorted by soldiers. The principal thoroughfares in the interior of the country were guarded by the king's soldiers and tolls were levied on these highways. The system of Government, which was far from despotic, also conduced to the public welfare.

The head of the Government was a hereditary monarch. His power was restricted by five councils, who were known as the " Five Great Assemblies." [1] They consisted of the representatives of the people, priests, physicians, astrologers or augurs and ministers. The council of representatives safe-guarded the rights and privileges of the people: the priests directed all religious ceremonies:

---

[1] Chilapp-athikâram iii. 1. 126—*Ibid.* v. 1. 157—*Ibid.* xxvi. 38. Mani-mekhalai l. 1. 17.

his legs cut off.[1]   Superstitious fears sometimes led the kings to
commit acts of great cruelty in the name of justice. The orders
of the king which concerned the people were proclaimed throughout his capital city with beat of drums, by officers riding on
elephants.[2]

Customs, tolls and land-tax formed the chief sources of
revenue. Customs were levied at all the sea-ports, where the
goods landed were impressed with a seal bearing the royal
emblem, and were removed to the merchant's warehouses after
payment of duty.[3] Tolls were collected on the trunk-roads
used by caravans and at the frontier of each kingdom.[4] The
land-tax was paid in money or in kind at the option of the farmer.
The tribute paid by vassal chiefs and princes, the booty gained in
border expeditions, and the profits of royal demesnes, such as the
pearl fishery, wild elephants and forest produce, also formed a
considerable portion of the king's income. One-sixth of the produce on land was the legitimate share of the king : and for water
supplied by the state a water cess was levied from the farmers.

The king was the head of society as well as of the Government. He freely mixed with the people, though surrounded as
usual by his bodyguards and other attendants. He took the
lead in every festivity in his capital; and in times of famine or
pestilence he was foremost to perform penances or sacrifices. He
shared the joys and sorrows of the people, or at least, the eti-
quette of the Court compelled him to do so. The people were so
much attached to some of their sovereigns, that there were
instances of the population of whole villages forsaking their
homes and fields, and settling within the territory of their own
king, when an invader had taken possession of their villages.[5] On
every festive occasion, whether in the public temples or in
private dwellings, prayers were offered by the people for victory
and long life to their king. " May (our king) Athan live for
ever ! may (our King) Avini live for ever ! So prayed my mother,"
says a maiden to her companion, on her return from the temple,

---

1 Ibid.
2 Chilapp-athikâram, xxiii. ll. 130, 131.
3 Paddinap-pâlai, ll. 125 to 185.
4 Perum-pan-arrup-padai, l. 81.
5 Kalith-thokai, s. 78.

"but, I prayed in silence, may (my lover) the lord of many a fertile field return home speedily."[1]

The distinction of the four castes Brahma, Kshatriya, Vaisya and Sudra, observed by the Aryas, did not exist amongst the Tamils. The expression "twice-born" applied by Aryans to those who were sanctified by the investiture of the sacred thread, was always used in Ancient Tamil literature to denote only the Brahmins, and it is evident therefore that the Kshatriya and Vaisya who wore the sacred thread were not known in Tamilakam. Amongst the pure Tamils the class most honoured was that of the *Arivar* or "sages." They pretended to know the three stages of time, that is, the past, present and future. They led a retired and religious life, dwelling outside the great towns. While the Brahmins were not unwilling to mix in the society of courtezans and prostitutes,[2] and acted as messengers between lovers, the "sages" strictly avoided them.[3]

Next in rank to the *Arivar* were the *Ulavar* or farmers. The Arivar were ascetics: but of the men living in society, the farmers occupied the highest position. They formed the nobility, or the landed aristocracy, of the country. They were also called the *Vellálar*, "lords of the flood," or *Karalar*, "lords of the clouds," titles expressive of their skill in controlling floods and in storing water for agricultural purposes. The Chera, Chola and Pandyan kings, and most of the petty chiefs of Tamilakam belonged to the tribe of Vellálas. The poor families of Vellálas who owned small estates were generally spoken of as the *Veelkudi-Ulavqr* or "the fallen Vellálas," implying thereby that the rest of the Vellálas were wealthy land-holders.[4] When Karikál the Great defeated the Aruválar and annexed their territory to his kingdom, he distributed the conquered lands amongst Vellála chiefs.[5] The descendants of some of these chiefs are to this day in pos-

---

[1] Ainkuru-nuru, ss. 1 to 10.
   Kalith-thokai, s. 103,104, 105,106.
[2] Tholkáppiyam, III. s. 503.
   Kalith-thokai, s. 72. ll. 17. to 20.
   Chilapp-athikáram, xiii. ll. 71 to 83.
[3] Tholkáppiyam III, s. 503.
[4] Chilapp-athikaram, v. l. 43.   Pura-náuuru, s. 230, l. 13.
[5] Thondai-nandalap-paddiyam.

15

session of their lands, which they hold as petty Zemindars under
the British Government.[1] They are now known as *Mudalis* or
" the First Caste." The Vellâla families who conquered Vadu-
kam, or the modern Telugu country, were called Velamas, and
the great Zemindars there still belong to the Velama caste. In
the Canarese country, the Vellâlas foundod the Bellâl dynasty
which ruled that country for several centuries. The Vellâlas
were also called the Gangakula or Gangavamsa, because they
derived their descent from the great and powerful tribe named
Gangâridæ which inhabited the valley of the Ganges, as mentioned by Pliny and Ptolemy. A portion of Mysore which was
peopled mostly by Vellâlas was called Gangavâdi in the tenth
and eleventh centuries of the Christian era. Another dynasty of
kings of this tribe who ruled Orissa in the eleventh and twelfth
centuries was known as the Gangavamsa.

The *Aiyar* and *Veddurar*, or the shepherds and huntsmen,
were next in rank to the *Ulaver*.[2] Below the shepherds were the
artizans such as Goldsmiths, Blacksmiths, Carpenters, Potters,
&c., and after them came the military class that is the *Padai-
ddchier* or the armed men. Last of all were the *Valayar* and *Pula-
yar* or the fishermen and scavengers.

When men of the higher classes passed in the streets, the
lower classes made way for them.[3] The Pulayan or scavenger
on meeting a nobleman bowed before him, with both his
hands joined in a posture of supplication.[4] Slavery was however unknown amongst the Tamils, and this is strong evidence
of their superior civilisation in this early period.

The division of classes amongst the Tamils as described
above bears a striking resemblance to that of the people of the
ancient Magadha Empire as recorded by Megasthenes. According to him, the population was divided into seven classes. The
first in rank were the philosophers: but in point of number they
formed the smallest class. They were engaged by private persons to offer sacrifices and to perform other sacred rites. The
king invited them at the beginning of the year to his palace, and

---

[1] The Zemindars of Cheyar, Chanampet, &c., in the Chingleput District.
[2] Kalith-thokai, s. 105, l. 7.
[3] Chilapp-adikâram, xvi. l. 107.
[4] Kalith-thokai, s. 55, ll. 18 and 1.

Venkadam

ARUVA-
-VADATHALA · Eyitpaddinam
Kanch · R.Palar

Koval
Kova
ARUVANADU
R.Pennal

MALADU

R.Kaviri

KAVIRIPPADDINAM

PUNALNADU
Uraiyur · Nagapaddinam

PANRI-
NADU

MATNURA Manippallavam
PANDINADU Saliyur
R.Vaigai

LANKA

THEN PANDI Korkai

EASTERN COAST
OF
TAMILAKAM.

Kumari

13

12

11

10

9

8

78   79   80   81   82

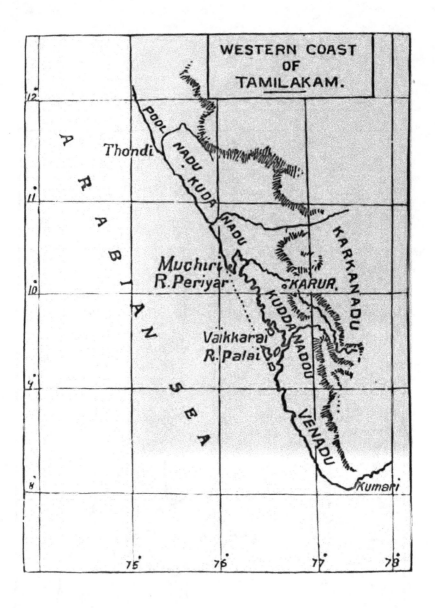

WESTERN COAST
OF
TAMILAKAM.

ARABIAN

Thondi

POOL

NADU

KUDA

NADU

Muchiri
R. Periyar

KARKANADU

KARUR.

KUDDANADOU

Vaikkarai
R. Palai

SEA

VENADU

Kumari

their rank in society and the race to which they belonged. Men
of the middle classes, amongst the pure Tamils, ordinarily wore
two pieces of cotton cloth, one wrapped round the loins, and reaching to the knees and the other loosely tied round the head.[1]
They did not cut their hair but allowed it to grow to its natural
length, and gathered it up on the crown of the head or tied it in
a large knot on one side. Coloured strings of silk with glittering
blue beads were used by the higher classes to fasten the head
knot, and the ends of the strings were allowed to hang like a tas-
sel.[2] A Marava chieftain who belonged to the Naga race wore
a cloth bound to his waist by a blue strap, and had peacock
feathers stuck in his head.[3] Brahmins cropped their hair leaving
a small tuft on the top of the head. A Tamil poet compares the
tuft of hair on a horse's head to the short hair on the heads of
Brahmin youths.[4] The soldiers employed to guard the public
thoroughfares, and the servants in the king's palace wore coats.[5]
In this ancient period, a full dress appears to have been the out-
ward sign of a servant rather than of a master: and the nobles
put on only so much clothing as can be worn without discomfort
in a hot climate.

In the ordinary dress of the Tamil woman, the shoulders,
arms and body down to the waist were entirely bare, the drapery
descending from the loins downwards to the ankles.[6] The
part of the body which was left uncovered was generally adorned
with sandal and other fragrant powders.[7] The Naga women
appear to have been almost naked like those depicted in the
Amaravati sculptures. The courtezans wore a piece of muslin
which covered their body from the waist to the middle of the
thigh: but it was of such fine texture that it hardly concealed
their person.[8] The women of the hill tribes wore bunches of

---

[1] Pura-nânuru, s. 189.
[2] Ibid., s. 150.
[3] Ibid., s. 274.
[4] Tholkâppiyan, III, p. 470. Thamotharam Pillai's edition.
[5] Perum-pânârrup-padai, l. 69.
    Chilapp-athikâram, xvi. l. 107.
[6] Kalith-thokai, ss. 111 and 115.
[7] Ibid., s. 18, l. 3.
[8] Chilapp-athikâram, ri. l. 88.

green leaves tied to a string round their waist.[1] The wives of wandering minstrels called Pânar, who accompanied their husbands during their travels, are described as perfectly nude.[2] In fact, nudity does not appear to have been a disgrace in ancient India.

The Tamil women wore their hair in a peculiar fashion. They divided it into five parts, twisted or plaited each part separately, and tied up the five tufts allowing the ends to hang down the back of the head in the manner they considered most graceful. They seem to have bestowed much care on the training of the hair, for it is stated that it was the custom for young girls to crop their hair with scissors, so close as to expose the skin of the head leaving five small tufts far apart from each other: and as the girls grew up, they gradually extended the tufts till they covered the whole surface of the head.[3] This custom of women dividing their hair into five parts, before tying it up, still exists, as I understand, amongst the Burmese. It was never adopted by the Aryan women, and has now disappeared altogether amongst the Tamils. .

All classes, both of men and women, applied oils to their hair. The women frequently used scents in dressing it, and ornamented it with a variety of flowers and jewellery.

Both sexes perfumed their persons with different kinds of fragrant oils, and adorned their skins with a variety of powders, of a red or yellow colour.[4] The women painted their eyelids with a black pigment.[5] In the houses of the higher orders, incense of benjamin, and other odoriferous. gums was generally burnt.[6] Although their clothing was scanty, the Tamil people indulged in a profusion of ornaments. Various ornaments worn round the neck, arms and waist formed the most splendid part of their costume. The chieftains and wealthy landholders wore a necklace of precious gems or pearls, and massive armlets made

---

[1] Kuriñcbippâdpa, l. 102.
[2] Porunar-arrup-padai, l. 39.
[3] Kalith-thokai, ss. 32, 55.
[4] Chilapp-athikaram, l. 69. Ibid., viii. 21.
[5] Ibid., iv. 53.
[6] Ibid., xiv. 98, 99.

of gold. Men of royal descent and petty chiefs wore in addition an anklet on their leg, as a mark of special distinction. The attire of the son of a chieftain is described as follows:— "On his feet are anklets made of a row of tiny bells, hanging from a double cord or twist of gold. Round his waist are a belt of golden coins, and a string of bright coral beads, and over these a piece of fine muslin tied round the loins. On his arms are two arm-rings, handsomely engraved, with fret-work raised like the eyes of a crab. From his neck hangs a double cord of gold with a toy sword and a toy axe, and a brooch bearing the figure of a bull, strung on it. On his head is a triple cord of pearls and golden beads, and above it a wreath of flowers, wound with a string of shining blue beads."[1]

Amongst the lower classes, the women wore bracelets made of the conch shell, and a necklace made of white and blue beads, and other cheap trinkets: while those of the middle classes used mostly golden ornaments, silver being very rare in Southern India at this period. The jewels worn by wealthy families were very costly, and those used by public actresses were most magnificent. The following description of the apparel of an actress which occurs in the Chilapp-athikáram, will convey some idea of this luxury and display of jewels. She bathed her tresses in a perfumed oil, which was extracted from the juice of 32 kinds of plants, 5 scents and 10 astringents: and having dried them over the smoke of the *Aghil* she parted them into five tufts, and applied a fragrant ointment made of musk. She painted her feet with red cotton, and put pretty rings on her little toes. On her feet she wore an ornament resembling a string of petals overlapping each other, and extending from the ankle to the big toe: and on the ankle itself she wore four anklets, one of which consisted of a row of little golden bells, and another of golden wire plaited in a beautiful design. On her thighs she tied the thigh clasp. Round her waist she wrapped in graceful folds a piece of fine blue coloured muslin, and over it she fastened a girdle of two and thirty strings of lustrous pearls. Above her elbows, she wore superb armlets made of brilliant gems and pearls chased in gold, and on her fore-arms, various bracelets, some made of polished

---

[1] Kalith-thokai, s. 85.

shells, and some of coral ; some of plain gold and some exquisite-ly engraved and set with diamonds and emeralds. Rings of various patterns she put on her fingers : one shaped like the mouth of a *makara*, and another which had a big emerald in the centre and a row of diamonds set round it. On her neck she wore many kinds of necklaces (which covered her bosom from the neck to the navel) : one of them was like a golden chain ; another like a twisted cord ; another was a string of beautiful beads, and another a string of pendant golden leaves. A splen-did clasp, which covered the back of her neck, held the necklaces in their position. Her ear-rings were set alternately with large diamonds and sapphires. On her head she fastened a net-work of ornaments which exceeded in beauty all her other jewels."[1]

Women mixed freely though modestly in the business and amusements of social life. In towns and cities, women of the poor classes were employed as hawkers, vendors, and shopkeepers or as servants in rich households ; and in the villages they worked in the fields and gardens along with men, and shared their hard-ships. The ladies of the higher classes were more confined to their homes, but they were not secluded from Society. From the queen downwards every woman visited the temples. During the evenings they came out on the terraces of their houses, and saw the scenes in the street : and on festive occasions, they joined the processions, and went out to invite their friends and rela-tions.[2] Owing to the freedom enjoyed by women, it was pos-sible for young people to court each other before marriage. It was not considered improper for a young lady even to elope with her lover, provided they returned to their relations afterwards; and entered into a married life. Love, and not the greed of gold, ruled the court, the camp and the grove, in those days ; and the behaviour of the sexes towards each other, among the Tamils, was far more polite and courteous than it is at the present day. It is no matter for wonder, therefore, that much of the poetry of this ancient period treats of love, and that rules for writing amatory poems were already in use. The courtship of young people was such an old and established custom with the Tamils

---

[1] Chilapp-athikaram, vi. 76 to 108.
[2] Ibid., i. 36, 37.

that in the great treatise on moral and social ethics,[1] composed by the poet Tiruvalluvar, during this period, one of the
three parts of the work is devoted to love affairs. The custom
has not yet died out entirely in Tamilakam, as it still survives to
some extent on the Malabar Coast. The relations of the sexes
can best be described in the words of the ancient poets themselves, and I therefore give below a translation of a few extracts
from love poems.

The following words are addressed by a girl to her friend, who
questions her on her conduct towards her lover:—" Askest thou
whether, as my neighbours say, I have given my heart to that
noble youth, who watches me while I bathe in the river, visits
me at my house, attends on me tenderly, sets right the jewels
that I wear, and paints my shoulders with sandal paste? Listen
to what I tell thee! Long I have strayed with him on the seashore, plucking the stout weeds that grow there, till the tips of
my fingers became red, thou sayest: but it was all for a doll which
he made with the weeds for me. It is strange that thou art so
simple as to believe the tales of my neighbours, who are never
happy when they cannot talk scandal. Afraid to meet thy curious
eye, I retraced my steps from my house, and he, finding me
come back, culled some flowers growing in the marsh and formed
them into a garland, and offered it to me. Is it for this trivial
mark of attention on his part that thou, without chiding those
who sent thee here with false tales, hast come to question me?
He did paint on my shoulders beautifully, with sandal paste, the
figure of a stalk of sugarcane, telling me that I knew not how
to paint it. Is it for this little act of courtesy, that thou gave
ear to the idle gossip of my playmates, and worried thyself?"[2]

Here is an example of a wayward and mischievous youth
who develops into a violent lover, and of whom a girl speaks to
her companion—" Listen to me, my friend! Knowest thou that
wicked youth, who knocks down our toy houses, tears the garlands from our hair, snatches away the ball with which we play
in the street, and gives us no end of trouble? One day, while
I and my mother were busy in our house, he came in and said
he was thirsty. 'Give him a cup of water,' said my mother,

---

and I, forgetting his evil ways, took a cup of water to him.
Suddenly he seized me by the arm and tried to embrace me, but
I cried out 'Lo! mother, behold what this youth has done.'
Hearing my cry, my mother rushed to the place where we were
standing, and I told her (a lie) that he was choked while drinking water. Then, as my mother stroked his back, that son of a
thief darted a look at me, as if he would stab me, and made me
laugh."[1]

There is more of romance in the love scenes in the hill and
sylvan tracts. "While I and my mistress were bathing one day
in a stream which was swollen with freshes, she slipped into the
middle of the stream and unable to stem the current, she was
being carried down the river, when a gallant youth who saw
the danger, leaped into the flood, decked as he was with garlands,
and bore her safely to the bank. Others who stood by, observed
that they had seen her swelling bosom rest on his broad shoulders,
and hearing these words my mistress vowed that she would be
ever faithful to that youth. He was the son of a chief of a powerful clan of the hill-tribes. "Never," said I, "will a Kurava girl
be false to her lover, and never will the arrow shot by a Kurava
be false to its mark. If ye, mountaineers are false, the valli
creeper would not yield its edible root, the honey bees would not
form their hives, and your hill farm yield no harvest." Her mother
who heard my words, told them to her fathers,[2] who had thought
of seeing her wed another youth of their choice. Their wrath
was kindled and with eyes aflame they chose their arrows
and their bows, and a whole day they thought of deeds of ven-
geance. But when they found that there was no fault in either
party they cooled down and consented to their daughter wedding
her lover. Then with joined hands we danced the Kuravai......
.........Later on the elders of the clan gathered in our hamlet, led
by the Arivan, to celebrate the wedding."[3]

The above is an instance of a chaste and noble-minded
maiden, and what follows is an illustration of a wanton and
forward girl of the period.

---

[1] Ibid., s. 51.
[2] In Tamil, the brothers of the father are called fathers, and not uncles.
[3] Kalith-thokai, s. 39.

" Thou damsel whose eyes are as dark as the flower of the Kaya! Many a day has a youth, decked with pretty garlands and armed with a bow, appeared before me, as if he was chasing some game, and gazed at me long and fondly, and vanished from my sight without ever uttering a word. The thought of him has driven sleep from my eyes, and I am pining with grief. He speaks not of his love, except with his eyes, and I being a woman am too shy to let him know how deeply I love him. Unable to bear the pangs of a secret love I did an act of which I am ashamed. One day while I was seated on a swing, by the side of our farm, he appeared before me as usual, and I called out to him and said, " Sir, swing me a little while." "I will do so, sweet maid " replied he, and was swinging me, when I pretended to slip from the swing, and fell on his shoulder. He caught me up in his arms at once, and I lay on his shoulder as if in a swoon. He held me fast and when at last I awoke, he bade me go, caressing me fondly and making me happy in the assurance that he loved me fervently." [1]

One of the most curious customs alluded to in ancient love poems is that of a disappointed lover proclaiming his love in the public streets and committing suicide. When a youth who had fallen desperately in love with a girl, found that she did not return his affections, he took the long stalk of a palmyra leaf and adorned it, like a horse, with a bell and peacock-feathers and garlands, and tying a string to one end of it, in the form of a bridle, he rode on it through the streets singing the praises of the girl he loved.[2] Seeing this, the girl herself sometimes relented or her relations persuaded her to marry him ; but if, notwithstanding this public exposure of his love, the girl remained indifferent towards him, he put an end to his life by throwing himself down from a precipice.

Every town and village had its street of harlots, and in the great cities, there were also courtezans who were educated and accomplished women and were the mistresses of wealthy nobles. The courtezans honoured by the special regard of the king were allowed to travel in carriages or palanquins, to visit the royal parks, to use betel boxes made of gold and fans made of the

---

[1] Ibid., s. 37.   [2] Kalith-thokai, 138, 139 and 141.

white tail of the yak, and to be escorted by guards armed with scimitars, when going out of their houses.[1] Though intercourse with other's wives was treated as a serious crime and severely punished, it was not considered indecent for a youth to visit harlots or courtezans, to stroll with them in the parks, or to bathe and sport with them in the public bathing places.

Boys were considered marriageable at sixteen and girls at twelve years of age.[2] The love poems of this period furnish many instances of young girls, who had not given up their toys and dolls, being courted by lovers. It was doubtless this custom of early marriages which Megasthenes exaggerates when he relates that "the women of the Pandian realm bear children when they are six years of age."[3] Amongst the higher classes marriages were solemnized with Brahminical rites. A few days before the marriage, young girls decked with jewels and mounted on an elephant, went round to their friends and relations and invited them to attend the ceremony. In the front of the bride's house, a spacious and lofty shed was erected and the ceiling was covered with blue cloth and decorated with strings of flowers. On the auspicious day fixed for the marriage, a Brahmin priest lighted the sacred fire under the shed, while drums and pipes and chanks sent forth their music; and the bride and bridegroom were led round the sacred fire three times. A number of damsels bearing lighted lamps and trays of incense, flowers and fragrant powders then strewed flowers on the wedded pair and escorted them with songs and blessings to their bridal chamber.[4] Among the lower classes residing in towns and among the hill tribes, who had not come under Brahmin influence, the marriage ceremony was performed by the *Arivar* or Tamil priests.[5]

Except during marriages and other domestic occurrences, there was, as a rule, no family gathering at meal time and each individual took his meals at the time most convenient to

[1] Chilapp-athikaram, xiv. ll. 126-131.
[2] Ibid, Canto i.
[3] McCrindle's Ancient India, Megasthenes and Arrian, p. 14. See also p. 202. " The women when seven years of old are of marriageable age."
[4] Chilapp-athikaram, Canto i.
[5] Kalith-thokai.

himself. The diet was extremely plain. Rice was the staple
article of food, and milk, butter and honey were in common
use. The various kinds of food on which different classes of
society subsisted are given in the following account of a wandering
minstrel. " The *Eyinar* or hunters served him with coarse rice
of a red colour and the flesh of the Guana, on the broad leaf of
the teak tree. The shepherds gave him maize and beans and
millet boiled in milk. In the agricultural tracts the laborers
invited him to a meal of white rice and the roasted flesh of the
fowl. On the sea coast, the fishermen fed him with rice and
fried fish in dishes made of palmyra leaves. The Brahmins
gave him fine rice with mango pickle and the tender fruits of the
pomegranate cooked with butter and the fragrant leaves of the
Karuvembu; and the *Ulavar* or farmers feasted him with sweetmeats and the fruits of the jack and plantain and the cooling
water of the cocoanut. In the toddy shops he was regaled with
toddy and the fried flesh of the male pig which had been fattened
by being confined in a pit and fed for many days on rice flour." [1]
Toddy drawn from the cocoanut palm was drunk by the poor
classes such as labourers, soldiers and wandering minstrels.[2]
Scented liquors manufactured from rice and the flowers of the
Thathaki (Bauhinia Tomentosa) and other fragrant substances
were used by the richer classes.[3] Cool and fragrant wines brought
by Yavana (or Greek) ships, which must have been therefore very
costly, were the favorite drink of the kings.[4]

Quail fights, dances, musical entertainments and religious
festivities appear to have been the chief sources of amusement to
the masses of the people. Women amused themselves at home
with teaching parrots, singing the *Vallai* or *Ammanai*, rocking
on swings and playing the games of *Thayam, Kalanku* or *Panthu.*
Thayam was the same as the modern game of dice ; but the
blocks of dice used were circular in shape, like the shell of a crab
marked with black spots, and not rectangular cubes like those
now in use. The game of Kalanku was played with seven tiny
balls, each of the size of an areca-nut and the players who remain-

---

1 Perum-Panarru, ll. 99 to 362.
2 Mani-mekalai, III. 99-89
3 Ibid, xxvii. 260 and 261.
4 Puram, a. 56, l. 18.

ed seated, threw up the balls first one at a time, then two, then three and so on up to seven at a time and caught them either on the palm or on the back of the hand. In the game of *Panthu*, balls of the size of a lime fruit were used, and the players struck the balls with their hands running forwards and backwards or wheeling round, according to the motion of the balls.[1]

The science and practice of the fine arts were highly developed amongst the ancient Tamils. The study of music was an essential part of a liberal education : and the Tamils excelled in soft melodies which had a gentle and soothing effect. The gamut consisted of seven notes which were named, *Tharam, Ulai, Kural, Ili, Thutham, Vilari* and *Kaikkilai*.[2] The principal tunes or airs were four in number :—*Palai, Kurinji, Marutham* and *Chevvali*[3]—and each tune had many variations, making in all 103 distinct tunes which were recognized in the musical treatises of the period. The different parts in music, bass, tenor and treble were also understood ; they were not however sung together but one after another in succession. A great variety of wind instruments were in use. Chank shells which gave a deep swelling sound were used in temples and in marriage and funeral processions. The flute which had eight holes in it was capable of considerable modulation. Single and double faced drums and pipes of various kinds, accompanied the lute in every musical concert. There were four kinds of lutes. The smallest in size and one most commonly used had seven wires :[4] the other kinds had fourteen, seventeen and twenty-one wires each.[5] While being played, the lute was held, in the left hand, four fingers of which rested on the screw pins and the wires were sounded with one or the other of the fingers of the right hand, excepting the thumb.[6] Tamil and Aryan systems of music are alluded to, showing thereby that the two systems were dis-

[1] Kalith-thokai, ss. 57 and 136.
[2] Chilapp-athikaram, viii. ll. 31-32.
[3] Ibid.
[4] Ibid.
[5] Ibid, page 81.
[6] Ibid.
Chilapp-athikaram, xxvii. 245.
Ibid, xxix.
Akam, s. 17

tinct from each other ; and that both were studied by those who wished to perfect themselves in music.

Dancing was cultivated as a fine art and there were text-books already composed, in which rules were given in detail for the performance of the several kinds of dancing then in vogue. These books are not now extant ; but much information regarding dancing is available in the *Chilappathikaram* from which it appears that there were two kinds of plays, Aryan and Tamil. Of the Aryan plays eleven are mentioned and they represented the following mythological events :—[1]

(1) Siva burning Tripura.

(2) Siva mounting the chariot brought by Brahma to take him to Tripura.

(3) Krishna crushing the elephant sent by Kamsa.

(4) Krishna wrestling with and killing Bânâsura.

(5) Skanda defeating the Asura in Lanka.

(6) Skanda fighting with the Asura army.

(7) Krishna destroying the fort of Bânâsura.

(8) Kâmadeva disguised as a eunuch entering the fort of Bânâsura to save his son Aniruddha.

(9) Durga crushing the Asuras.

(10) Lakshmi deceiving the Asuras.

(11) Ayrani, the wife of Indra, appearing before the northern gate of the fort of Bânâsura.

Of the Tamil plays there were numerous kinds :—Some of them were in praise of the gods or kings and of their achievements ; some in mimicry of men or animals ; and some represented love scenes. Besides these the *Kuravai* dance, in which, seven, eight or nine persons danced together, standing in a ring, and clasping each other's hands, was a favourite form of amusement. Both men and women joined in this dance and accompanied it with songs of love cr war.[2] Most of these plays were acted by dancing girls or actresses. The education of an actress commenced as early as her fifth year and was continued for seven years. The curriculum of her studies, as given in ancient poems would do credit to any accomplished lady of the present day. She was taught to dance and sing and carry herself

---

[1] Ibid.   [2] Ibid.

gracefully. In addition to this she was taught to play on the lute,
the drum and the flute, to sing songs composed in foreign
tongues, to draw pictures, to sport in the bath, to adorn the person
with powders of bright colors, to make pretty garlands, to deck
herself with jewels, to arrange and beautify the bed, to calculate
the divisions of time, to know what was appropriate for each
season, to discuss the chief points of the various sciences, to
propose puzzles, to solve problems and to read the thoughts of
others![1] In short she learnt everything that was calculated to
amuse and please, to dazzle and captivate the minds of men. In
her twelfth year she made her first entry on the stage, in the
presence of the monarch and the noblemen of the city. She was
accompanied by a poet who could improvise verses suited to the
occasion, a music master who could set the poet's words to music,
a lute-player, a flute-player, and a drummer who were all trained
men in their respective callings. The stage was in the form of
a platform two feet high, fourteen feet broad and sixteen feet
long. At a height of eight feet above the platform, was
erected a canopy which rested on pillars. Figures of guardian
deities were set up above the canopy, and painted curtains were
hung up on all sides of the platform. The performance commenced after nightfall when the theatre was brilliantly lighted.
The front part of the platform to the breadth of 6 feet was
reserved for the actress ; behind her stood two or three old actresses who prompted her in her performance ; and behind these
stood a few songsters, who sang at intervals to relieve the actress.
The musicians such as the drummer, the lute and flute-players
stood in the last row. As the curtains were drawn up, the actress
appeared on the stage, decorated in her best costume, and literally blazing with jewels, in which burnished gold and brilliant
diamonds seemed to emit a thousand rays. She began the performance with a hymn which she sang in silvery tones, invoking
the gods for their blessings and for their aid to ward off all evil.
Then she went through a choice programme of songs and dances,
throwing her body and limbs into every graceful attitude which
the most flexible form was capable of exhibiting. Her youth
and beauty, her witching voice and graceful person, the brilliant

---

[1] Mani-mekalai, ii ll. 18-31.

lights and the soft strains of music won the audience and the king presented her with a gold necklace of the value of 1,008 gold coins which was the highest award given on such occasions.[1]

In the arts of painting and sculpture also the Tamils had acquired a considerable degree of proficiency. Figures of gods, men and animals were painted with a variety of colors on the walls of private houses and public buildings, such as temples and palaces.[2] The curtains used in bedrooms and theatres, and the cloth cases used for the lute and other musical instruments were beautifully painted in imitation of flowers and creepers.[3] Very pretty dolls were made out of wood or the soft pith of the *Kidai*.[4] In the temples and monasteries, there were images of gods and goddesses made of mortar and painted so exquisitely that the superstitious worshippers believed that the cunning hand of the painter had endowed them with the power to grant their prayers. No mention is made however of images or statues made of such enduring materials as stone or metal! ; and this accounts for the total absence in the Tamil-land of any relics of sculpture more ancient than those at Mamallaipuram, which were executed in the seventh or eighth century A. D.

The houses of the poor classes were built of mud and thatched with grass or with the leaves of the cocoanut or palmyra palm : and their walls were painted with red earth. Most of the houses in the towns were built of brick and had tiled roofs : the walls were plastered with lime, and small windows shaped like the eye of the deer admitted light and air into the inner compartments. The gateway or portico, which was always a conspicuous part of the house, was approached by a flight of steps from the streets ; and wide piazzas erected on both sides of the entrance afforded seats for visitors or the inmates of the house, during their leisure hours.[5] The gateway was generally distinct from the main building, and in the open space or court-yard between it and the house, stalls were erected for the shelter of the sheep, cows and other cattle belonging to the owner of the house. The man-

---

[1] Chilapp-athikaram, Canto iii.
[2] Manimekalai, iii. 127-130.
[3] Chillap-athikaram, vii. 1.
[4] Ibid., v. 33.
[5] Paddinap-palai, ll. 140-145.

sions of the wealthy citizens, had terraces and towers and separate bed rooms for the summer and winter seasons. Furniture
of various descriptions was in use, such as raised seats, cots with
canopies and cushions stuffed with swan's down, lamps borne by
statues, and swings for the amusement of women and children.
The temples and palaces were also built of brick : and no buildings of stone are alluded to in the literature of this period except
some of the great fortresses, the walls, ramparts and towers of
which were constructed with rough hewn stone and mortar.

All the villages and towns were more or less fortified against the
attacks of robbers and enemies. Every village was defended by
a thick fence of thorny trees : and every town fortified with
a wall and ditch and a broad belt of thorny jungle surrounding
the ditch. In the great forts of Madura, Karur and Kanchi,
many curious engines were mounted on the battlements to shoot
arrows or to fling stones on those that besiege them. There were
machines like the fishing rod and angle to catch and drag up
those that approach the wall : and like iron fingers to seize and
tear them to pieces. There were, besides, furnaces from which
hot oil and molten metal might be poured on those that attempt
to scale the wall : and iron spokes and spears to shove down
those that might succeed in mounting the ramparts.[1] The
arsenals in the fort were stocked with daggers, swords and lances,
bows and quivers full of arrows, shields and breastplates and
chariots and harness for horses and elephants.

In besieging a fort the method adopted by the Tamils was
first to cut open a wide passage through the jungle which enclosed
the fort : then fill up the ditch to enable the army to approach the
walls and finally scale the wall with ladders, or burst open the gates
with the help of elephants trained to the work.

When the line of battle was drawn up, the elephants were
placed first, the chariots and horsemen were ranged behind
them, and the infantry occupied the rear. The ordinary foot
soldiers carried in their left hand large bucklers made of ox-hide
and in their right hand a lance or a battle-axe. The archers
carried long bows in their left hand and quivers suspended
at their backs. Both lancers and archers were armed with

[1] Chilapp-athikaram, xv. 207-217.

swords which were broad in the blade and about a yard long. The cavalry carried lighter arms and shorter bucklers than those supplied to the infantry. Those who rode on chariots or elephants were the generals who led the army and were invariably men of noble birth. They carried lances or swords, and shields adorned with gold and wore coats of mail. The war chariots were light cars raised on two low wheels with a railing of stout rattan round the stand, which afforded room for only two men, the charioteer and the warrior. Each chariot was drawn by a pair of horses. Large and heavy chariots drawn by four or seven horses were used only in processions or festive occasions. When attacking an enemy, the archers discharged their arrows aiming at the elephants in the opposing army and at the generals who rode on them. If the men were skilful archers and sufficiently strong in number, the first shower of arrows compelled the enemies' elephants to beat a retreat and threw their army into confusion : but if the elephants withstood the attack, the mounted soldiers threw their javelins at them and the infantry also attacked them with their long spears ; and then engaged the enemy at close quarters fighting with their swords and battle axes. The elephants always formed the most formidable part of an army and hence, to cut down a soldier or any number of soldiers was not esteemed so great a feat of valour as to kill or disable an elephant. To fly from the battlefield or to receive a wound on the back was considered a great disgrace.

The fighting men who belonged to the military caste among the Tamils were very loyal to their kings. "Thou Lord of the handsome chariot and troops of elephants," says a bard to his chief, pointing to a young warrior, "share with this youth the toddy thou drinkest, for his father's father gave up his life to save thy father's father in a fierce fight : and this youth so full of valour, will throw himself between thee and thy foes, when they aim their lances against thee."[1] Even the women of the fighting classes were animated by the same martial spirit which the soldiers possessed. "Alas! how bold is she, the worthy matron of the warrior tribe!" exclaims a bard, "It was only the day before yesterday that her father cut down an elephant on the

[1] Puram, 290.

battle-field and fell bravely fighting with the foes, and yesterday her husband routed a whole array of elephants and was slaughtered on the same field, and yet to-day, when she heard the war drum, she seemed to be filled with joy and gave her only son a white cloth to wear, combed his hair and putting a lance into his hand, bade him go to the battle-field."[1] " The old mother with trembling frame and withered arms," says another bard speaking of a woman of the military caste, "hearing that her son had fled from the battle-field, swore that she would cut off her breasts that nursed him, if he had really turned his back on the foe, and armed with a sword went to the battle-field and finding among the slain, the mangled body of her son, rejoiced more than she did when he was born."[2]

Warriors believed that their souls would ascend to the heaven reserved for heroes if they died in battle and this superstition had such a hold on them, that they seldom flinched from sacrificing their lives in the service of their kings. The kings too had the same superstitious belief and it is said that when severely wounded in battle, or about to die a natural death from old age or disease, they preferred to be laid on sacred grass spread by the Brahmins, and to be ripped open with a sword, so that they may die a warrior's death.[3]

The frequent skirmishes and fights with his neighbours in which each king was engaged, kept the soldiers in constant practice and fostered their martial spirit. The bards and minstrels who always formed part of the retinue of a king contributed in no small degree to create and strengthen a thirst for military glory. In times of peace they amused the king and his soldiers with tales of the heroic deeds of their ancestors, and in times of war they marched with the army, and with their war-songs stirred the soldiers and generals to emulate the valiant feats of their forefathers. There are four classes of bards mentioned in ancient Tamil poems—the Panar, Kooththar, Porunar and Viraliyar. The Panar were a very low caste and lived in the outskirts of the towns among the harlots, and when they wandered about

[1] Ibid, 279.
[2] Ibid, 278.
[3] Ibid, 93.   Manimekalai, xxiii. 13.14.

from town to town, they were accompanied by their wives and
children who carried with them their begging bowls and cooking
utensils. The Kooththar were actors, who sang as well as acted
plays, which were more of the character of a ballet than of a
regular dramatic exhibition. The Porunar or war-bards were
generally members of the suite of a chief or king. They carried
a small drum to which was tied a short stick with which
they sounded the drum. "Each time I strike my drum with the
short stick which is attached to it, your enemies tremble," says
the bard Kovur-kilar addressing the Chola king Nalank-Killi, for,
when the war-bard sounds his drum it is generally the signal for
an army to march.[1] Female bards of this class were known
as Viraliyar. It is these war-bards that were the authors of a
considerable portion of the literature of this ancient period.

We have a vivid picture of Madura in the verses left by the
poets of this period which may well conclude this Chapter on the
social life of the Tamils.[2] " Long before dawn Brahmin students
begin to recite Vedic hymns; musicians tune their lutes and
practise upon them; pastry cooks clean the floors of their shops;
and toddy sellers open their taverns for early customers.[3]
Minstrels go round, singing their morning blessings. In the
temples, in the monasteries and in the palace of the Pandya conch
shells boom, and big drums resound with deafening noise.[4] The
rays of the morning sun now gild the tops of the fort towers and
reveal the proportions of the city. The main streets " are long
and broad as rivers " and the buildings on either side of the main
streets are, most of them, lofty mansions with upper stories, furnished with many windows.[5] At every temple a flag is hoisted
Over each liquor shop floats a merry steamer. Each trader's ware-

---

[1] Puram, 382.

[2] Mānkudi Maruthanar's Mathuraik-kānchi—Nakkirar's Nedu-nal-vādai and
Ilanko-adikals' Chilappathikāram.

[3] Mathuraik-kānchi, line 654 and f. Two very interesting articles on the
"Ten Tamil Idylls" which appeared in the Christian College Magazine, from the
pen of Mr. Sundaram Pillay, M.A., have been of much use to me, as they contain
translations of extracts from the Nedu-nal-vādai and Mathuraik-kānchi—C. C.
Magazine Vol. VIII No. 9, page 661 and Vol. IX No. 2, page 114.

[4] Chilapp-athikāram, XIV—7 to 14.

[5] Mathuraik-kānchi, 357 and f.

house is distinguished by a special banner. For every victory gained by the king's forces gorgeous colours are unfurled. So many, and of such divers shapes and colours are these flags that the city looks as if it has been decked for a grand festival. Detachments of the king's troops return to the city from their raids into enemies' territories, bringing with them such booty as horses and elephants, and beautifully carved gates removed from fortresses which they had stormed. Other parties of soldiers return with herds of cattle, lifted at night, in the light of burning villages, and driven with their long spears, which now serve as goading sticks. Feudatory chiefs follow with their tributes to be presented to the king. Later, flower-sellers with trays full of loose blossoms and garlands suspended on their arms, and vendors of fragrant powders, of aracanuts and betel leaves, stroll in the streets or sit in the shade of the lofty buildings. Elderly women with tempting dainties and sweet smelling flowers, go from door to door, offering the articles for sale to the inmates of each house. The wealthy classes drive in chariots drawn by horses or ride on ambling steeds which are trained to special paces. The poor pedlars and petty dealers now run hither and thither, excited and terror-stricken, as a fierce elephant, which had burst its chains and killed its guards, rushes through the street, while men run before and behind it, blowing conch-shells to warn passengers off the road. Now and then the brawls of drunken soldiers also disturb the peace of the street. In the great market which is held in an extensive square, are exposed for sale [1] "carts, chariots and ornament chariot tops; coats of mail and metallic belts which cannot be cut; leathern sandals and fly wisks made of the white tail of the yak; strong spears and curved clubs; elephant goads and shields to protect the face of elephants; various articles made of copper and of brass; saws and lathes and other tools; pretty garlands of flowers and fragrant pastes to be burned as incense or rubbed on the body, and other articles too many to be set forth." In the jewellers street are sold diamonds of the four kinds then known to merchants, emeralds, rubies, sapphires, topaz, lapizlazuli, onyx stones, lustrous pearls and bright red coral beads. The gold merchants who dwelt in a separate street, sell the four varieties of

[1] Chilapp-atʾikâram, XIV—168 to 211.

that precious metal known as Satharupam, Kilichchirai, Adakam and Sambunatham. Cloths of various colours and patterns, made of cotton, wool or silk are exposed to view, folded and neatly arranged in rows, to the number of several hundreds, in each of the clothier's shops. Sacks of pepper and the sixteen kinds of grains, such as paddy, millet, gram, peas, sesamum seeds, are heaped in the grain merchants' street; and the brokers move to and fro with steel yards and measures in their hands, weighing or measureing the pepper and grains purchased by the people. In the Courts of Law preside learned Judges, who carefully avoid all anger and levity, and weigh the evidence and expound the law, without fear or favour.[1] In the Ministers' Courts are seated the sage councillors of the king, honored with the high title of Kavithi, who with a keen foresight prevent all that is evil and promote what is good for their prince and for the people over whom he rules.

On a spacious lawn enclosed by a wall stands the palace of the Pandya.[2] The gateway is so high as to allow elephants to enter with banners erect on their backs. "The tower over the gateway" says the poet "is like a hill and the passage underneath like a tunnel bored through the hill." The folding gates are strongly rivetted with iron and provided with massive bolts and bars. They are painted with vermillion, and on the door-posts are carved images of the guardian deities. In the courtyard which is covered with white sand, gambol "the long-haired yak and the short-legged swans." In another part of the enclosure are the royal stables where superb steeds are ready for the king's use. The stately apartments reserved for the use of the queen and her attendants, which no male but the king can approach, are decorated with flags of all the colours of the rainbow. The walls are of the hue of polished brass, and are at intervals plastered with white mortar which shines like silver. The beautiful creepers, painted on the walls, and the blue colour of the pillars blend to make a harmonious picture of the whole.

In the audience hall is seated the handsome Pandya. He wears only a single piece of clean starched cloth on his waist.[3]

---

[1] Mathuraik-kânchi, line 489 and *f.*
[2] Nedu-nal-vâdai, lines 76 to 114.
[3] Mathuraik-kânchi, 716 to 752.

Over it is clasped a jewelled belt. On his bare arms, above the elbow, are armlets of pure gold beautifully wrought. On his broad shoulders, fragrant with sandal paste, is a priceless necklace of brilliant pearls, besides a wreath of flowers. Around him stand a group of sturdy warriors, his trusted Captains, heroes who had captured many a fortress or slaughtered fierce elephants in battle, veteran chiefs, whose coats of mail have been battered and bruised in many a fight. Actors and minstrels and lute-players display their skill in the presence of the monarch and receive chariots and elephants as presents.

In the cool hours of the evening, the noblemen drive out in splendid chariots drawn by horses, each attended by a number of his footmen who run by the side of the chariot.[1] They are clad in red coloured garments. Their swords hang by their sides, in scabbards ornamented with gold, and on their breasts are wreaths of flowers. Their ladies wearing sounding ankle rings and golden bracelets, appear on the high terraces, of their mansions, and their perfumes spread fragrance through the streets. The public walks are filled with a motley throng of chank-cutters, beadmakers, goldsmiths, coppersmiths, tailors, weavers, painters and dealers in perfumes and flowers, who move about the streets and dispose of the things they have brought to sale.[2] The hotels and restaurants are all now crowded by visitors who feast upon luscious fruits such as the jack, mango or plantain and on sugar-candies, tender greens, edible yams, sweetened rice or savoury preparations of meat. Above the hum of voices is presently heard a flourish of trumpets and other instruments of music, which summons the people to their evening worship. Women wearing glittering jewels, accompanied by their husbands and children, carry incense and flowers to the Buddhist monasteries. In the retreats of the Brahmin ascetics, which are like excavated blocks of rocks, is heard the chant of Vedic hymns. Nigranthas crowd the cool cloisters of the monks of their sect, the walls of which are exceedingly high, and painted red, and are surrounded by pretty little flower gardens. Others visit the Brahminic temples and offer the evening sacrifices to the gods, "the chief of whom is He

[1] Mathuraik-kânchi, lines 431 and *f*.
[2] Ibid lines.511 and *f*.

who is the creator of the five elements and who is armed with the battle-axe" (Siva).[1]

As the shades of evening darken, lamps are lit in each house. Youths gaily attired, and harlots decked with jewels and flowers, walk the streets. Drunken soldiers go reeling, not minding even the sharp pointed caltrops strewn in the streets to keep off elephants. Young mothers escorted by their relations, proceed with lights, singing sweet melodies to the accompaniment of the lute and the tabor, and present boiled rice and other oblations to the goddess who is supposed to ensure the safe delivery of children, and with the priestess they partake of the offerings. In the suburbs, among the lower classes, at the bidding of soothsayers, festivals are held in honor of Muruga, and they dance hand in hand, wild and uncouth measures, with noisy songs and loud cries, while shrill cymbals and rattling drums keep up a discordant music.

Little by little the dancing and singing parties disperse. The petty traders close their shops; the dealers in sweetmeats go to sleep in front of their stalls; and silence reigns in the city. The night guards now patrol the streets. Armed with bows and arrows, unerring archers as they are, they go their rounds with fearless hearts and sleepless eyes, " not failing in their duty even in dark and rainy nights when the high streets overflow with water." [2]

---

[1] Mathuraik-kânchi-lines 453 and *f*.

[2] Ibid., lines 646—650.

CHAPTER X.

THE KURAL OF TIRUVALLUVAR.

Many of the poems of this period are still extant in a complete form. The most popular of these poems and one which has exercised the greatest influence on succeeding generations is the Muppâl or Kural composed by Valluvar. Very little authentic is known of the life of Tiruvalluvar : but he is generally believed to have been a native of the ancient town of Mailapur which is now a suburb of the town of Madras. He went to Madura with his great work to submit it for the approval of the Pandya and his college of poets. Some of these poets were natives of Madura, while others hailed from Uraiyur and Kavirip-paddinam in the Chola kingdom, from Chellur in the Kongu-nâd, from Venkatam in the Thondai-nâd and from other parts of Tamilakam. There was in that conclave of poets Poothan-chenthanar, author of the small poem Iniya-nârpatu : there was Nallâthanar, author of the moral epigrams called Tirikadukam ; there was Nallanthuvanar who compiled the Kalith-thokai ; there was Iraiyanar who wrote the Akapporal or grammar of erotic poetry ; there was Kapilar to whom we owe the charming little poems, Kurinjip-paddu and Inna-narpatu ; there was Mankudi-maruthanar who addressed the ode Maduraik-kanchi to the Pandyan king Nedunj-cheliyan, victor of Alankânam ; there was the learned Nakkirar who has left us the beautiful idylls, Nedu-nal-vâdai and Thirumurukârruppadai ; there was the profound Buddhist scholar Cheethalaich châthanar, who composed the interesting epic Manimekalai ; there were besides, others who were styled professors of medicine, of astrology or of literature, but whose works have not come down to us. In this galaxy of the eminent poets and scholars of the period and in the presence of the Pandya Ugrap-peru-valuthi, the greatest patron of letters in the Tamil-land, Valluvar must have stood with an anxious heart when he submitted his work for their criticism. The Muppâl consisted, as implied by its name, of three parts which treated of virtue, wealth and love. It was a code of morals expressed in poetical aphorisms. Though a firm believer in the tenets of his own religion the Nigrantha faith, the author appears to have been a freethinker and held that true wisdom is the science of happiness. " To receive charity is bad

though it may serve your need," said he, " to bestow alms is good
even if there is no heaven." " Dauntless valor is heroic, but far
nobler than that is kindness to an unlucky being." He described
eloquently the charms of a happy home and exalted a faithful
wife to the rank of a saint. " The pipe is sweet, the lute is sweet,
say those who have not heard the prattle of their own children."
" The rain will fall at the bidding of her who serves no god but
her husband." He held up to scorn the life of those who seek
the company of prostitutes. " The false embrace of a harlot,"
said he, " is like the clasping of a corpse in a dark room."
Among the different callings of mankind he preferred that of the
husbandman. " Those who till the ground are truly happy, all
others live by serving and following (the great)." He laughed at
fatalists and declared that greatness can be achieved by labor.
" Those who toil with untiring energy will overcome even fate."

" Be not faint-hearted fancying that a work is very difficult
to accomplish. It is diligence that brings greatness." He recommended learning to all and said that the life of the ignorant
was not worth having. " The ignorant live, but are like the sterile
ground that yieldeth nothing." " Like beasts to men are the
ignorant to the learned." " The wise have all that they want,
but the ignorant, though having all, are ever poor." Being a
Nigrantha, he considered it the greatest virtue, not to take the
life of any living thing, and spoke with contempt of the bloody
sacrifices of the Brahmins. " Better is it to avoid the killing of
one living being, than to pour ghee and perform a thousand
sacrifices." He believed in the existence of what is called Neme-
sis. " If thou dost evil to others in the forenoon, evil would
befall thee in the afternoon." " If thou dost love thyself truly, do
not even think of evil deeds." He warned the learned to live
laborious days, not to be proud of their learning, to attempt
nothing which will not lead to good, and to revere and obey the
Supreme Intelligence which governs the Universe. " He that
doth not court pleasure, can never feel pain." " Never be proud
of thyself : never attempt any work that will lead to no good."
" Alas ! of what use is learning, if the learned worship not the
blessed feet of Him who is all-knowing ? "

A work of this kind had never before been written in any

language then known to the Tamil poets. They accepted it therefore as a very creditable performance, and each of the poets expressed his opinion in a stanza addressed to the king. Irayanâr very truly predicted that the work of Valluvar will live for ever and be a source of instruction to many generations to come. Kalladar was surprised that the six religious sects which ever wrangle with one another, for once agreed in accepting as true the Muppâl composed by Valluvar. " Nedu Mâra, that wieldest the sword of victory which has cut down thy enemies !" exclaimed another poet " having heard from the mouth of Valluvanar, what we never heard before, we know what is virtue, what is wealth, and what is love and clear to us is the way to eternal bliss." " The Brahmins " observed another poet " preserve the Vedas orally and commit them not to writing, being afraid that they would then be less valued. But the Muppâl of Valluvar though written on leaves and read by all would never lose its value." " The Sun, Moon, Venus, and Jupiter swiftly dispel darkness from the face of the earth" remarked an astronomer " but the light which illuminates the minds of men is the Kural of the learned Valluvar." "Thou (king who exultest in thy strength,) like the elephant which batters rocks with its tusks ! all are relieved of their headache by smelling the seenthil salt and sliced dry ginger mixed with honey : but Chathan was relieved of his headache by hearing the Muppâl of Valluvar," said a physician who took this opportunity of publishing his *recipe* for headache, and cracked a joke at his fellow-poet Chathanar, who had a habit of striking his head with his iron stylus, every time he heard an incorrect or inelegant expression, but who did not even once strike his head during the whole of the time that the Kural was being explained to the Sangha or College. " Faultless in verse, in language and in sense, is the sweet Kural which embodies in itself the wisdom of all authors, and all ages " said another poet. Hearing the praise unanimously bestowed on the Kural, the king Ugra Pandya eulogised the author and his great work as follows:—" The four-faced Brahma disguised as Valluvar has imparted to us the truths of the four Vedas, in the Muppâl, which should therefore be adored by the head, perused by the mouth, listened to by the ear and studied by the mind.".

CHAPTER XI.

The Story of Chilapp-athikaram.

Far more interesting than the Muppal, are the epic poems Chilapp-atbikaram and Mani-mêkalai, which contain very full and vivid accounts of ancient Tamil Society. The Chilapp-athikaram relates the tragic story of Kovilan and his wife Kannaki, and the Mani-mêkalai gives a romantic account of Kovilan's daughter who became a Buddhist nun. The story of the Chilapp-athikaram may be briefly told as follows :—

One of the most flourishing of the ancient cities of Jambudvîpa[1] was Pukâr or Kâvirip-paddinam, the great sea-port at the mouth of the river Kâviri. It was a mart of many nations. Caravans from inland cities, far and near, thronged its thoroughfares; and merchant vessels from distant lands, whose people spoke strange tongues, crowded its harbour. Among the merchant princes of this city there was one noted for his deeds of charity, Mânâykan, whose daughter Kannaki was warmly praised by all who knew her, for the charms of her person, and the purity of her mind. In the same city, lived another merchant Mâchâttuvan, master of untold wealth, whose son Kovilan was a most accomplished youth, gay and handsome as the God of War. The two merchants having agreed to unite their chidren in marriage, the wedding of Kannaki and Kovilan was performed with such pomp as was rarely seen even in the proud city of Pukâr. Shortly after their marriage, the young couple were installed by their parents in a spacious mansion furnished with every luxury that wealth could command. A numerous suite of attendants served them, and ministered to their comforts. Kovilan loved his young wife, and called her his darling and his beauty, his peerless pearl and priceless gem. He vowed that she was more graceful than the peacock, that she stepped more prettily than the playful swan ever did, and that her voice was sweeter than that of any parrot. He chided her servant maids for adorning her with

---

[1] That portion of Asia which is south of the Himalayan plateau was known as Jambudvîpa.

jewels and flowers, which could not add to her beauty, and whose weight, he complained, her slender waist could not bear. Beloved by her husband, Kannaki's joy was full, and she entered upon her duties as mistress of his house with infinite delight. To feast her husband's guests, to welcome the ascetics and Brahmins who visited the house, to feed the hungry and clothe the naked were duties always pleasant to her loving and tender heart. Ever busy in doing good to others, and beloved by all, her days were bright and unclouded ; and the first few years of her married life glided away happily.[1]

Karikâl the Great was then the monarch of the Chola kingdom. He had fortified Pukâr and made it his capital. As he was the most powerful and enlightened ruler in Dakshinapatha or Southern India at this period, his friendship was sought by the kings of Avanti, Mâlava and Magadha. His brilliant court was the scene of much revelry, and many an actress sang and danced in the presence of the monarch to amuse him and his courtiers. Mâthavi, a young and beautiful actress, who claimed descent from the celestial actresses in the court of Indra, made her first entry on the stage in the presence of the king, his nobles and the rich men of the city. She sang and danced with such exquisite skill and grace that the monarch awarded her the highest prize given on such occasions, that is, a necklace of 1.008 gold coins. Kovilan who was an accomplished musician, and passionately fond of music, was charmed by her performance and wished to make the acquaintance of the young actress. In a fit of enthusiastic admiration for the sweet songstress who ravished his ears, he purchased the prize necklace which was offered for sale, and presented it again to her. Admitted to her presence, he was struck with the beautiful and dazzling form of the actress, which appeared most attractive when least adorned. Her radiant face and sparkling wit were so fascinating that forgetting his faithful wife, he fell in love with the actress, and was unable to quit her society. Mâthavi accepted the young rich merchant as her lover, and day after day he spent in the company of the bewitching actress, and lavished upon her all the wealth amassed by his ancestors.[2] In course of time Mâthavi gave birth to a lovely daughter. On

---

[1] Chillap-athikaram, Cantos 1 and 2. [2] Ibid., Canto 3.

the fifth day after the birth of the child, one thousand dancing girls met at Mâthavi's house, and with great ceremony they blessed the child and named her Manimekalai, as desired by Kovilan, the favourite deity of whose ancestors was Manimekhala, the goddess of the ocean. Kovilan gave away handfuls of gold to the Brahmins who assisted at the ceremony.[1] The birth of the child seemed to strengthen the ties of affection between Mâthavi and Kovilan, and he became more attached to the actress than ever. A few years of the gay and luxurious life he led drained his resources. Having spent all his patrimony, he began to remove and sell one by one, the jewels of his wife, who willingly parted with them, in order to please her husband whom she continued to love as faithfully as she did in the days when no rival had estranged his affections.

The annual festival in honor of Indra was celebrtead with much pomp and splendour in the city of Pukâr. The joyous city put on its gayest appearance during the festivities which lasted eight and twenty days. On the first day of the festival the king attended in person the opening ceremonies. He started from his palace, surrounded by an imposing cavalcade consisting of the chief officers of State, the five great assemblies, the eight groups of attendants, and the nobility and gentry of the city, mounted on horses, elephants or chariots, and proceeded to the banks of the Kâviri. In the presence of the king, the sacred water of the river was filled in golden pots by youths of the royal family, and the procession then marched to the temple of Indra, where the image of the king of gods was bathed with the sacred water amid the acclamations of the multitude, and the flourish of musical instruments.[2] At the close of the festival, the princes and nobles with all their retinue bathed in the sea at the mouth of the river Kâviri. On the last night of one of these festivals, Mâthavi wished to see the spectacle at the beach, of people bathing and sporting in the sea. She decked herself with her magnificent jewels, in the most charming style, and drove in a carriage, accompanied by a few of her female attendants. Kovilan rode on a mule followed by a number of his footmen. They wended their way through the market road to the beach, where

---

1 Ibid—Canto XV., ll. 21—41.   2 Ibid—Canto 5.

were many gay parties bathing in the sea or seated in the open
air, and they rested themselves on a sofa, which had been placed
by their attendants, within an enclosure of painted canvas, under
the shade of a *Punnai* tree, which was then in full blossom. After
resting a while, Måthavi received from the hands of her maid
Vasantamålai, her favorite lute.[1] It was beautifully painted
and polished and a garland of fresh flowers was wound round its
handle. She tuned the instrument and handed it to her lover,
begging to know his wishes. Kovilan who was tempted by the
gay scenes around him to give vent to his joyous feelings in song,
began to play on the lute, and sang, in a fine melodious voice, a
few sonnets in praise of the river Kåviri, and the ancient city of
Pukår. Then he poured forth a number of love songs describing
the alluring beauty of a girl of the fisherman tribe, whose eyes
were as sharp as arrows in piercing the hearts of men, and who
was herself a cruel murderess, for those who set their eyes on her
died broken-hearted. Måthavi, who listened with pleasure to the
masterly manner in which Kovilan sang and played on the lute,
fancied that the verses were meant to refer to herself, and that
her lover was beginning to dislike her. Receiving the lute from
her lover's hand, she began to sing in a voice so sweet and enchant-
ing that it soothed and gladdened the hearts of every one who
had the good fortune to listen to it. She too sang of the river
Kåviri and of the city of Pukar, and then a few songs which describe the lament of a girl of the fisherman tribe for her absent
lover, as follows :—

Pretty flower! bright and blooming,
　Oh! how happy art thou sleeping :
While with sleepless eyes and lonely,
　Waiting for him I am weeping.

Lovely flower! full of honey,
　Art thou dreaming that my lover,
In this moonlight soft and pleasant,
　Cometh back into my bower?

The birds have flown away to roost
　The glowing sun has set :
But still I wait with streaming eyes
　Where last my love I met.

---

[1] Ibid., Canto VI.

> The moon doth shed its light so mild
> All over land and sea
> This pleasant eve, our trysting time
> Doth not my lover see ?

> The wild pine shades the sandy banks
> Where he my love did woo:
> Now, all my sports I have forgot,
> And all my playmates too.

> Though he has gone forsaking me,
> I hold him in my heart :
> His dear image shall not fade,
> Till death my life doth part.

These verses were sung with such deep pathos, that Kovilan who was all attention and intoxicated with the thrilling music of her voice suspected that Mathavi had set her heart on another man, and wild with jealousy, he quitted her abruptly, observing that it was very late, and went away followed by his attendants. Mathavi, who was grieved at the strange conduct of her lover, returned home immediately in her carriage.[1]

It was early summer now, a season in which Love reigns supreme in the Tamil-land. The southern breezes which set in at this season carried his messages throughout Love's chosen realm : and the cuckoo which warbled in every flowery grove acted as his trumpeter. Mathavi who was unhappy owing to the absence of her lover, went up to her summer bed room, in the upper storey of her mansion, and seated on a couch tried to console herself with the charms of music. She took the lute in her hand and essayed to sing, but such was the agitation of her mind that she could not hum more than a few words. She began to play on the lute, and struck a mournful tune; and even in this she failed. Longing to meet Kovilan, she took the thin bud of the *Piththikai*, and dipping it in red cotton paint, wrote a missive to her lover on the fragrant petal of a flower of the wild-pine. "Mild summer," she wrote; "who turns the thoughts of all living creatures to Love, is now the prince regent. The silvery moon who appears at sunset frowns at lovers who are parted from each other. And the great monarch Love will not

---

fail to shoot with his flowery darts every maiden who is not
united to her lover. Bear these in mind, and have mercy on me."
Calling her maid Vásanta-Málai, she gave the letter into her
hands, bidding her to present it to Kovilan. Vasanta-Málai
took the epistle accordingly, and meeting Kovilan in the market
road, offered it to him. He declined however to read it, and told
her "I know your mistress too well. Trained to act any part
on the stage, she is capable of every kind of dissimulation, you
may take the letter back to your mistress." Vasanta-Málai retraced her steps with grief and informed her mistress that Kovilan had declined to receive her letter: and Mathavi retired to
bed, sorrowfully saying to herself, " He is sure to come in the
morning, even if he does not appear to-night." [1]

On that same evening, Kannaki was seated in her mansion
alone and gloomy, she was now a prey to melancholy. Her eyelids were not painted : her hair was not combed and she wore no
ornament save the marriage badge on her neck. [2]

Devanti, a Brahmin woman who came to console Kannaki,
sprinkled grass and rice on her, and blessed her saying "may
you regain the love of your husband." " Alas! I fear I shall not
enjoy that happiness again," said Kannaki, "I dreamt that my
husband took me to a great city, and while we were there, strangers accused us of a grave crime. My husband met with a
serious misfortune, and I went to plead his cause before the king.
Evil befell the king and his great city ; but I and my husband
attained a bliss which you would not believe, if I told you."
" Your husband does not hate you," rejoined Devanti, " In your
former birth, you failed to keep a vow. The evil effects of that
sin may be removed, if you bathe in the two tanks sacred to the
Sun and Moon, at the mouth of the river Kaviri, and worship the
God of Love at his temple. We shall go one day and bathe in
those tanks."

" It is not proper for me to do so," said Kannaki. A servant-
maid then announced that Kovilan had entered the house, and
Kannaki hastened to meet her lord. Kovilan entered his bedroom, and drawing his wife near to him, noted her sad look and
thin body worn by grief.

---

[1] Ibid., Canto VIII   [2] Ibid., Canto IV, ll. 47 to 57.

"I am ashamed of myself" said he,. "I have wasted all the wealth given to me by my parents on a deceitful actress." "There is yet a pair of anklets" .said Kannaki smiling, "you can have them." "Listen to me, dear girl," he said, "with these anklets for my capital, I wish to trade again and recover my fortune. I intend going to the famous city of Madura, and thou shalt go with me." Kannaki's joy was great to see her husband come back to her, renouncing the actress, and she was prepared to accompany him to any corner of the world. [1]

Long before daybreak the husband and wife quitted their home without the knowledge of their servants. In the dark and still night, they drew the bolt of the outer gate without noise, and came out into the street. They passed the temple of Vishnu, and the seven Buddhist Vihâras believed to have. been erected by Indra, and approaching the pedestal of polished stone on which Nigrantha monks used to sit and preach their doctrine, they reverently went round it, and walked down the broad. road leading to the fort gate. Coming out of the fort they passed through the royal park and reached the bank of the river Kaviri : then turning westwards along the northern bank of the river, they walked on for a distance of about a *kavatham* and arrived at a nunnery of the Nigrantha sect. Here they halted in. a grove : and Kannaki who was panting, after her unusual exertion, gave rest to her aching feet. She then asked her husband in her artless way, " where is the ancient city of Madura ? "

"It is five, six *kavathams* beyond our country, it is not far,". replied Kovilan, laughing at the ignorance of his wife. He ought to have said it was five times six or thirty *kavathams* away : but being afraid that she may be frightened at the distance, he disguised the expression, so that she may.believe it was only 5 or 6 *kavathams*. It being daylight now, they both entered the nunnery and saluted a *kavunthi* [2] or nun, who was lodging in it. The nun observed with surprise the handsome features and noble appearance of the pair, and enquired why they had quitted their home, and like destitute persons journeyed on foot.

---

[1] Ibid., Canto IX.

[2] Kanti is the designation of a Nigrantha nun or female devotee.

"I have nothing more to say than that I wish to go to Madura to seek my fortune there," said Kovilan.

"It will be no easy task for this delicate lady," said the nun, pointing to "Kannaki to walk over rough roads and through wild woods, the long distance you have to go. I beseech you to desist from this adventure: but you seem bent on going to Madura. I too have been for some time past wishing to visit Madura, and to learn the doctrines of Argha as taught by the wise and learned men of that city. I shall therefore accompany you: and we shall start together."

"Reverend nun!" said Kovilan thankfully, "if thou art pleased to go with us, I need not feel any anxiety for the safety of my wife."

The nun dwelt on the dangers and difficulties of the road to Madura, and warned Kovilan specially to be on his guard against causing pain or death to living creatures, however small or insignificant, as it was a sin denounced as heinous by the Nigranthas. Praying to Argha for a safe journey, she slung her alms-bowl on her shoulder, and taking a bundle of peacock feathers in her hand, she too started on the journey. By short marches they travelled through a fertile country where fields covered with waving corn, luxuriant plantations of the sugar-cane, and green woods with hamlets nestling in their shade met their eyes on every side. They forgot the fatigue of their journey, when they heard the roar of floods rushing through sluices and locks into the channels branching from the Kaviri, the joyous chorus of women working in the fields, and the merry songs and shouts of men driving the oxen yoked to their ploughs, or urging the buffaloes which were treading the sheafs of corn reaped from the fields. After travelling for many days they arrived at an island in the middle of the Kaviri, where in a garden which was full of sweet-scented flowers, they met a Nigrantha monk, at whose feet they fell and prayed for his blessing. The sage, who could read by the light of his serene mind the past and future lives of those who stood before him, addressed the nun in the following manner: "Mark my words, thou pious nun! No one can escape the effects of his good or evil deeds. Even like the seeds which are sown and yield a harvest of their kind, our deeds react upon us. Like lights set upon a plain which go out when the wind blows, our souls go out of our bodies. Only those whose minds have been enlightened by the truths preached by Argha can save themselves from this prison of re-births."

"To the end of my life," replied the Kavunthi reverently, "I will worship none but Argha and believe in no precepts but those revealed in his Agamas." The monk was pleased with the words spoken by the nun and blessed her and her fellow passengers saying, "May you be freed from the bonds of desire!" The travellers then got into a boat and landing on the southern bank of the river entered the city of Uraiyur. '

They lodged in a Nigrantha monastery at Uraiyur, and worshipped the resplendent image of Argha, which was placed under a triple umbrella, beneath the shade of an Asoka tree. They stayed one whole day in the monastery, and on the next morning they started with the early dawn, and travelling till sunrise they arrived at a pleasant garden surrounded by cool tanks and verdant meadows. While they were resting in this garden, a Brahmin pilgrim also happened to arrive. He said that he was a native of Mankadu in the Chera country; that he had travelled through the Pandyan land and was going to worship the images of Vishnu at Arankam or Venkadam. Kovilan enquired of him the different routes to Madura and the nature of the roads. In reply to him the Brahmin said, "It is a pity you have come with this lady at a season when the fierce rays of the sun dry up and heat the surface of the earth: and travelling is far from pleasant. The road from Uraiyur up to the great tank at Kodumbai ' lies through rocks and narrow defiles; and thence there are three routes to Madura. The route on the right hand will take you through a wild region, where water is scarce, and lawless tribes harass the passengers. On that road you will see the Sirumalai hills, on which every kind of fruit tree grows in abundance. Keeping to the left side of the mountain you will arrive at Madura. If you take instead the route on the left hand, from Kodumbai, you will have to travel

---

· ¹ Chilapp-athikâram, Canto X.
² Now known as Kodumpâlur.

through fields and jungles and weary wastes to the mountain, whose summit is crowned with a temple of Vishnu, and whose base is washed by the river Silambu. Near that mountain, there is a valley, which is guarded by a goddess who may give you trouble. Praying to Vishnu for help, you should pass through this valley and reach Madura. Between these two routes there is a middle path which is more convenient, as it passes through woodlands and hamlets, and you may safely take that road." Having ascertained the easiest route, they pursued their journey to Madura. In the course of their journey, Kannaki having complained of her sore feet and fatigue, one day they had to stop at a Kali temple, in a village inhabited by Vedas.[1] Here they witnessed the weird dance of the priestess of Kali, who, attired like that dread goddess, stood up in the village common, and trembling all over as if she was possessed by a devil, declared in terrific tones that the goddess Kali was incensed, as the Maravar had not offered any sacrifice at her temple, for some time past, and that they should now bestir themselves, and attack the herds of cattle in neighbouring villages.[2] Having learnt that in the land of the Pandyas, there was no fear of robbers or wild beasts on the highways, Kovilan proposed that they should travel at night instad of during the day, as Kannaki was unable to bear the heat of the sun or to walk on the hot ground. The nun having agreed to this plan, they started from the Vedar village after sunset. Though there was a bright moon, the timid Kannaki, afraid to walk out at night, followed close to her husband, resting one hand on his shoulder, while the Kavunti beguiled the way with many a story which she had learnt from her religious books. Travelling all night, they arrived early in the morning at a Brahmin village. Leaving his wife with the Kavunti in a garden, he lifted the thorny branches which formed its fence, and went towards a pond. Kausika, a Brahmin who approached the pond at the same time, being doubtful as to whether he was Kovilan, exclaimed as follows, pretending to speak to a flowery creeper : " Thou creeper, why art thou faded ? Dost thou suffer from the heat of this early summer, like thy

[1] Chilapp-athikaram, Canto XI.
[2] Ibid., Canto XII.

namesake the long-eyed Mathavi,[1] who pines for her absent lover Kovilan?" Hearing these words Kovilan asked Kausika what he meant by his exclamation. Recognizing Kovilan at once that Brahmin informed him that as soon as it was known that he and his wife had left their home, his servants were sent out in all directions to search for him and bring him home. His aged parents were sunk in profound grief and all his relations were unhappy. Mathavi having come to know of his disappearance was overcome with grief. Hearing of her distress, the Brahmin went to visit her and she entreated him to carry a letter to her lover, who was dear to her as the apple of her eye. Taking charge of the letter he went to many places, in search of Kovilan, and had the good luck to meet him there. Saying thus, the Brahmin handed to him a roll of palm-leaf. The perfumed leaf reminded him of the fragrant tresses of the actress, and with no little tremor he unfolded the palm-leaf and read it. "I fall at thy honoured feet," wrote Mathavi, "and beg you will graciously read my simple words. I know not any fault on my part which could have led you to quit thy home in the night, with thy gentle wife, and without the knowledge of thy parents. May thy pure and noble heart be pleased to remove our sorrow." He read it with pleasure and felt relieved, as he was now satisfied that his suspicions against Mathavi were ill-founded. "Make haste" said he to the Brahmin, "and let my parents know that I am safe, and tell them not to grieve for my absence." Returning to the garden where his wife and the nun were staying, he joined a band of musicians, and pleased them by his skilful play on the lute. From them he learnt that Madura was within a few hours' journey and that they could travel without any fear. As on the previous day, the three again travelled at night, and in the early dawn they were delighted to hear the distant sounds of drums. Walking on, they heard the trumpeting of elephants, the neighing of steeds, the chant of Vedic hymns, and the songs of war-bards coming to their ears in a mingled roar, like the noise of waves on the seashore. Their hearts were elated with joy, and when they approached the classic stream of the Vaigai, the theme of many a poet's song, they felt they were treading on sacred

---

[1] Mathavi is also the name of a flowery creeper.

ground. Avoiding the public ferry where a continuous stream of passengers crossed the river on boats whose prows were shaped like the head of a horse or a lion or an elephant, they went to a small ferry, which was less frequented, and crossing over on a raft they reached the southern bank of the river. Keeping to the left of the city, they went round to the eastern gate, and entered a village, which was outside the walls of the city, in the midst of groves of areca and cocoanut plams, where only ascetics and men devoted to religion resided.[1]

Early on the next day when the sound of the morning drum at the palace and at the various temples in the city was heard outside the city walls, Kovilan approached the nun and saluting her reverently, said "Pious nun! Having forsaken the path of virtue, I was the cause of much misery to my poor wife, and we have suffered great hardships in travelling through unknown countries. I shall now go into the city and make the acquaintance of the merchants there. Until I come back, may I leave my wife in thy care?"

"Many have suffered in the past for the woman they loved" replied the nun, "Know you not the story of Rama who obeying the commands of his father, went into exile with his wife, and losing her, was for a long time a prey to intense grief. Another king played at dice and lost his kingdom: then fleeing into a forest with his wife, deserted her at midnight. You at least are not so unfortunate as those kings. You have still got your wife with you. Be not disheartened, therefore, but go into the city, and enquire where you can find a suitable lodging and return."

Having taken leave of the nun, Kovilan entered the city passing through the gate which was guarded by Yavana soldiers who stood with drawn swords. With wonder he beheld the grand city, its broad streets, and the storied mansions of the opulent classes. Till midday he strolled through the market, the merchants' streets and the public squares, and unable to bear the heat of the noon-day sun, he walked back under the shade of the numerous flags which lined the streets.[2] While he was describing to the nun the grandeur of Madura, the happiness of its

[1] Chilapp-athikaram, Canto XIII.
[2] Ibid., Canto XIV.

population and the power of the Pandyan king, Madalan, a
Brahmin pilgrim from Thalaich-Chenkanam, a village near
Pukar, arrived at the grove where they were staying. Kovilan
who had known him before saluted him. The Brahmin was
surprised to learn that Kovilan had travelled on foot, with his
wife, to Madura. He praised the many generous acts done by
Kovilan while at Pukar, and wondered why one, who had been
so kind and benevolent to the poor and the unlucky, should himself suffer misfortune. Both he and the nun advised Kovilan to
enter the city before sunset and secure suitable quarters among
the merchants' houses, as it was not proper for them to stay outside with ascetics and religious mendicants. During their conversation, Mathavi, a shepherdess, who was returning to Madura,
after worshipping the image of a goddess outside the city, saluted
the nun.

"Listen to me, Mathavi!" said the nun who thought it best
to entrust Kannaki to the care of the shepherdess, "If the merchants of this city come to know the name of the father of this
lady's husband, they would hasten to welcome him to their house,
and deem it an honour to have him as their guest; but until he
makes their acquaintance and finds a proper lodging I entrust
this lady to thy care. Take her to your house, and let her
bathe and change her dress. Paint her eyelids, and give her
flowers to wear in her hair. Take care of her as if she was
your own daughter. Brought up in affluence, her soft little feet
had seldom touched the bare ground in her native city: and
yet in the long journey she has now made she felt not her own
fatigue, but grieved that her husband exposed himself to the hot
sun, and was ever attentive to his wants. So loving and faithful
a wife I have not seen. Take her with you, and do not tarry."
Mathavi was only glad to render any assistance to so amiable a
young lady as Kannaki; and about sunset when the shepherds
were returning with herds of lowing cows from their grazing
grounds, she accompanied by Kannaki, and followed by a number of shepherdesses, entered the city, and led Kannaki to her
house.[1]

Mathavi, who was really proud to have such noble guests as

---

[1] Ibid., Canto XV.

Kannaki and her husband, vacated for their use a neat little cottage, which was fenced round, and the walls of which were painted with red earth. She assisted Kannaki in bathing and changing her dress, and introducing her daughter, said ' Fair lady ! my daughter Ayyai shall be thy maid-servant, and we shall see that thou and thy husband are in want of nothing while you stay here.' On the next morning, she provided new vessels for cooking, fine white rice, vegetables such as the tender fruits of the mango, pomegranate and plantain, and milk fresh drawn from her cows. Kannaki set to work at once to prepare the morning meal. She sliced the fruits carefully, and Ayyai assisted her in lighting the oven. She cooked the rice and vegetables to the best of her knowledge, and as she exposed herself to the heat of the oven, her eyes became red and drops of sweat trickled down her face. Having finished the cooking, she invited her husband to take his meals, and placed a small mat, prettily made of white dry grass, for his seat. After he had washed his hands and feet and taken his seat on the mat, she sprinkled water and cleansed the floor in front of his seat, and spreading out a tender plantain leaf on the clean floor, she served upon the leaf the food prepared by her. Kovilan offered the usual prayers which are prescribed to the merchant caste, and then ate the food set before him. When he had refreshed himself, and taken his seat apart, Kannaki offered him betel leaves and areca-nuts to chew. Inviting her to come near him, Kovilan said, " How much our aged parents must have suffered at the thought that thy tender feet could not walk over the rough paths we have travelled? Is this all a dream or the effect of my sins? I shudder at the thought what fate yet awaits us. Will heaven yet smile on a sinner like me, who loved the company of idlers and rakes, who scorned the advice of my elders, who failed in my duty to my parents, and caused no little pain to so young and virtuous a wife as yourself ? Never did I pause to think what evil course I pursued : and yet you readily followed me when I asked you to venture on this distant journey. Alas! what have you done?"

" Your revered parents," replied Kannaki," whenever they visited me, and found me receiving them with a smiling face, praised my patience, and consoled me with kind words, as they

knew that heavy sorrow weighed down my heart and that I neglected even the household duties in which I had once taken great
pleasure. Because I did not express my grief, and tried to conceal
it from them, they appeared all the more distressed. Though
you led a life which no one liked, I had not the heart to refuse
even your slightest wish and I could not but follow you when
you asked me to do so."

"You left your dear parents, and your devoted servants and
friends, and with only your virtues for your safeguard, you followed me and shared my sorrows. You have been indeed a
ministering angel to me in my distress. Let me now take one of
your anklets for sale, and until I return, stay you here and be not
afraid that I leave you alone," said Kovilan, and embracing her
tenderly, he took one of her anklets, and left the cottage. Tears
dropped down his manly cheeks, but he brushed them aside before any one could notice it ; and with staggering steps he walked
through the shepherd street and passed on through the road
where courtezans reside, and reached the market road. He met
there a man coming up the road, followed by a number of workmen and distinguished by his dress which consisted of a long coat
in addition to the usual dress of a Tamil. Learning that he was
the chief jeweller to the Pandyan king, he approached the goldsmith and enquired " Can you value an anklet fit to be worn by
the queen ? "

"Your servant " replied the jeweller saluting Kovilan with
both his hands, " may not be able to estimate the value correctly,
but he manufactures crowns and other jewels for the king."

Kovilan took the jewel out of the cloth in which he had
folded it, and showed it to the goldsmith, who was amazed to find
it to be a superb anklet set with emeralds and diamonds and
engraved most beautifully. " None but the queen is worthy of
wearing this jewel," exclaimed he, " Stay here near my humble
abode, I shall inform the king and let you know his wishes."
Kovilan took his seat accordingly within the enclosure of a temple
adjoining the goldsmith's house. The goldsmith thought to himself, " this jewel resembles exactly the queen's anklet which I
have stolen ; I may therefore accuse this stranger of having stolen
it, before the king finds any reason to suspect me of the theft"

and went direct to the palace. He approached the king as he was about to enter the queen's apartments, and falling at the king's feet reported as follows:—" The thief who without a crowbar or a shovel, but with only the help of his incantations, caused the palace guards to fall asleep, and stole the queen's anklet : and who eluded the vigilant search of the city guards hitherto, is now in my little cottage." The king called some of the guards and commanded them to see if the anklet is in the thief's hands, and if it is, to kill the thief and bring the jewel. The goldsmith, glad to find that his scheme succeeded so well, led the guards to Kovilan's presence, and told him, " These soldiers have come to see the anklet under the orders of the king." Kovilan showed the jewel to them. They looked at the jewel and at Kovilan, and taking the goldsmith aside, said " This man's appearance is noble : he certainly is not a thief."

" Thieves are armed with spells and drugs," said the cunning goldsmith " if you delay carrying out the king's orders, he may make himself invisible by his incantations, or he may throw you into a profound sleep by the use of his drugs. In any case, you will incur the displeasure of the king and suffer punishment."

" Have any of you," he further asked them, " traced that thief, who during the day sat at the palace gate, attired like the courier of a foreign king, and after nightfall entered the palace in the disguise of a servant maid and walking along the shadow of the pillars, found his way into the bedroom of the king's brother and removed the necklace from the prince's person : and who, when the prince awoke and drew his sword to cut down the thief, defended himself with the scabbard, and disappeared dexterously behind a pillar, leaving the prince to wrestle with that pillar of stone." " Thieves are extremely cunning," said one of the soldiers, " I remember on a dark and rainy night, when I was going my rounds in the city, there appeared before me suddenly a burglar armed with a crowbar, and prowling like a hungry tiger. I drew my sword, but he snatched it from my hands and in the darkness of the night I found neither him nor my sword again. Comrades! we must decide quickly what to do: or we shall be surely punished by the king." Scarcely had he ceased speaking when another soldier, an illiterate youth, drew his sword, and with one stroke of the shining blade beheaded Kovilan. His body dropped down and the crimson blood gushed out on the earth.[1]

Meanwhile, in the shepherd's quarter of the city, the shepherd lasses held a sacred dance for the good of their cattle and for the amusement of Kannaki. One of the girls personated Krishna, their national hero, another represented Baladeva, his elder brother, and a third appeared as the shepherdess, who was the favourite mistress of Krishna. Seven of the shepherd lasses stood in a ring clasping each other's hands, and danced and sang merrily for some hours.[1] When the dance was over, one of the lasses went with flowers, incense and sandal to bathe in the Vaigai river, and to worship the feet of the God Vishnu. She heard a rumour in the city that Kovilan had been killed, and hurried back to Kannaki's lodging. She whispered to her neighbours what she had heard, but stood mute in Kannaki's presence, unwilling to break the sad news to her. Kannaki who had been eagerly waiting for the return of her husband, enquired of her "what is it, friend, that my neighbours whisper? It is long since my husband went out, and I am alarmed about his safety."

"Your husband," replied the shepherdess, "has been killed, because he had stolen an anklet from the palace."

Kannaki who heard these words, burst into tears and sank to the ground crying "Oh my husband! my husband!" Wild with anguish, she stood up again and cried out "Listen to me all ye girls who danced the Kuravai! Thou Sun, who knowest all that takes place on this wide earth! be my witness. Is my husband a thief?"

"He is no thief," said a voice in the air, "this city is doomed to be destroyed by fire."[1]

Taking the other anklet in her hand, she walked out of the shepherd's quarter, with tears streaming from her eyes. She told the people that followed her that her husband was not a thief, and that he had taken for sale one of her own anklets and had been unjustly killed. As she went sobbing and crying through the

[1] Ibid., Canto XVI.
[1] Ibid., Canto XVII.
[1] Ibid., Canto XVIII.

streets, men and women rushed out of their houses, and gazed
pathetically at her, expressing their consternation and horror for
the unjust execution of her husband. The sun had set when she
approached the place where her husband lay a corpse. She embraced her husband's body and was shocked to find it cold. She
fell down weeping by the side of the corpse, and her lament was
heard throughout the long night.

"See'st thou my sorrow," cried she, "alas! thy handsome
body now rolls in the dust. Alone and friendless, I am weeping
by thy side, in the dark night, and thy body lies on the bare earth.
Tears flow from my eyes, when I see blood dropping from thy
wound, and thy body covered with dust."

In the frenzy of her despair, she again embraced the body
of her husband, and fancied that he stood up and wiped the tears
from her face, and as she clasped his feet he told her to remain,
and his spirit ascended to heaven. She had hoped to be the
faithful companion of his life, to be the partner of his joy and
sorrow and to solace his grief, but these hopes were now dashed
to the ground. She thought of her dream which had come to pass
all too soon. She had no wish to live; but one burning passion
now possessed her, and it was to prove her husband's innocence,
and curse the wicked king who had caused his death.[1]

During the same night, the Pandyan queen had frightful
dreams and saw bad omens. She hastened, therefore, on the
next morning to the king's presence, surrounded by the dwarfs,
eunuchs, hunchbacks and women who were her usual attendants.
She found the king already seated on his throne and related to
him her dream. While she was relating it, Kannaki appeared at
the palace gate, "Thou guard!" said she addressing the sentinel
at the gate, "Thou guard who servest the stupid and senseless
king who knows not his duty to his subjects! say to your king
that a woman who has lost her husband is come, carrying an
anklet in her hand."

One of the guards went to the royal presence and making the
usual obeisance, addressed the king: "Long life to our king of
Korkai! long life to the lord of the Pothiya hill! long life to the
Cheliya! long life to the sovereign of the southern region! long

life to the Panchava that never stoops to an unjust deed!
Furious as the goddess Durga or Kali, a woman who has lost
her husband is at the palace gate and seeks an audience, holding
a golden anklet in her hand."

"Let her come, bring her here," said the king. Led by the
guard Kannaki entered the hall, where the king was seated on the
throne with his queen. Her long flowing hair hung loose and in
disorder; her body was covered with dust, and tears flowed fast
down her cheeks. The king, who was moved with pity at the
sight of her, enquired graciously "Who art thou maiden, that
appearest before me bathed in tears?"

"Rash king! I have to speak to you," began Kannaki,
utterly unable to control her anger, her voice broken by sobs " I
come from Pukár, the kings of which city are famous for their
impartial justice. One of them cut off the flesh from his own body,
to save a dove : another drove his chariot over his dear son, because he had killed a calf. My name is Kannaki, and I am the
widow of Kovilan, the son of that well-known merchant Macha-
thuvan, who came to thy city to earn a livelihood, and was killed
under your orders, when he went to sell one of my anklets."

"Lady," responded the king, " it is no injustice to kill a
thief ; but it is the right of the ruler of a country."

"Thou erring king of Korkai! my anklets are filled with
diamonds," said Kannaki. "Well hast thou spoken," exclaimed
the king, "our anklets are filled with pearls. Bring the anklet and
let us examine it."

The anklet was placed before the king, and as Kannaki broke
it, the diamonds which were in it, spattered out, some striking
even the king's face. The king was unnerved, when he saw the
sparkling gems. He was now convinced that he had been
deceived by his jeweller.

"No-king am I," said he with deep humility and remorse,
"who believed the words of my goldsmith. I am the thief: I
have done an act which sullies the fair fame of the long line of
kings who ruled the southern land. Better for me is it to die than
to bear this disgrace," and swooned on the throne. The Pandyan queen fell at the feet of Kannaki, praying for pardon, knowing that she could offer no consolation to a woman whose

husband had been killed.[1] "This king shall die and his palace shall be destroyed by fire," said Kannaki in the bitterness of her anguish, and invoked the wrath of the god of fire. The palace was soon enveloped in flames. The guards were astonished to find dense smoke issuing from the palace gates. Elephants and horses burst from their stables and rushing out of the palace, escaped from the fire. The high priest and ministers and other officers of state hastened to the palace not knowing that the king and queen had died, and tried in vain to put down the flames.[2]

The goddess of Madura then appeared to the vision of Kannaki and beseeched her to appease her wrath and save the city from total destruction. "Your husband was killed," said the goddess, "by the effect of the sin he had committed in a former birth. Vasu and Kumara, kings of Simhapura and Kapilapura respectively, in the Kalinga country, were once waging a fierce war with each other, and none approached their cities within a distance of 6 *Kavathams.* Sangaman, a merchant, greedy of large profits, secretly entered Simhapura with his wife, during the war, and was selling his goods, when Bharata, an officer in the service of king Vasu, seized Sangama and reporting to the king that he was a spy, had him unjustly executed. That Bharata was reborn as Kovilan and suffered for his former sin."

Kannaki broke her bracelets at the temple of Durga, and went out of the city by the western gate, saying to herself, "With my husband I entered this city by the eastern gate, and alone I go out, by the western gate." The unhappy widow found no rest by day or by night. Distracted with grief and unable to eat or sleep, she walked along the northern bank of the Vaigai river and ascended the hills sacred to Murugan. There in the midst of the villages inhabited by Kuravas, on the fourteenth day after the death of Kovilan, her pure spirit, which had harboured not a single evil thought, but had drunk deep of the cup of misery in this life, ascended to heaven.[3]

When the sad news of the execution of Kovilan and the departure of Kannaki reached the ears of the nun, she was so over-

[1] Ibid., Canto XX.
[2] Ibid., Cantos XXI and XXII.
[3] Ibid., Canto XXIII.

whelmed with grief that she declined all food and died soon
afterwards. The Brahmin pilgrim, Mâdalan, conveyed the
news to Pukar on his way to his native village. Kovilan's
father was so shocked with the tragic fate of his son that
he renounced the world and took the vow of a Buddhist
monk ; and his mother died broken-hearted. Kannaki's father
gave away all his property in charity and joined the ranks of Ajivaka ascetics : and her mother died of grief. The actress Mâthavi, who heard of these events, vowed that she would lead a religious life, and devoted her daughter Manimekalai also to the life
of a Buddhist nun.

From that memorable day on which Kovilan was beheaded,
there was no rain in the Pandyan kingdom; and famine, fever
and small-pox smote the people sorely. Verri-vel-Cheliya, who
held his court at Korkai, believing that these misfortunes were
brought on by the curse of Kannaki, sacrificed one thousand goldsmiths at her altar and performed festivals in her honor. Copious
showers of rain then fell and famine and pestilence disappeared
from the kingdom. Kosar, king of Kongu, Gajabâhu, king of
Lanka, and Perunk-killi, the Chola, erected temples and performed festivals in her honor, and their kingdoms were blest with
never-failing rain and abundant crops.

The Chera king Chenkudduvan conducted an expedition
personally to the banks of the Ganges, and with the help of the
Karnas, kings of Magadha, obtained stone from the Himalayas,
bathed it in the Ganges and brought it to his capital Vanji,
where it was fashioned into a beautiful image of Kannaki. He
consecrated the image with grand ceremony in the presence of
the kings of Kongu, and Malava and of Gajabahu, king of Lanka.

In conclusion the author points the moral of the tale that the
laws of morality are inexorable : no prayer, no sacrifice, can atone
for our sins : we must ourselves suffer the reaction of our deeds.
" Beware, therefore, ye people of this world ! youth and riches
and our life are fleeting. Waste not your days : but take heed in
time, and acquire the merit of good deeds, which alone will help
you in your future life ! " .

CHAPTER XII.

The Story of Mani-mekalai.

The Mani-mêkalai, or more properly, [1]Mani-mêkalai-thura-vu, as it is named by the author himself, is an epic poem describing the circumstances under which Mani-mêkalai, the daughter of Kovilan, renounced the world and took the vows of a Buddhist nun. The work is specially valuable as a record of the extent to which Buddhism had spread in Southern India, Ceylon and Sumatra, in the early part of the second century A.D. : and its value is enhanced by the fact that it is much older than the Chinese works of Fa Hian and Hwen Thsang, and the Pali chronicles Dipawanso and Mahawanso of Ceylon. It is, I believe, the earliest record extant in any language, with the exception of the Buddhist sacred texts, which furnishes information regarding the objects of worship, the peculiar beliefs and superstitions, and the abstruse philosophy of the followers of Buddha. We learn from the poem that Buddhist monks were numerous in the Tamil-land, and that some of them, at least, claimed wonderful powers, such as the ability to know the past and foretell the future ; and that they believed in charms and incantations, and in the existence of spirits which could communicate with human beings. The author, Cheeththalaich-châttanar, who appears to have been a learned and zealous Buddhist, following the traditions then current regarding the journeys of Buddha through the air, and his knowledge of previous births, describes the heroine of the poem also, as travelling through the air and performing various other miracles. I shall now give briefly the story of the Mani-mêkalai, reserving the references to Buddhism till I come to describe the religions which prevailed in Tamilakam.

The yearly festival held in the city of Pukâr in honor of Indra, the king of the celestials, was drawing near. Ever since the festival had been founded by the Chola king, Thodi-thôd-chembiyan, renowned as the hero who destroyed the wondrous

---

[1] Mr. V. Saminatha Iyer, Tamil Pandit of the Kumbakonam College, has lately published an excellent edition of this poem with explanatory notes.

hanging castles, it was performed most punctilliously by successive Cholas. In accordance with the time-honoured custom, the reigning king Killi-valavan issued orders for the commencement of the opening ceremonies. A brilliant band of warriors, mounted on horses, chariots and elephants, and foot soldiers armed with shining swords, started from the temple of Indra, escorting the big drums of the temple which were placed on an elephant, and marched through the main streets of Kaviripaddinam, announcing with beat of drum the approach of the grand festival. "Sweep the streets and squares" shouted the public-crier who proclaimed the royal commands "and cover them with fresh sand. Plant along the streets sugar-canes and pretty creepers and plantain trees and areca-palms bearing bunches of fruits. Hang out flags and banners. Arrange in front of your houses lamps borne by statues and vases filled with water. Adorn the pillars with strings of pearls and garlands, and set up ornamented gateways. Ye Brahmins! perform your services in all your temples, from the great shrine of Siva to the small fanes of the local deities. Ye preachers of virtue! attend the pavilions erected for you. Ye teachers of the religious sects! ascend the public halls of debate. Let there be no fight, no brawl during the eight and twenty days of the great festival, when even the gods will visit this city in disguise, and mix with mortal men! May there be abundant rain and rich harvests! May our great city prosper for ever! May our sovereign ever wield his sceptre with justice!"[1]

Chitrápati who heard this announcement with a pang of regret, knowing that her daughter Máthavi and grand-daughter Mani-mékalai will not prepare as usual to take part in the festivities, called her daughter's maid-servant, Vayanta-málai, and bid her tell Máthavi what her friends thought of her entry into a convent. The maid went to the Buddhist convent, where Máthavi was seated in a hall, with her daughter Mani-mékalai, stringing flowers, and touched with pity at the altered appearance of the once gay actress, told her how people ridiculed the absurd idea of an accomplished courtezan like her becoming a nun.

"Alas! my maid," replied Máthavi mournfully, "cursed is

[1] Mani-mekalai, Canto I.

my soul which did not quit this body the moment I heard of the unhappy fate of my lover. The married women of this land will, on the death of their husbands, die instantly unable to bear their grief, or willingly give up their lives on their husbands' funeral pyre, or by fasts and prayers seek to rejoin their husbands in their future births. Unlike them, the saintly widow of my lover, furious with wrath at the unjust execution of her husband, devoted to the flames the great city of Madura. My daughter Mani-mêkalai, who stands in the relation of a daughter to that chaste widow, shall never lead a wicked or worthless life, but all her lifetime she shall be a zealous devotee to virtue. Listen to me further, my maid! I visited the Buddhist monastery in this city, and falling at the feet of the venerable abbot, related to him the sad story of my lover. He consoled my afflicted mind, revealing to me the noble truths that:

Those who are born suffer endless sorrow.
Those who are not born rest in bliss.
It is desire that causeth birth.
Those who have no desire cease to be born.

He explained to me, besides, the five kinds of purity which lead to salvation. Tell my mother Chitrâpati and her friends that I have resolved to follow his advice." Hearing these words, Vayantamâlai returned home with a heavy heart, like one who had dropped a precious gem in the sea.[1]

Mani-mêkalai who had been closely listening to the conversation between her mother and her maid, was moved to tears when she thought of the tragical fate of her father and stepmother. Her tears flowed fast, and falling on the garland which she was preparing, spoilt its brilliancy. Mâthavi, who saw that her daughter was weeping, comforted her, and wiping the tears from her eyes with her dainty fingers, observed, " This garland is now unfit for an offering, as it is bedewed with your tears. I wish you will go and gather fresh flowers." " Will you allow Manimêkalai to go out alone?" enquired Sutamati, who was also making a garland to be offered at the monastery. " Her pretty face and dark eyes will surely attract every one who sees her. Beyond the royal park, she may meet the princes of the

---

[1] *Ibid.,* Canto i.

Chola family, and hence it is not safe for her to go either to Champâti-vanam or Kavêra-vanam: but there is Uva-vanam which, under the blessing of Buddha, is ever full of flowers, and in it there is a crystal alcove, which contains a sacred seat of Buddha. Your daughter may safely go to that garden, and I shall go with her." Mâthavi having expressed the assent, Manimekalai and Sutamati left the convent, and walked along the chariot road towards Uva-vanam. The festival of Indra having begun, there were crowds of revellers on the public roads. A drunkard stood before a naked Nigrantha monk, who carried a rattan in his hand, a pot slung on his shoulder, and addressed him " Welcome, thou reverend Sir ; I worship thy feet. Pray listen to me. The soul which dwells in thy unclean body pines like a prisoner confined in a close cell. Drink therefore of this toddy which is drawn from the spaltre of the cocoanut palm, and which will give you pleasure both in this world and see if my words are not true." In another part of the street, a madman, clad in rags and bunches of leaves, daubed with sandal paste, and decked with the flowers of the wild *alari* and *erukkai*, was shouting and dancing and running to and fro, to the great merriment of the rabble. In another quarter, a man was acting the pantomimic play, of the eunuch who danced before the son of Krishna, in Bana's great city. Groups of people strolled in the streets looking at these scenes, or at the children adorned with tiny jewels, who were riding on toy elephants set on wheels, or at the beautiful lifelike paintings on the walls of buildings, representing gods and human beings, and animals of all kinds. As the groups one by one caught sight of the slender and graceful form of Manimekalai, an unspeakable tenderness seemed to light up every face. Struck with her wonderful loveliness they gathered round her, and admired the exquisite beauty of her face and figure. Many of them could not help following her, and expressed their sorrow at the heartless conduct of Mâthavi in devoting her beautiful daughter, in the bloom of youth, to the dull and joyless life of a nun. Both Sutamati and Manimekalai passed these crowds silently, the latter stepping so lightly that her footprint was scarcely visible on the soft ground ; and they entered the Uva-vanam, which stretched before them like a sheet of canvas painted with glowing colours, by a skilful artist. Here the cassia, the laurel, the orange tree, the wild lemon, the screwpine, the sweet-scented jassamine, the ever-green *asoka*, and the silk-cotton trees with their brilliant scarlet flowers, seemed to vie with each other in the profusion of their blossoms, and presented such a picturesque scenery that Manimekalai and her companion spent a long while wandering through the delightful garden.[1]

While Manimekalai and Sutamati were in the park, a huge elephant had broken out of the royal stables, and rushed through the palace road, the chariot road and the market road, scaring the populace who fled for their lives in every direction. Elephant-keepers and drummers ran after the animal, and with their shouts and beat of drum warned the people to keep out of its way. Udayakumaran, the son of the Chola king Killi-valavan, having heard of the accident, mounted a fleet steed and over-taking the elephant, stopped its mad career, and delivered it into the hands of its keepers. He then got into a chariot and, followed by an escort of soldiers, was returning to his palace, through the actresses' street, looking as handsome as a god, when his eyes fell on a merchant of noble rank seated motionless in the mansion of an actress, near a window facing the street apparently in great distress of mind. The prince stopped his chariot opposite the gilded doorway of the house, and enquired " What ails you ? Why are you and the actress so dejected ?" The merchant accompanied by the actress approached the prince, and making a profound obeisance, wished him a long life, and said " I happened to see just now Mâthavi's charming daughter Manimekalai going to the flower-garden Uva-vanam. Her beauty seems to fade in the close air of the convent like that of a flower shut up in a casket. Her appearance and the recollection of her father's sad death affected me so much that I sat still unable to play on the lute."

" I shall take the lovely girl in my chariot and bring her here," said the prince joyously, and drove towards the park. Stopping his chariot and his attendants at the park gate, he jumped down and entered the park alone, scanning with his eager eyes

---

[1] Ibid.

every nook and corner of the shady groves. Manimekalai who heard the tinkling bells of the prince's chariot, as it came near the park, told Sutamati, in her sweet voice, " I have heard Chitrapati and Vayantamalai informing my mother that Prince Udaya Kumara had set his heart on me. The bells we hear appear to be those of his chariot. What shall I do?" Sutamati was very much frightened, and told Manimekalai to enter at once the crystal grove, and to conceal herself in the central chamber. She then stood at a distance, within sight of the building: and the prince who came up to her a little later, said " Though you are standing alone, I know quite well why you are here. Tell me why has Manimêkalai come out of the convent. Is she old enough to feel the passion of love?"

" How can I, a woman, advise a prince who is descended from that illustrious king, who ashamed of his youth, assumed the disguise of an old man and dispensed justice?" said Sutamati, greatly agitated, " Yet shall I speak to thee, valiant prince! Our body is the result of our deeds in former births, and the cause of our deeds in our present birth. Formed of flesh, it decays by age : it is the seat of disease, the haunt of desire ; the den of every vice ; the hiding place of anger ; and in it dwells the mind which is oppressed with grief, distress, despair and lamentation. Therefore, thou noble prince ! view this body with contempt." Before Sutamati finished her speech, the youthful Manimêkalai came out of her chamber, and stood within the crystal alcove appearing outside like a statue made of coral.

The prince who saw her through the walls of crystal, at first thought her to be a beautiful statue newly placed in the alcove, but afterwards suspecting it to be Manimêkalai, attempted to enter the building, and examined it on all sides, but failed, the crystal door being bolted on the inside.

" There are beautiful sculptures in this building, where is your young companion hiding herself?" asked the prince.

" She must indeed be a saint," replied Sutamati, evading an answer, " if she does not wish to see your god-like figure."

" Who can resist surging floods," remarked the prince, " who can conquer love? If she does love me, let her come to me;" and was about to go away, when he turned to Sutamati again and enquired, who she was, and why she accompanied Manimêkalai to the park. On hearing her reply, he observed " I shall obtain Manimêkalai yet, through Chitrâpati " and left her. As soon as he had gone Manimêkalai came out of the alcove, and said " I was' not offended with him, although he seemed to think lightly of me as a common harlot, who has no sense of chastity, who has no regard for caste, and who is ready to sell herself for money : but my heart went after this stranger. Can this be the effect of love?" While they were thus conversing the Goddess Manimêkalai assuming the form of a woman residing in the city, visited the garden, and reverently went round the sacred seat praying to Buddha.[1]

The sun had now set, and the full moon rose in all its effulgence, and shed its soft silvery light on the park. In the bright moonlight, the goddess met Sutamati and Manimêkalai and enquired why they were staying in the park after nightfall. Sutamati related to her the meeting between herself and Udayakumâran, and the goddess said, " The prince is deeply in love with Manimêkalai and although he left you here, deeming it improper to press his suit in this park, which is assigned to Buddhist devotees, he will not fail to meet you on the public road outside the park. If you leave this garden by the gate in the western wall, you will find, near the public cemetery, a large monastery where many monks reside ; and you will be safe from all danger, even if you stay there during the whole night." She then gave a long account of the origin of the monastery which was called Chakra-vâlak-kôddam. Sutamati fell asleep during her recital, and watching the opportunity, the goddess took hold of Manimêkalai and lifting her into the air carried her to Manipallavam, an island thirty *yojanas* south of Kavirip-paddinam.[2]

Meanwhile Prince Udaya-kumaran who returned to his palace from Uva-vanam, remained sleepless, tossing in his bed, thinking of Manimêkalai, and devising plans to obtain possession of her. The goddess Manimêkalai appeared to his startled vision and said, " Thou son of the king ! if the king fails in his duty, the planets will not move in their orbits : if the planets do not keep in their usual course, seasonable showers will not fall on the earth : if the

---

[1] *Ibid.*, Canto v.   [2] *Ibid.*, Canto vi.

rains fail, men will die of famine: and the saying that the life of all human beings is the life of the king will prove to be untrue. Do not therefore seek to ruin a girl who has devoted herself to a religious life." The goddess then entered Uva-vanam, and awaking Sutamati informed her " Be not afraid ; I am the goddess Manimêkalai and I came to this city to witness the festival of Indra. As it is now time for your young companion Manimêkalai to become a devotee of Buddha, I have removed her to the island of Mani-pallavam where she is quite safe at present. She will there come to know her former birth, and will return to this city on the seventh day. Though she may appear in disguise in this city, she will not forsake you, and many wonderful events will happen here on her return. Inform Mâthavi of my visit, and the holy path into which her daughter has been led. She knows me. Tell her that I am the goddess of the ocean, whose name was given to her daughter as desired by Kovilan. On the day on which the child was named after me, I appeared to Mâthavi in her dream, and told her that her daughter would grow into a most beautiful maiden, and that she would become a most sincere and pious devotee." Having said this, the goddess left her, and flying up in the air disappeared from her view. Grieved at the mysterious disappearance of Manimêkalai, Sutamati arose and quitting the park through the western gate, entered the wide portals of the adjacent monastery. As she went in and sat inside the gate, she heard with trembling and fear, a voice from one of the statues sculptured on the gateway, addressing her, " Thou Veerai, daughter of Ravi-varman and wife of King Duchchayan ! Thou, who killed thyself on hearing of the death of thy sister Thârai ! Thou art now born as Sutamati, daughter of Kausikan of Champai, and come into this town with Mâruta-vekan. On the seventh day from this, your younger sister Lakshmi will return to this city at midnight, after knowing her previous birth." Sutamati, half dead with fright, left the monastery at early down, and hastened to Mâthavi's residence and related to her the strange occurrences of the previous day ; and Mathavi, who was already dreadfully alarmed about the safety of her daughter, swooned away, overwhelmed with grief.[1]

---

[1] Ibid., Canto vii.

Manimêkalai awoke in the island of Mani-pallavam, and was
astonished to find herself alone on a strange seashore. The sun
was rising above the broad blue sea, spreading its countless rays.
The rippling sea-waves threw up on the sandy beach pearl-chanks
and pieces of coral : and close by were deep pools, on the margin
of which bloomed the lily and the violet. She wondered whether
it was a part of Uva-vanam or whether Sutamati had deceived
her and brought her to a strange place. She called out "Sutamati l Sutamati l come to me l answer me wherever you are l"
But no answer came. No house or human being was seen. As
she walked over the hillocks of sand, she found only troops of
swans, cranes and sea-ducks swarming on the marshes, and
standing in long rows, like opposing armies arrayed on a battle-
field. Frightened at the thought that she had been abandoned
on a lonely island, she burst into tears ; but as she walked on,
along the sea-shore bemoaning her helpless condition, she saw a
sacred seat of Buddha built of polished crystal.[1]

The young maiden was beside herself with joy at the sight
of the sacred seat. With joined hands raised above her head and
tears of ecstasy rolling down her cheeks, she walked round the
seat thrice, and prostrated herself in front of it. When she stood
up again strange memories of her former birth seemed to flash
upon her mind, and she spoke as follows :—

" Thou venerable sage Brahma-dharma l who could foretell
coming events, I realise to-day that what thou predicted on the
banks of the river Kâyankarai, has come to pass. Thou warned
thy brother Attipati, king of Pûrvadesam in the Gândhâra country, that on the seventh day, a frightful earthquake will destroy
his capital city Idavayam, and that it should therefore be vacated.
The king proclaimed the impending catastrophe to his subjects,
and ordered them to quit the city in all haste, with their cattle,
and he too left his palace and encamped with the whole of his
army, in a grove near the banks of the river Kâyankarai, on the
road to Vasanti, north of his capital. On the day mentioned by you,
the city was destroyed by an earthquake as foretold, and when the
grateful sovereign and his subjects crowded at thy feet and
praised thee, thou preached the Law to them. I was then born as

[1] Ibid., Canto viii.

Lakshmi, the daughter of Ravi-varman, king of Asodhara, and of his wife Amuta-pati ; and had married Râhula, son of the king Attipati and of his wife Nilapati, who was the daughter of Sri-dhara, king of Siddhipura. Myself and Rahula also fell at thy feet on that occasion, and thou foretold that Râhula will die on the sixteenth day from the effects of the bite of a venomous snake and that I will ascend his funeral pyre. Thou told me further that I shall be re-born at Kavirip-paddinam, and that when I am in a serious peril, a goddess will remove me at night from that city to an island in the south : and that I shall there worship the sacred seat where Buddha had once sat and preached the law, and purified the hearts of the Naga kings, who had been furiously fighting with each other for possession of the seat. I then beseeched thee to tell me what will be the re-birth of my beloved husband, and thou told me that the goddess who brought me here will point him out to me. Will not that goddess appear before me now ?[1]

The goddess Manimêkalai who knew that her namesake had learnt her previous birth at the sacred seat of Buddha, and that she was now a fit person to receive further favours, appeared before her and said " In your former birth, when you were seated with your husband Râhula, in a pleasant grove, a Buddhist saint Sâdhu-chakra who was returning from Ratna-dvîpa after 'turning the wheel of Law,' alighted from the clouds in your presence, and you gave him food and water. The effect of that good deed will save you yet from re-births. Your former husband Râhula is now re-born as Udayakumâra, whom you met at Uva-vana : and hence your heart was attracted towards him. Târai and Veerai, your elder sisters in your former birth, were both wedded to Thuch-chaya, king of Kachchayam in Anga-desa. When they were stay-ing with their husband on the banks of the river Gangai, a Buddhist monk visited them, and at his advice they worshipped the sacred feet of Buddha, on the hill where the Buddha had for-merly taken his stand and preached his religion. By virtue of this good deed they are now born as Mâthavi and Sutamati. Before being instructed in the true Law, you shall have to learn the tenets of other religions ; and the teachers of those faiths may not

[1] Ibid., Canto ix.]

be willing to impart instruction to you as you are a young girl. I shall therefore teach thee the incantations which will enable you to assume any form you like or to fly through the air, wherever you wish to go.. Rest assured that you shall attain the true knowledge of Buddha, on the holiest day of the Buddhists." Having said so, she taught the spells to Manimêkalai, and ascended to the sky : but returned immediately to the earth and said "I have forgotten to teach you one thing more. This mortal body is sustained by food. Learn therefore the great charm by which you can remain without food." She then taught her the third charm, and then flew away out of her sight.[1]

"After the departure of the goddess, Manimêkalai walked about the island, admiring the strange scenery of the sand hills, flowery groves and glassy lakes. She had hardly gone the distance of a Kâvatham when a Buddhist nun appeared before her, and enquired "who art thou maiden, that appearest on this island like a shipwrecked passenger ? "

"In which birth do you ask ?" replied Manimêkalai, "In my former birth I was Lakshmi, wife of Prince Râhula, and in this birth, I am Manimêkalai, the daughter of the actress Mâthavi. The goddess, whose name I bear, having brought me hither, I have learnt my former birth, by worshipping the sacred seat of Buddha. May I ask who art thou ?"

"Close by this island, in Ratnadvîpa, is the high mountain Samantam, on the top of which are the impressions of the sacred feet of Buddha, the worshippers of which will be freed from the bondage of births. I worshipped the feet and am now returning— thence. I guard the sacred seat of Buddha in this island, under the orders of Indra, the king of the celestials, and my name is Deeva-thilakai. Opposite the sacred seat is the tank Gomuki, where an alms-bowl which was once the property of Aputra comes up to the surface of the water, once a year, on the birth-day of Buddha, that is on the day of the 14th Lunar asterism, in the month of Idapam. To-day is that auspicious day, and that alms-bowl is, I believe, destined for your use. Out of that bowl you may give alms to as many as may appear before you, and

---

[1] Ibid., Canto x.

yet it will ever be full. You may learn further about it from the venerable Buddhist Abbot of your native city."

Manimêkalai gladly accompanied Deeva-thilakai, to the tank Gomuki, and as soon as she reverently came round it, and stood near the edge, the alms-bowl sprung out of the water and entered her hands. Overjoyed at this miracle, Manimêkalai praised the Buddha's sacred feet which were conspicuous by the side of the tank, under the shade of a Bodhi tree. Taking leave of Deeva-thilakai Manimêkalai quitted the island, carrying the alms-bowl in her hand and ascending into the air, flew through the sky and descended at Kavirippaddinam, in the presence of her mother, who was counting the days of her separation and anxiously awaiting her arrival. To her mother, and her friend Sutamati, who received her with joy, she related her adventures. "I worship your feet," said she at last, " you who were my elder sisters in our former birth, when we were born as the daughters of Amutapti, who was the wife of king Duchchaya and daughter of king Ravivarman. You shall, under the guidance of the reverend Abbot of this city, be able to lead a pure life." She then went to the residence of the Buddhist Abbot accompanied by Mâthavi and Sutamati.[1]

They approached the grey-headed old monk, and bowing thrice at his feet, Manimêkalai introduced herself, and recounted to him all that had transpired from her meeting with Udaya-kumara at Uva-vana up to her return from Manipallavam. His aged face brightened, and he seemed hardly able to contain his joy. "I met Duchchayan, king of Kachchayam, again, on my way to the sacred hill of Buddha," said he with trembling accents, " and enquired after the welfare of his queens. He wept bitterly and said that Veerai having gone in front of a wild elephant, newly caught, was killed by that animal, and Târai who loved her sister dearly, unable to bear her loss, died by throwing herself from a lofty terrace. How wonderful! Like actors who change their dress and appear again on the stage in new characters, you are re-born and appear before me in your present bodies."[2]

"Listen, thou maiden!" he continued, " to the history of Aputra, whose alms-bowl thou carriest. There was a teacher of

[1] Ibid., Canto xi.   [2] Ibid., Canto xii.

the Vedas at Vâranâsi, whose name was Apanchika. His wife
Sâli having proved faithless to him, and afraid of punishment,
joined a company of pilgrims, who were going to Kumâri, and
while returning from Kumâri gave birth to a child and abandoned
it in a dark wood. Attracted by the cries of the babe, a cow
approached and licked it, and fed it with its milk for seven days.
A Brahmin from Vayanankodu happened to pass with his wife by
the wood, and hearing the cry of the infant, he searched for the
child and found it. Pitying its helpless condition he and his wife
carried it to their home. He brought up the child as his own son
and taught him the Vedas and other sacred texts. When he grew
up into a young man he happened to go into a neighbouring house
occupied by a Brahmin, and was surprised and grieved to find a
cow which was tied to a post, lowing piteously like a deer caught
in a hunter's net. It was decked with flowers and intended to be
sacrificed on the next morning. Feeling deep horror for the cruel
fate that awaited the cow he determined to save it: and in the
midnight he stole the cow and led it out of the village. His theft
was however discovered, and the Brahmins chased and arrested
him, and thrashing him soundly, asked him to confess why he
had stolen the cow. Meanwhile the cow burst from its captors,
and having gored the master of the sacrifice, fled into the jungle.
The boy prayed to the Brahmins not to beat him, and asked
them to tell him why they wanted to kill a harmless cow, which
had from the day of its birth done no injury to any one: but had
eaten of the green grass growing on meadows, and had given its
sweet milk for the use of man.

"Not knowing the sacred books revealed to us by Brahma,"
said the Brahmins, "you have reviled us. You are verily the son
of a beast."

"Asalan was the son of a deer: Siringi was the son of a cow:
Vrinji was the son of a tiger: Kesakambalam was the son of a fox:
and these you honor as your sages. Why do you spurn me as
the son of a beast?" retorted the youth.

"I know the birth of this boy," said one of the Brahmins, in
indignant tones. "He is the son of Sâli, the wife of a Vedic
teacher of Varanasi, who having behaved in a manner unbecoming a Brahmin woman and afraid of punishment, came away

with pilgrims bound to Kumári, and there gave birth to a child, near a shepherd's village, and abandoned it. This boy is that child. Touch him not: he is a bastard."

"I shall tell you the origin of the Brahmins," replied the boy with a scornful laugh. "Were not two of your first patriarchs the sons of Brahma, by a celestial courtezan? Is this not true? How can you then speak ill of Sáli?"

"Astounded at these words, his foster father declined to receive the youth into his house: and the Brahmins set up a hue and cry after him as the thief who had stolen the cow. The youth therefore left the Brahmin village and came to the great city of Dakshina Mathura, where he begged food from door to door, and out of the food so collected he fed the blind and the lame, the old and the infirm, and himself ate the remainder. At night, he took his bed in the hall outside the temple of Chinta-devi, with his alms-bowl for his pillow; a beggar in all else, but rich in his boundless love for all living creatures.[1]

"On a dark and rainy night, when he lay fast asleep in the temple of Chinta-devi a few beggars who were weary with travelling arrived there, and being very hungry awoke him and asked for food. The poor youth having no food to give was greatly distressed. The goddess Chinta-devi then appeared to him and handed to him a cup saying, "Grieve not, but take this cup. You will never find it empty though the whole land may be famine-strirken." The youth praised the goddess and receiving the cup fed the travellers out of it. The wonderful cup was never empty although he fed myriads of poor people who flocked to him, owing to the famine then prevailing in the Pandyan kingdom. Favourable seasons soon followed, and Aputra found that no one came to him for charity. He left Madura and travelled to other towns in search of poor and starving people. He heard from merchants who arrived by sea that there had been no rain in Chavakam, and that the inhabitants of that country were dying from want of food. Hence he resolved to visit Chavakam and relieve the distress of the people of that land, and went on board a ship bound to Chavakam. As a storm came on during the voyage the ship anchored at Mani-pallavam, and

---

[1] Ibid., Canto xiii.

Aputra went ashore on the island. But during the night, a
favorable breeze rose, and the captain set sail, not knowing that
Aputra was still on the island. The latter finding that the ship
had sailed away, and that the island was uninhabited was plunged
in grief. Annoyed at the thought that his wonderful cup
will remain useless in his hands, he threw it into the tank
Gomuki praying that it should appear once a year on the surface
of the tank, and go into the hands of a pure minded and charitable person. Unwilling to feed alone out of the cup which had
fed thousands of people, he decided to starve himself to death.
I happened to visit Mani-pallavam just then and learnt from his
own mouth his unhappy tale.[1]

Aputra was reborn in Chavakam in the hermitage of Man-
muka. The king of that country being childless obtained the
child from Man-muka and brought him up as heir to his throne.
In course of time Aputra succeeded his father, and is at present
king of Chavakam. His miraculous cup should not remain useless in your hands, and you should therefore feed the beggars
of this city, out of the cup, for there is no greater charity than
that of feeding the poor."

Manimêkalai took leave of the monk reverently, and as desired by him wished to begin at once the work of charity. When
she appeared in the street with the alms-bowl in her hand, in the
attire of a *Bikshuni* or religious mendicant, the people passing
in the street gathered round her, wondering why she who was
courted by the son of the king should have put on a mendicant's
garb.[2] Being a mendicant, she deemed it proper that she
should first receive alms from a married woman, and going to the
house of Athirai, the wife of a merchant, accepted alms from her
in the miraculous cup.[3]

She then commenced giving out food from the cup, and the
first person who received food was Kaya-Chandikai, wife of a
Vidyadhara. She had been suffering with a disease which caused insatiable craving for food, and this strange malady was cured
by her eating the meal served out of the cup. She blessed
Manimekalai most fervently and desired her to go to the

[1] Ibid., Canto xiv.   [2] Ibid., Canto xv.   [3] Ibid., Canto xvi.

Buddhist monastery and feed the poor who collect there in large numbers.[1]

Having heard that Manimêkalai was in the dress of a *Bikshuni* or mendicant in the Buddhist monastery, her grandmother Chitrapati was in a furious rage. Vowing that she would induce prince Udaya-Kumara to bring back Manimêkalai in his golden chariot, she hurried to the prince's palace, accompanied by a few of her servants. Entering the palace, she came into the presence of the Prince who was seated on a throne supported by shining figures of lions, and fanned with chowries by servant maids who were standing on both sides of him. As she bowed low at his feet, the Prince enquired with a smile "Are Mâthavi and Manimêkalai still disposed to remain in the monastery?"

"Long life to thee brave Prince," said Chitrapati. "Manimêkalai is now in the public hall attached to the monastery outside the city. I pray you will take her with you and enjoy the pleasure of witnessing her skill as an actress."

"When I last saw her in the crystal alcove, she stood with her arms folded on her bosom, and her dark eyes seemed to melt with love. Her coral lips revealed the lustre of her pearly teeth, and her smile thrilled through me. That sweet smile and fairy form entered my heart at once never again to leave it. But what puzzles me yet is that, on the following night, a goddess appeared in my sight and warned me not to think of her. Was that a phantom of my imagination, or was it a real goddess that warned me so gravely," said the Prince.

"Let not such doubts disturb your mind," replied Chitrapati, "surely, you ought to desist, if Manimêkalai was a girl born in wedlock: but she is an actress trained to display her charms on the public stage and to allure and captivate the rich. Need I tell you that it is the duty of a king to bring her back to the profession to which she was born."

Encouraged by Chitrapati, Udaya-kumara mounted his chariot, and urging the steeds harnessed to it, arrived in no time at the monastery. He saw Manimêkalai appearing in her marvellous beauty, like the divinity of the place, and feeding the poor

who flocked to her, out of the alms-bowl in her hand. All his love
for her seemed to swell in his heart. Going near her, he addressed
her, with a look of passionate and adoring love, "Ah! You siren
who has stolen my heart, why do you torment yourself with
penance, and lead the life of a mendicant? Dearest maid! tell
me why you wish to be a nun?"

"I shall answer thee," said Manimêkalai who trembled lest
her own heart should be weak enough to give way to love for him
who was her dear Rahulan in a former birth, "If thou hast pro-
fitted by the converse of the wise, Listen! Knowing that this
body is the seat of suffering: that it suffers in birth, in disease,
in old age and in death, I have embraced the life of a nun, what
more can a woman tell a valiant prince like thee? If thou feel-
est the truth of my words, do as thy heart bids thee to do."

She then entered the hut which had been occupied by the
mendicant Kayachandikai, and repeating the incantation by which
she could transform herself, she assumed the form of Kaya-
chandikai and returned to the presence of the Prince. He was
amazed at the disappearance of Manimêkalai. He searched the
hut and not finding her there, he vowed that he will not leave
that place till he sees again the dear girl whose sweet speech and
surpassing beauty have made him a captive.[1]

A voice proceeding from one of the statues of the temple
warned him not to make foolish vows. Udaya-kumara was awe-
struck and did not know what further he ought to do to win
Manimêkalai. The sun had set and the shades of evening were
growing darker. He quitted the temple therefore reluctantly,
sighing as his attempt to take Manimêkalai with him was un-
successful. Being certain that the Prince would not leave her if
she appeared in her own form, Manimêkalai determined to continue in the disguise of the mendicant Kaya-chandikai. She was
anxious to continue her work of charity, and deeming it proper
that she should not wait till the poor seek her assistance, but
should herself search for them and relieve their distress, she went
to the City Jail, where criminals were confined. With great
pleasure she entered the building where the unhappy prisoners
were ill-fed and pinched with hunger: and began to feed them

[1] Ibid., Canto xviii.

to their hearts' content. The warders were astonished to see
that she had only one cup in her hand but was able to feed
hundreds out of that single cup. They thought it such a wonder
that they should report it at once to the king and proceeded to
the palace. The Chola king Ma-van-killi had then gone out for
a walk in the royal park with his queen Cheerthy, who was the
daughter of a king descended from the illustrious Mahabali.
Followed by the queen's attendants, the king and the queen
stepped slowly along the well-laid-out walks admiring the charming scenes. They were delighted to see, in a cool spot, a peacock spreading its gorgeous tail and dancing on the green turf,
while the cuckoo warbled and the honey bees hummed on the
wide spreading branches overhead. In a shady bower a female
monkey was seated on a swing and the male was swinging it.
The king and queen and her ladies burst out laughing at this
queer sight, and their merry laughter rang through the park.
They invited the deer and mountain goats to come near them ;
and the king pointed out to the queen, the quails and hares that
fled through the shrubberies, frightened at their approach. They
ascended the artificial hills and looked at the waterfalls. They
enjoyed the balmy breeze blowing around the cool grottoes and
romantic fountains, and wandered through labyrinths. Tired
with the excursion, the royal party then returned to the palace,
and the king entered the throne hall. The guards having announced that the warders of the City Jail were waiting for an
audience, the king commanded that they should be admitted.
They came and, standing at a distance, made a profound obeisance, and said "Long life to thee, Mighty King Ma-van-killi !
thou, whose army, led by thy son, routed the forces of the Pandya
and Chera in a battle at Kâriyâru! Know great king that a
maiden who wandered in this city as a beggar has now visited
the jail and fed countless people out of a single cup ! May your
Royal Highness reign for ever."

"Let her come to me, I would be glad to see her," said the
king eager to see the maid. The guards led her into the royal
presence, and she exclaimed, "Wise king! may thou be ever
merciful ! "

"Thou pious maiden ! Who art thou," asked the king, "and
whence is this miraculous cup ? "

"I am the daughter of a Vidyadhara," replied the maiden, "I have lived in this city for some time past. This cup which was given to me by a goddess has wonderful properties. It has cured insatiable hunger; and it will feed any number of people. May Your Majesty prosper for ever."

"What can I do for the young maiden," enquired the king pleased with her demeanour.

Emboldened by the king's courteous enquiry, she said, "Let the City Jail be assigned for a public charity hall, may thou be blessed for ever!"

The monarch graciously acceded to her prayer.[1] The prisoners were set free and Buddhist monks occupied the prison and used it as a charity hall and hospital. These news soon reached the ears of Udaya-kumara who was still infatuated with the love of Manimêkalai. He determined now to seize her wherever she may be found outside the monastery, and to convey her to his palace in his chariot. With this intention, he entered the monastery. Kanchanan, the husband of Kaya-chandikai, who had in the meantime come to Pukar in search of his wife, found Manimêkalai in the disguise of Kaya-chandikai, and believing her to be his own wife, he went up to her and fondly asked whether she had been cured of her disease, and wondered from which God she had obtained the miraculous cup. But Manimê-kalai did not care to converse with him: she met prince Udaya-kumara however, and to him she addressed a few words of wisdom. "Mark this aged matron, thou Prince!" said she pointing to an old woman "her tresses which were once raven black are now turned grey: her shining forehead is now wrinkled: her arched brows are now shrunk like dry shrimps: the eyes bright as the lotus are now dim and dropping rheum: her pearl-like teeth are now decayed and lustreless: her coral lips have lost their colour: such is woman's beauty" she spoke in this strain and tried to turn the prince's thoughts from the fleeting objects of worldly desire, to things of eternal moment for his spiritual welfare. Kaya-chandikai's husband, who followed Manimêkalai, was fired with jealousy at seeing his wife indifferent to himself, but anxious to engage the attention of the prince. He resolved

---

[1] Ibid., Canto xix.

therefore to watch her conduct further and concealed himself in a dark corner of the temple. Udaya-kumara was now convinced that Manimêkalai herself was in the disguise of Kaya-chandikai, but could not understand why Kanchanan dogged her steps, and he too made up his mind to observe their behaviour at night. He returned therefore quietly to his palace and at midnight came out alone and entered the temple. The perfumes on his person however spread through the temple and revealed his presence to Kanchanan who was awake. Finding that it was the Prince who stole into the temple at that late hour, his worst fears regarding his wife's constancy were confirmed. He got up wild with jealousy and drawing his sword beheaded the Prince upon the spot. He then attempted to enter the room where Manimêkalai was asleep; but a voice from one of the images warned him not to enter the apartment. It said, "Your wife Kaya-chandikai, cured of her disease, went in search of you and died on the Vindhya hills. Although Udaya-kumara has now paid his life as a penalty for his former sins, you have committed a great sin in murdering him, and the effect of this sin will not leave you." Hearing these words, Kanchanan left the temple gloomy and disheartened.[1] Manimêkalai who had awoke and overheard the words of warning uttered by the spirit, rushed out of her room, crying in tones of deep anguish, "Oh my beloved! for whom I mounted the funeral pyre, when you died of a snake-bite in your former birth; for whom my heart yearned when I saw you first in the Uva-vana: for whom I assumed the disguise of Kaya-chandikai to instruct you in wisdom and to lead you in the path of virtue. Alas! have you fallen a victim to the sword of the jealous Vidyadhara?" Crying thus, she was about to approach the corpse of her lover, when she heard the voice of the same spirit cautioning her, "Don't go, don't go, young maiden!" said the spirit. "He was your husband and you were his wife in many former births. Do not give way to your passions, you who seek release from the prison house of re-births!"

"I worship thee, wise spirit!" said Manimêkalai, "knowest thou why he was bitten by a snake in his former birth, and

[1] Ibid., Canto xx.

now killed by the sword of the Vidyadhara? If you do know it, tell me graciously so that it may console my sorrowing heart."

"Listen to me maiden!" the spirit replied. "In your former birth, when Brahma-dharma was preaching the Law, you wished to feast him on a certain day, and asked your cook to be ready by early dawn. But when he came in the morning and tripped and fell on the cooking utensils and broke them, enraged at his carelessness, your husband killed the cook. It is that sin that still haunts you. I shall now tell you what is to happen to you in the future. Hearing of the murder of his son, the king will cast you into prison, but the queen will intercede for you, and releasing you from jail, will keep you with her. The venerable Buddhist monk will then plead for you with the queen, and you will be set at liberty. You will then go to Aputra, who is now king of Chavakam, and with him you will again visit Manipallavam. Leaving that island, you will in the guise of a monk visit Vanji, and there learn the tenets of other religions. You will then proceed to Kanchi and feed the poor during a famine in that city. There you will meet the Buddhist abbot and from him you will learn the Buddhist doctrine and become a nun. In future births, you will be born as a man in Uttara Magadha and eventually become one of the foremost and favorite disciples of Buddha." Knowing her future, Manimêkalai was greatly relieved in mind and deeply thankful to the spirit.[1]

On the following morning, the visitors to the temple of Champa-pati saw the corpse of Udaya-kumara and reported it to the monks of Chakra-valak-kôddam. They questioned Manimêkalai, and having ascertained from her, how and by whom he had been killed, they concealed the prince's body in a separate room and proceeded to the palace. Having obtained permission through the guards, they appeared before the Chola king who was seated on his throne, majestic like Indra. "Hail monarch! may thy reign be prosperous! may all thy days be happy!" said one of the monks, "even in former days, many men have died in this city for the women they loved. When Parasurama was killing all the kings of Jambu-dweepa, in days of old, Kanthan then reigning at Pukâr, deemed it prudent to conceal himself

---

[1] Ibid., Canto xxi.

and left the kingdom in charge of his illegitimate son, Kakanthan, who being the son of a courtezan could not succeed to the crown, and therefore would not be attacked by Parasurama. Kakanthan's son, having made an immodest proposal to the wife of a Brahmin who was returning alone through the city gate, after bathing in the Kaveri, was killed by his father. Another son of the same king was also killed by the father, for having insulted similarly a chaste and beautiful woman who was the daughter of a merchant."

"Is there any misfortune of the kind which has occurred now?" enquired the king: and the monk related to him that Prince Udayâ-kumâra had been of late courting Manimêkalai although she had become a nun: that to avoid him she assumed the shape of Kâya-chandikai: and that the husband of the latter killed the prince out of jealousy, as he attempted to enter his wife's apartment at midnight. The king was shocked and grieved to hear of the melancholy end of his son, and looking at his prime-minister, Choliya-enâti, said, "The punishment that I should have meted out to my wayward son, has been inflicted by Kanchanan. Let the prince's body be cremated at once and the daughter of the actress be confined in prison."[1]

The Queen, Raja-maha-devi, bereaved of her beloved prince was disconsolate. She was however bent on taking revenge on Manimêkalai for having been the cause of her son's death, and said to the king that it was unjust to confine in prison a pious and intelligent maiden like Manimêkalai. The king having consented to her release, she sent for Manimêkalai and directed her to lodge with her in the palace. She then plotted to disgrace Manimêkalai, and inviting an illiterate youth gave him a handful of gold coins, and told him to seduce Manimêkalai, whom she also tried to render unconscious by administering drugs. But Manimêkalai was unaffected by the drugs, and assumed the form of a man, when the youth came to her; and he fled out of the city, afraid that the Queen had attempted to entrap him in some dangerous intrigue. The Queen then shut up Manimêkalai in a room, on the pretence that she was unwell, and gave her no food. Manimêkalai repeated the incantation which could save her from hunger, and remained

---

[1] Ibid., Canto xxii.

as lively as ever. Disconcerted in all her attempts, and astonished
to find that Manimékalai was not in the least affected by want of
food, the queen was now convinced that she was a virtuous and
saintly character. She prayed for Manimékalai's pardon for ,
having persecuted her under the belief that she was the cause
of her son's death. Manimékalai who was ready to forgive
her said, " When you were Queen Nilapati in your former birth,
your son Rahula died, bitten by a venomous snake, and I
who was then his wife gave up my life on his funeral pyre.
Your son had in a fit of rage killed his cook in his previous
birth, and the effect of this sin reacted on him now and he was
murdered by the Vinchayan." She related further to the Queen
all the events that occurred since she met prince Udayakumara
at Uya-vana and explained to her how she was able to preserve
her life, with the help of the spells taught to her by the Goddess
of the ocean, notwithstanding the persecutions of the Queen.
"I could have with the aid of my spells, gone out of the prison,
but I did not do so; because, I wished to stay and console you,
who are the mother of my departed lover. Those only know
true happiness who never cease to love all sentiment beings."
Consoled with these words, the Queen rose and made a profound
obeisance to Manimekalai, but the latter would not allow her to
do so. "You are the mother of my husband in a former birth :
and now you are the great Queen of the Monarch of this land.
It is not proper that you should bow to me," she said and bowed,
low to her in return.[1]

Chitrapati who had heard of the murder of Prince Udaya-
kumara and of the imprisonment of her grand-daughter Manimekalai and her subsequent release, went to the palace and
falling at the feet of the Queen represented to her all her misfortunes, and implored that Manimekalai be restored to her.
But the Queen informed her that Manimekalai hated intensely
the life of a courtezan, and would not therefore reside with her
hereafter. Meantime Máthavi accompanied by the Buddhist
abbot also sought an audience of the Queen. When they saw
the venerable monk, the Queen and her attendants rose and went
forward to receive him. The Queen greeted him respectfully,

---

[1] Ibid., Canto xxiii.

and having led him to a seat, washed his feet, and courteously
said, " It is my good fortune that you are pleased to pay me this
visit, although this short walk must have given your aged feet
no little pain. May you be blessed with health for many years
to come !"

"Listen to me Queen ! " said the monk " although my life is
devoted to religion, I am now like the setting sun." He then
began an eloquent exposition of the teachings of Buddha regarding the cause of birth, ignorance, good and evil deeds and
their consequences. He exhorted the Queen and all who listened
to him to keep in the path of virtue : and turning to Manimêkalai, he said, " you young maid, who know your former birth !
you shall have to learn first the doctrines of other creeds, and
then I shall teach you the principles of Buddhism." As he rose
to depart, Manimêkalai bowing at his feet, said "If I stay any
longer in this city, every one will curse me as one who caused
the death of the king's son. I shall therefore visit the country
of Aputra : thence I shall go to Manipallavam, and to Vanji
where a temple has been erected to Kannaki." Looking at her
mother and grandmother, she said, " my dear relatives ! be not
concerned about my safety," and left them. Proceeding to the
temple of Champa-pati, she worshipped the Goddess, and flying
through the air, descended in a grove in Chavakam,[1] outside
the great city of the king, who is a descendant of Indra. She
saluted a monk, who was living in that grove, and asked " what
is the name of this city and who is its ruler ? " The monk replied
" This is Naga-puram, and the reigning king is Punya-raja,
son of Bhoomichandra. From the day of the birth of this king,

---

[1] Chávaka or Chávaka-dvípa is the island of Sumátra. The king of Chávaka
appears to have ruled over also Java and the small islands adjacent to Sumátra.
Ptolemy speaks of the Greater and Lesser Chávaka, referring to Sumátra and Java.
I have not been able to identify Nágapura, because the information available
regarding Sumátra is at present very scanty. The most important seaport on the
East Coast which traded formerly with the Coromandel Coast is Sri Indrapura. It
is the capital of a kingdom. See J. Anderson's Acheen and Coast of Sumátra., pp.
231 and 172. Dr. B. Heyney's Account of India and Sumátra, pp. 395 and 396.
That Buddhism and Brahminism spread to Sumátra and Java, at a very early
period, is attested beyond a doubt by extensive remains of ancient temples and
sculptures on these islands.

24

the rain has never failed, and harvests have been plentiful, and no pestilence has visited this country." [1]

Soon after the king happened to visit the monk Dharma-sravaka, with his family, to listen to his preaching of the Law. Surprised to find a young and beautiful maiden in the company of the monk, he enquired " who is this maiden of matchless beauty, who seems to be a mendicant and listens to the preaching of the Dharma ? " One of the king's officers replied, " There is none equal to this maiden in all Jambu-dvîpa. I learnt the history of this maid when I went in a ship to Kavirip-paddinam and paid a friendly visit to the Chola-king Killi-valavan. The Buddhist monk then told me all about this maid. She is now come here from that city."

" The alms-bowl which once belonged to you is now in my hands," said Manimêkalai to the great astonishment of the king. " You do not remember your former birth, nor do you know your present birth. Unless you worship the seat of Buddha at Mani-pallavam you cannot understand the nature of this prison of re-births. I would advise you to come there." She then quitted the city, and flew through the air to Mani-pallavam. The king returned to his palace and learnt from his foster mother, Queen Amara-sundari, that he was not her son but was born in the hermitage of the Buddhist monk, and that the late king Bhoomi-chandra obtained him from the monk, and, brought him up as his own son. Having thus ascertained the truth of Mani-mêkalai's statement, he was anxious to lay down the crown, and to lead the life of a recluse. He disclosed his intention to his minister Jana-mitra, who being alarmed at the sudden change which had come over the monarch's mind, said, " My king! may thou live for ever ! Before you were born, this kingdom suffered from severe famine for twelve long years, mothers abandoned their babes, and myriads of people died of starvation. Like rain in the midst of scorching summer, you were born, and from that time forward showers have fallen in due season, crops have been abundant, and none felt the want of food. If you leave this country, I fear our prosperity will vanish and famine will again appear in the land. Tenderness to other lives is the first duty

---

[1] Ibid., Canto xxiv.

preached by the great Buddha. You seem to forget this duty
which you owe to your subjects."

"Anyhow I am so eager to visit Mani-pallavam that I will
not be satisfied unless I go there. You ought to look after the
Government and the palace for the period of a month," said the
king, and commanded at once that arrangements be made for his
voyage. As soon as a ship was ready, he went on board, and
with favourable winds, the ship arrived at Mani-pallavam.
Manimêkalai received the king with sincere pleasure, and took
him to the sacred seat of Buddha. The king reverently went
round the seat and worshipped it, and at once, his former birth
came to his recollection as clear as if it had been reflected in a
mirror. "I know my former birth and my sorrow is removed,"
exclaimed the king, "Thou Goddess of Learning! of Dakshina-
Mathura in the Tamil-land : on a rainy night when a number
of beggars came to me, at thy shrine, for food, and I was at a
loss to find meals for them, you were pleased to place in my
hands a miraculous cup out of which any number of people
could be fed. Ever in my future births I shall worship thee
as I have done in the past." He then left the seat with Manimêkalai and rested in the shade of a *Punnai* tree. Deepa-thilakai,
the guardian deity of the sacred seat, appeared before them and
accosted the king. "Welcome! thou pious man who brought
the wonderful cup and died on this island. Behold the skeleton
of thy former body which lies at the foot of yonder tree, under a
heap of sand thrown up by the waves of the sea." She then
addressed Manimêkalai as follows : "Thou good maid, who
now holds the miraculous cup in thy hand! your native city has
been destroyed by an eruption of the sea. I shall tell you the
cause of the calamity. Peeli-valai, the daughter of the king
of Nâga-nâd, visited this island with her son, to worship the
Buddha's seat, which had been placed here by Indra. When
she was staying here, a ship belonging to a merchant of Kavirip-
paddinam happened to anchor at the island. The princess having
ascertained that the ship was to sail to Kavirip-paddinam, en-
trusted to the merchant's care her son, to be taken to his father,
the Chola-king Killi-valavan. The merchant received the prince
with great pleasure on board his ship, and sailed immediately.
But violent winds wrecked the ship on an adjacent coast at

midnight, and the merchant and some of the crew who escaped reported the sad occurrence to the king. Killi-valavan went in search of his son and neglected to perform the annual festival in honor of Indra. The goddess of the ocean enraged at this insult to the king of the gods, sent a huge sea-wave, which submerged Kavirip-paddinam. The venerable Buddhist monk accompanied by Mâthavi and Sutamati has gone to Vanchi, and you should go there and meet them." The goddess then departed, and the king desirous of seeing the body in which he was previously born, scooped out the sand at the spot indicated by the goddess and discovered a skeleton in perfect order. At the sight of this skeleton, the king fainted, and Manimêkalai comforted him by telling him that she came to his City and invited him to the island, in the hope that after learning his former birth, he will be the model of a pious and good king, and establish his fame throughout the many islands over which he rules. "If kings themselves wish to turn monks who will help the poor?" she said. "Remember! true charity is to give food and clothing and shelter to living beings."

"Whether in my own country, or in other lands, I shall perform the charity which you have indicated. You have reformed me by giving me a knowledge of my former births. How can I part from you who have been so kind to me?" replied the king.

"Grieve not for this parting. Your kingdom calls for thee and your presence is needed there. Return therefore at once on board your ship. I shall go to Vanchi" said Manimêkalai and flew into the air.[1]

She arrived at Vanchi and visited the temple erected in honor of her father Kovilan and step-mother Kannaki.[2] Having worshipped them she changed her form to that of a monk, and inspected every temple and hall and platform where men devoted to religion were congregated. She sought instruction from the professors of the Vedic, Saiva, Vaishnava, Ajivaka, Nirgrantha, Sankya, Vaiseshika and Lokayata religions.[3] She met Kovilan's father who had become a Buddhist monk, and from him she learnt that the Buddhist abbot of Pukar had

---

[1] Ibid., Canto xxv.   [2] Ibid., Canto xxvi.   [3] Ibid., Canto xxvii.

to go to Kanchi and feed the poor of that city, as a famine was raging in that part of the country. She took her miraculous cup and flew through the air to Kanchi, and visited the Buddhist Chaitya which had been built by king Killi, the younger brother of Killi-valavan. Her arrival having been reported to the king by his officers, he visited her accompanied by all his ministers. "Thou pious maid!" said the king "my kingdom groans under a severe drought, and I am glad therefore that thou hast appeared with this wonderful cup. I have built a tank and planted a grove just like those at Mani-pallavam," and pointed out the place to her. At her request, the king built a sacred seat for Buddha, and temples for the goddesses Deepa-thilakai and Mani-mêkalai. She then fed all the deformed and aged and destitute persons who came to her. The Buddhist monk arrived later on, with Mâthavi and her friend Sutamati: and Manimêkalai received them with every mark of respect and feasted them.[1] Then she sat at the feet of the venerable abbot and learnt the doctrines of Buddha.[2] When she was convinced that the doctrines were true, and was prepared to take refuge in the threefold gem, the Buddha, Dharma and Sangha, the monk initiated her further in the duties of a nun, and she was admitted into the order, with due ceremony, amidst a grand display of lights.[3]

---

[1] Ibid., Canto xxviii.   [2] Ibid., Canto xxix.   [3] Ibid., Canto xxx.

CHAPTER.

TAMIL POEMS AND POETS.

Another poetical work of this period which deserves special mention is the Kalith-thokai.[1] It consists of 150 love songs composed in the *Kali* metre, said to have been collected by Nall-anthuvanar, a Professor of Tamil in the city of Madura. The names of the authors of these songs have not been recorded, but judging from the varying style of the verses, and the different scenes described in them, it appears most probable that all of them are not the production of one and the same author. The songs are mostly in the form of a dialogue, the speakers being chiefly a lady, her servant maid, and her lover. They are remarkable for a refined sentiment of chaste and chivalrous love which runs through most of them, so different from the gross sensuality which pervades the amatory poems composed in Tamil in later periods. The love scenes described in them depict most vividly the social relations between the sexes, and the mode of courtship and marriage peculiar to the Tamils. Some of the scenes are as follow:—A youth going out a-hunting, meets a maiden who is seated on a swing in a shady grove, or bathing in a stream, or mounted on a loft in a cornfield and engaged in scaring away the birds which come to steal the corn, and struck with her beauty he visits the place frequently on pretence of following game. If he finds favor in the lady's eyes, she allows him to visit her at her house, to take long walks with her, to accompany her to the river and even to assist her in her toilet,[2] and finally he marries her. If however the lady is very coy and does not encourage his suit, he speaks to the lady's maid, praises her mistress' exceeding beauty and beseeches her aid to procure a meeting. The maid gently broaches the subject to her mistress.[3] She tells her with pride of the noble look of the youthful and handsome stranger

[1] The Kalith-thokai was published in print by Rai Bahadur C. W. Tamotharam Pillai in the year 1887.

[2] Kalith-thokai, 76.

[3] Ibid., 47.

who is smitten by her charms. The lovers meet in a grove outside the village in which she resides, at first during the day; but later on they have stolen interviews at night.[1] The lover proposes to the father of the lady to marry his daughter, and obtains his consent, or he informs the lady that they must separate at least for a time, as he has to go on a distant journey. The lady's maid tries to persuade him to stay: she warns him of the dangers of the road which is infested by wild beasts and robbers more cruel than wild animals. She asks him to remember that youth is fleeting: that it returns to no man: and that it is the season for enjoying the pleasures of life. She relates to him how sorry her mistress is if he absents himself from the trysting place even a single day, and expresses the fear that she may die of grief if her lover deserts her. If he is still determined to go, the lady entreats him to take her with him: but he pleads that timid and delicate as she is, she cannot undertake a long and difficult journey. She replies that, even in the forest, the hind follows the stag. "I shall neither eat nor drink, but ever thinking of thee, I shall die," says she, "my heart is now a captive in thy bosom: keep it and let it not return to me lest it cause me grief"[2] He is silenced, and the lady elopes with her lover. The mother of the young lady going in search of her, enquires of the pilgrims whom she meets, whether they had seen a girl following a young man on the road. The pilgrims console her with the advice that her daughter had not acted improperly in having eloped with the youth who loved her. "Of what use is the pearl" they say, "to the sea in which it was born? Of what use is the sandal to the mountain on which it grew? Of what use is the coral to the reef on which it was formed? They are useful only to those who would wear them. Even so, has thy daughter gone with the young man of her choice."[3] After some days' absence, the daughter returns to her mother's house accompanied by her lover, and the youthful couple are married with the usual rites. If the lover hastily departs on a long journey in the service of the king, the lady is distracted. She gives up the society of her friends. She laughs and weeps by turns. She fancies that her sorrow is shared even by the inanimate objects around her: the

---

[1] Ibid., 49.   [2] Ibid., 23.   [3] Ibid., 9.

sea moans, the sand hills shiver : the leaves on the trees droop, and she feels like a ship-wrecked sailor at sea, who sees no means of escape.[1] She sees the *Ilavu* put forth its crimson flowers, and the *Kongu* its flowers of gold, and all the trees on the river banks in blossom : the honey bees hum and fit about busily from flower to flower: the cuckoo warbles : and all nature is gay : but her heart is sad as her lover is still absent.[2] She dreams that her lover had returned to her and that, touched by her sad look, he knelt at her feet and prayed to be forgiven : that she playfully struck him with her flower garlands ; and that he begged with trembling accents to know what offence he had committed. She is therefore cheerful on the next morning ; hoping that she should soon meet her lover.[3] Her maid recalls to her mind the noble qualities of her lover and assures her that he will not forsake her.[4]

I have given a brief summary of four of the larger poems of this period, *viz.*, Muppal, Chilapp-athikaram, Mani-mêkalai, and Kalith-thokai. The smaller poems may be conveniently mentioned under the names of their authors, which I shall give in the order of their date.

Kalath-thalai (A.D. 30—60) was a war bard attached to the court of the Chera king. He was present in the battle in which both the contending kings Cheral-Athan and the Chola Killi fell mortally wounded. Subsequently he was present in the battle of Vennil in which another Cheral-Athan was defeated by Kari-kal Chola. The poet Kapilar speaks of him as an older poet and states that the town of Araiyam, the capital of Irunko-Vêl, was destroyed as that prince did not honor Kalath-thalai. Six stanzas composed by this bard are preserved in the Purananuru.[5]

Uriththirank-kannanar (A.D. 40—70) was the author of two poems, Perumpanarrup-padai and Padinappalai. The former was composed about A.D. 50, when Thirayan, King of Kanchi, was in possession of the Chola kingdom. Though professedly a panegyric on king Thirayan it partakes more of the nature of a pastoral

---

[1] Ibid., 134.
[2] Ibid., 86.
[3] Ibid., 128.
[4] Ibid., 150.
[5] Purananuru 62, 65, 270, 288, 289, 366.

poem, and describes the various scenes in the territory of that king, such as the long lines of bullock carts in which salt dealers travel with their families : caravans of asses carrying sacks of pepper : the toll-gates guarded by soldiers : the villages inhabited by hunters, shepherds and farmers : the seaports which were crowded with ships and the capital city of Kanchi. The latter poem appears to have been written about the year A.D. 70, when Kârikal Chola was settled on his throne and was already the father of several children. The poem is in praise of Kavirip-paddinam, the capital city of Kârikal Chola. It describes at length the fertile region watered by the Kaviri : the fields and groves around the city : the sea-port and its spacious wharfs : the market place and its wide avenues : the fortifications of the city and the prowess and victories of the King Tiru-mâvalavan *alias* Kârikal Chola.

Mudath-thámak-Kanniyar (A.D. 60-90) composed the poem Porunar-ârrup-padai in praise of Kârikal Chola. He alludes to the escape of Kârikal from prison while young : his victory at the battle of Vennil : his subsequent career as a king and warrior : and his courteous and generous treatment of the bards and minstrels who visit his Court.

Kapilar (A.D. 90-130) was a Brahmin by birth and a poet by profession. He resided for some time at the Court of the Chera King Athan, who married the daughter of Kârikal Chola : and the king was so pleased with him that he bestowed on the poet several villages as a free gift.[1] Attracted by the fame of Pâri who was noted for his liberality to poets, he visited that chieftain and was soon installed as his favorite bard and boon companion. Being a perfect master in the art of flattery he was a general favorite wherever he went. The verses which he has left in praise of his patrons, show that he had a wonderful facility of expression and subtlety of thought which enabled him to compose felicitous verses extolling the bravery and generosity of his patrons, apparently with perfect truth, but in fact, in a highly exaggerated strain. After the death of Pâri, he took his daughters to be married to Vichchík-kon and Irunko-vel ; but not succeeding in his mission, he bestowed the girls on Brahmins,

---

[1] Pathirupp-pattu, 61 to 70.

and starved himself to death unwilling to survive his generous patron Pâri.[1] His poem Perunk-Kurinchi narrates a story of love among the hill tribes in Tamilakam : and is said to have been composed for the instruction of an Aryan King Prahasta. Another poem composed by him entitled Inṇanârpatu is a didactic poem consisting of 40 stanzas treating of four unpleasant things in each stanza. Three of the stanzas are translated below as a specimen of the work :—

"Bitter is (life) to those who do not worship the feet of the three-eyed god (Siva). Bitter is it not to pray to the fair god (Baladeva) whose flag bears the device in gold of a palmyra palm. Bitter is it to forget the god (Vishnu) who wields the Chakra. Even so is (life) bitter to those who do not adore the god who is armed with the lance (Muruga)—(Stanza I.)

"Bitter is it to witness the distress of a friend. Bitter is it to see the pride of a foe. Bitter is it to reside in a town which is not fortified. Even so is it bitter to gamble with the dice.—(Stanza 26.)

"Bitter is the folly of lusting after another's wife. Bitter is the bearing of a cowardly king on the battle-field. Bitter is it to ride a fiery steed without a saddle. Even so bitter is the work under a kenby a slothful man.—(Stanza 39.)"

One hundred verses composed by him form part of the Ainkkuru-nuru : and ten of his verses in praise of the king Cheral-Athan are included in the Pathirrup-pattu. He was present at the convocation of poets at the court of Ugra Pandya at Madura when Tiruvalluvar first recited his Muppâl, and warmly approved of the work. He visited the Malayamân Kâri at Mulloor.[2] In company with the poets Paranar, Arisîl-Kilâr and Perunk-kunrur-kilâr, he paid a visit also to Nalli and Pekan, the chief of the Aviyar, who were famous in his time as patrons of poets.[3] As specimens of his eulogistic verses I give below two of the stanzas composed by him in praise of his patrons Pâri and the Chera King Athan.

"Most generous Pâri ! Lord of the land of mountains, where jack-fruits as large as drums, torn open by monkeys, serve as

---

[1] Puranânurû, 200, 201, 20% and 236.
[2] Ibid., 121 to 124.
[3] Ibid., 143 to 147.

food for hunters of the Kurava tribe! Thou wert really no friend of mine, but an enemy, during the many years that thou supported me, for, out of my intense love of thee, I would have gladly died with thee: but thou prevented it; and having survived thee, I feel I have not been faithful to thee. Yet, I pray that in the next world, I may enjoy thy friendship for ever, as I did in this world." [1]

"Thou wouldst obey none but Brahmins. Distinguished for dauntless bravery, thou fearest nothing but to offend thy friends. Thy perfumed breast on which the bow ever rests, throbs before none but beautiful women. Thou wouldst not be false to thy promise even if the earth should change its position. Swift and terrible as the thunderbolt which shakes hillocks to their base, thou hast with thy valiant Tamil soldiers, routed the armies of thy two rival kings, and won thy laurels as a warrior: and now thou hast added to thy triumphs by conquering my poverty. Thou, Chelvak-ko! scion of the Cheralas! If good deeds are rewarded on this earth which is surrounded by the mighty ocean, Thou, Athan! wilt prosper for countless thousands of years! and be blessed in all thy undertakings!" [2]

An elegant versifier, an amiable companion, and a consummate courtier, he was beloved alike by his patrons and brother poets. No poet of this ancient period, except Tiruvalluvar, appears to have been so popular as Kapilar, if we are to judge by the many complimentary allusions to him in the verses of contemporary authors. Nakkirar speaks of him as "the eloquent and famous Kapilan who is praised by many throughout the world." [3] Poruntil-ilankkiranar refers to him as "the learned and famous Kapilan, whose elegant verses are full of deep meaning": [4] and Marokattu-Nappasalaiyar alludes to him as "the pure minded Brahmin who has sung thy praises so fully that other minstrels have nothing new to say," while addressing Kari, the Malayaman. [5]

Nakkirar (A.D. 100—130) was the son of a schoolmaster of Madura. He alludes in his poems to the Chola kings Karikál and Killi-valavan, the Pandyan king Nedun-cheliyan and the

---

[1] Ibid., 236.　[2] Pathirapp patin, 63.　[3] Akananurû, 78.
[4] Purananuru, 53.　[5] Ibid., 126.

Chera king Vâna-varmman *alias* Athan. Only two of his poems are now extant, *viz.*, Tiru-murugaruppadai and Nedu-nal-vadai. In the former he praises Muruga, the god of war who had six faces and twelve arms, and who was worshipped at Parank-, Kunru, Alaivái, Avinan-kudi, Erakam, and Palam-utir-cholai. In the latter poem the long winter night at Madura is described. The chill north wind blows through the groves of areca-palms, and down the broad streets of Madura. Windows and doors are bolted and closed to keep out the cold air, and fires are lit in bed rooms. In the Pandya's palace, the queen lies sleepless on her couch thinking of her lord who had gone with his army to fight with neighbouring kings, and tears fill her eyes and trickle down her cheeks : while the Pandyan king encamped on hostile ground is also awake. He is not however thinking of his queen : but is busy visiting the wounded and issuing orders for their treatment and for the safety of the camp. Both the poems are well conceived and expressed in a polished style. Many stray stanzas uttered by him are found in the poetic collections known as Purananuru, Akananuru, Kurunthokai and Narrinai.

The poems of Nakkirar are full of allusions to contemporary events and show that he was no ordinary bard who cared only to flatter and please his patrons ; but was a fairly good scholar who strove to produce lasting memorials of his literary skill. It is from his verses that we know that Karikâl Chola settled the wandering tribes of Kurumbas[1] ; that seven kings, whose names he mentions, were defeated by the Pandyan king Nedunj-Cheliyan at A'lankânam ;[2] that the same Pandyan king invaded the Chera territory and went up to Muchiri (the Muziris of Ptolemy) on the western coast ;[3] and that Palayan Mâran defeated under the walls of Madura the large army with which Killi-Valavan had invaded the Pandyan territory.[4] He picks his words and uses the most appropriate expressions to convey his ideas, and his style is always dignified and elegant; but he tries to show off his learning and sometimes pushes his scholarship almost to the verge of pedantry. Besides the Tiru-Muru-kârrup-padai, nine small poems which are attributed to Nakkirar appear in the eleventh Book of the collection of Saiva hymns. The

---

[1] *Akam*, 140.   [2] Ibid., 36.   [3] Ibid., 57.   [4] Ibid, 345.

language of these poems is, however, so modern that no critical
student will hesitate to declare them to be forgeries.[1] The
legend regarding the origin of these poems is found in the Hâl-
asya Mahâtmya, a Sanscrit chronicle of the temple of Siva at
Madura, the pious author of which, who lived about the eleventh
century A.D., appears to have had little or no knowledge of
ancient Tamil literature.[2]

---

[1] The late Professor P. Sundaram Pillai, M.A., was of the same opinion.
Christian College Magazine for August 1891, p. 127. The names of the nine poems
are as follow:—

1. Kayilai-pâti-kâlatti-pâti-antâti.
2. Eenkôy-malai-elupata.
3. Valanchuli-mum-manik-kôrai.
4. Ein-kûrr-irukkai.
5. Perum-deva-pâni.
6. Kôpap-prasâtam.
7. Kâr-eddu.
8. Pôrrik-kali-ven-pâ.
9. Kannappa-devar-tiru-maram.

[2] The poem states that during the reign of the Pandyan king Vankya-
Sekaran 48 Pandits from Kâsi (Benares) travelled southwards and settled at
Madura under the patronage of the Pandya. His successor Vankiya-Chûdâmani
alias Champaka-Mârnn was one day seated in the royal park, with his queen, and
charmed by the fragrant smell of her tresses, wondered whether the fragrance was
natural or acquired. In a gay mood he sent word to the poets of his court offering
a purse of 1,000 gold coins to anyone who would guess his thought and solve his
doubt. The poets who were not thought-readers were at a loss to know what they
should do to satisfy their royal patron. A poor Brahmin who heard of this handsome offer thought it a good opportunity to enrich himself, and entering the
temple of Siva and falling at the feet of the image of the god, prayed fervently
that the god should help him to win the prize. Moved by his prayer the god gave
him a palm leaf with a stanza written on it. The Brahmin received it with joy and
hastened to the Poet's hall and presented the verse. It was a gem of poetry:
every one pronounced it beautiful in language and sentiment. It was taken to
the king who read it with pleasure and ordered that the purse of gold be given to
the Brahmin. He hurried back to the poet's hall to receive the prize: but
Nakkirar said that there was a fault in his verse, and that the prize ought not to
be awarded to him. The Brahmin, sadly disappointed, retraced his steps to the
temple of Siva and falling once more at the feet of Siva's image implored the
mercy of the god. Incensed at the presumption of Nakkirar in criticising his
verse, the god assumed the form of a bard, and appearing in the assembly of
poets, enquired which of them had dared to find fault in his verse. Nakkirar
replied that it was himself and that the fault was in the statement that women's
tresses were naturally fragrant, which he said was impossible. The god enquired
whether the tresses of Padminis, the highest class of women, were not naturally

Mámúlanâr (A.D. 100-130) : many verses composed by this bard are found in the Akananuru, and a few in the Kurunthokai and Narrinai. It appears from these verses that he was a great traveller and visited the Chera, Chola, and Pandya Kingdoms, Panan-Nadu (Wynaad), Tulu-Nad (South-Canara) and Eru-mai-Nadu (Mysore Province).[1] He frequently mentions "the festive and wealthy town of Venkadam (the modern Tirupathi) ruled by the generous Pulli," who seems to have been his patron.[2] He alludes also to several ancient kings : Perunj-Chôrru-Utiyanj-Cheral ;[3] Cheral-Athan who conducted an expedition by sea and cut down the Kadambu ;[4] another Cheral-Athan who was defeated at Vennil by Karikal-Chola ;[5] and the illegitimate Mauriyas who led their army up to Pothiya Hill, when Mohoor did not submit to the Kosar.[6]

Kallâdanâr (A.D. 100-130) appears to have been a native of Venkadam, which town he says he quitted with his family during a severe famine.[7] He travelled southwards and found

fragrant ? "No" said the defiant Nakkirar. " Are not the tresses of celestial women fragrant" enquired the god irritated. "No" repeated Nakkirar "unless they wore the celestial Mandhâra flower in their hair." "Are not the tresses of Parvati, the goddess whom you worship, naturally fragrant ?" asked the god with kindling anger. "No" asserted the obstinate Nakkirar. The wrath of the god was now uncontrollable. The eye in the centre of the god's forehead opened and emited flames. "It is false : even if thou openest a thousand eyes," said the dauntless Nakkirar, carried away by his blind zeal to maintain what was right. The divine eye flushed a ray of fire on Nakkirar, and the latter scorched by the heat fell instantly from his seat, into the tank of the golden lotus : and the god disappeared. In humble repentance the poet then composed the nine poems to appease the wrath of the god.

The Mahatmya names Kapilar and Paranar as the contemporaries of Nakkirar during the reign of Champaka Mâran. Continuing the narrative the poem states that fourteen kings reigned at Madura after Champaku Mâran ; and during the reign of the fifteenth king Kulena Pandya that is, after the lapse of about a century, it introduces again, with no little absurdity, the poet Kapilar and his friend Idaik-Kâdar.

See also Tiru-vilaiyâdar-purânam, chapters 51, 53 and 56.

[1] *Akam*, 15, 114.
[2] Ibid., 61, 294, 310, 393.
[3] Ibid., 233.
[4] Ibid., 346, 126.
[5] Ibid., 55.
[6] Ibid., 250.
[7] *Puram*, 391.

relief in the fertile regions on the banks of the river Kaviri, where the chieftains of Poraiyuru and Ambar welcomed him and treated with all the honor due to a minstrel.[1] He accompanied the Pandyan army to the battle of Alankânam, and when the battle was over he sang the praises of the Victor Nedunj-Cheliyan and received a share of the spoils.[2] He refers in his verses to the battle in which Kari, king of Mullûr, defeated and killed Ori, king of the Kolli Hills,[3] and to the battle in which Kalankâik-kanni-nâr-mudich-cheral defeated Nannan.[4] A commentary to the Tamil Grammar Tolkâppiyam is said to have been written by him, but it is not extant. The poem Kallâdam[5] which recounts the miracles performed by the god Siva at Madura is also ascribed to him; but the language of the poem and the numerous allusions to later events contained in it, stamp it as a spurious work.

Mânkudi-Maruthanâr (A.D. 90-130) or Maruthanâr of Man-kudi is the earliest poet laureate mentioned in Tamil literature. The Pandyan King Nedunj-cheliyan, victor of Alankânam, speaks of him as the chief of the poets of his court. A few stanzas composed by him are found in the Pura-Nânuru; but the work by which he is best remembered is the poem Maduraik-Kânchi,[6] which he addressed to the king Nedunj-cheliyan. It is a moral epistle, and the author appears in the character of a teacher and a moralist; but as it is addressed to a restless and ambitious warrior flushed with success, who is his own patron and king, the author has considered it proper to render the moral to be conveyed as agreeable as possible by a profuse panegyric on the king and his prosperous dominion. The poem opens with an eloquent apostrophe in which the justice and wisdom and martial glory of the ancient line of the Pandyas is set forth; then it relates in glowing terms the various exploits of the king which have extended his authority and increased his fame; and extols

[1] Ibid., 385.
[2] Ibid., 371.
[3] Akam, 208.
[4] Ibid., 198.

[5] This poem was printed some years ago with a commentary by Maiyil-êrum-perumal Pillai for the first 37 stanzas and by Subbraya Mudaliar for 62 stanzas.

[6] Published by the Tamil Pandit V. Sâminâtha Iyer in 1889; the sixth poem in the Pattup-pâddu.

the personal merits of the king, his love of truth and justice, his faithful friendship and fearless bravery, his high sense of honor and unbounded charity. The monarch is asked to bear in mind the fact that of the many kings, great and good men, who graced the throne of the Pandyas before him, not one is alive! The poem then proceeds to describe with considerable wealth of detail the extensive country which owns the sway of the Pandya, comprising fertile fields, pasture lands, wild wastes, hill-tracts and a sea-coast studded with busy ports where fishermen, salt merchants, chank-cutters, and pearl-fishers ply their trade. It describes very vividly the proud and wealthy city of Madura, the scenes in the streets and in the palace, the personal appearance of the Pandya, and the manner in which he receives and rewards his courtiers; and concludes with the advice that the king should follow in the footsteps of his pious ancestors, perform sacrifices, advance the welfare and secure the loyalty of his subjects, and enjoy the good things that the gods give. It will be seen from the poem that the author was an ardent lover of Nature, and a keen observer of men and manners. His descriptions are true to life; but his diction is not as polished and dignified as that of Nakkirar.

Tiru-valluvar (A.D. 100-130). His fame as the author of the Kural or Muppal will last as long as Tamil is a living language. I have already given a brief summary of the work and described how warmly it was approved of by the poets of the court of Ugra-Pandya. The immediate popularity of the Kural is proved by the fact that verses from it are quoted by contemporary authors such as Cheethalai-chattanâr[1] and Ilankô-Adikal.[2] After the lapse of eighteen hundred years it has lost none of its original favour among the Tamil people, and it is still considered the first of works from which, whether for thought or language, there is no appeal. No less than ten commentaries have been written on it at different times; but the commentary which is most studied at present is that composed by Pari-mel-Alakar.[3]

---

[1] Main-makalai, xxii, 208 and 209.

[2] Chillapp-adikaram, xxi, 3 and 4.

[3] Published by the late Arumuga Navalar. The names of the commentators are: Dharmar, Manak-kudavar, Thamattar, Nachohar, Pari-melalakar, Parnti, Triu-malaiyar, Mallar, Kavip-perumal and Kalinkar. According to the Kapilar-Akaval, which is a spurious poem, Uppai, Uruvai, Valli, Avvaiyar,

Kovur-Kilar (A.D. 100-130) was a war bard who was very influential in the court of the Chola kings. Several stanzas composed by him in praise of Ched-chenni-Nalank-killi-valavan are found in the Pura-nanuru. In the civil wars that raged during the reign of Nalank-killi, between him and his younger brothers, Kovur-kilar was in the camp of Nedunk-killi. When Nalank-killi besieged Uraiyur and afterwards Avur, where his brother Nedunk-killi had taken refuge, the bard tried to reconcile the brothers.[1] He saved the life of Ilan-thathan, a poor minstrel, whom Nedunk-killi was about to kill on the suspicion that he was a spy.[2] During the reign of Killi-valavan, when that king seized the sons of Malayaman and condemned them to be trampled by elephants, the bard saved the youths, by reminding the Chola-king of the deeds of mercy which had rendered the names of his ancestors celebrated in ancient song.[3] When that king invaded the Chera kingdom and besieged the capital Karur, Kovur-killar and two other bards, Alathur-killar and Marokattu-Nappasalaiyar, were in the Chola camp.[4] The following is a translation of one of the stanzas addressed by him to his patron Nalan-killi.

" We are the devoted bards of Nalan-killi, the fierce and brave warrior king of Chola-Nad, who riding on a steed with flowing mane and jewelled trappings leads an army as vast as a sea and lays waste the lands of his foes. We seek not rewards from the hands of others by singing their praises. Him alone we will sing and bless for ever! Thou lord of fleet steeds! Myself and my minstrel youths, who know not the pangs of hunger, but

Athikarman, Kapilar and Triuvalluvar were the issues of the illegitimate union of Bagavan, a Brahmin, and A'di, a Pariah woman. Their parents led a wandering life in the Tamil country, and abandoned each child as soon as it was born : but the children were brought up as foundlings by strangers, and lived to become famous. The story is palpably untrue : for if each child had been abandoned as soon as it was born, the story does not state by what means their common origin was afterwards discovered It is surprising that Mr. Simon Casie Chetty, author of the Tamil Plutarch and Mr. J. R. Arnold, author of the Galaxy of Tamil Poets, have accepted this story as true.

[1] *Puram*, 44, 45.
[2] Ibid., 47.
[3] Ibid., 46.
[4] Ibid., 36, 37.

have always feasted on sweets and rice and flesh fried in ghee (at thy palace) will never quit thy side ! Give up thy peaceful habits and start like the hooded white serpent (springing on its enemy) with sparkling eyes and forked tongue. Let thy victorious chariot proceed against the fortresses of thy rival kings, and the whole of this sea-girt earth shall be thine ! Every time I strike my war-drum with the short stick with trinkling bells tied to it, thy foes shall tremble !" [1]

Iraiyanâr (A.D. 100-130) author of a grammar of errotic poetry called Iraiyanâr-Akapporul. In later periods the author's name was confounded with that of Siva and his insignificant treatise of sixty Sutras was considered the incomparable production of the god Siva ! [2]

Paranar (A.D. 100-130). Like most of the minstrels of this period he appears to have travelled through the Chera, Chola and Pandyan kingdoms, visiting the mansions of petty chiefs as well as the courts of kings. He refers to a confederacy of nine princes, most probably Kurumbas, defeated by Karikal-Chola who had invaded their territories with a large army: [3] and to the defeat of Arya kings by Chenkudduva-Chera, the grandson of Karikal Chola. [4] He praises the valor and munificence of Thittan, king of Uraiyur, [5] of Uthiyan, chief of Pali, where gold mines were worked [6] and of Thithiyan, chief of the Pothya hill, who defeated the Kosar. [7] Ten stanzas composed by him in praise of the Chera king Chenkudduva, form part of the Pathirrup-pattu. The poetess Auvaiyar states that he was present when Kovalur, the capital of Kari, was stormed by Nedu-man-Anchi, chief of the Athiyar, and sang the praises of the victor ; but the verses uttered by him on the occasion are not now extant. [8] The following is a translation of one of the stanzas sung

[1] Ibid., 382.
[2] Published by Rao Bahadûr C. W. Thamôtharam Pillai, with the commentary Nilakandan.
[3] *Akam*, 124.
[4] Ibid., 396.
[5] Ibid., .
[6] Ibid., 257.
[7] Ibid., 195.
[8] *Puram*, 99.

by him on the battle-field in which both the rival kings Nedunj-
cheral-Athan and Peru-virar-Killi died after a most sanguinary
conflict.

" The elephants pierced by arrows are all disabled for ever.
The splendid chargers are all slaughtered with their brave riders.
The commanders who drove in their chariots all lie dead, their
faces covered with their shields. The big thundering drums roll
on the ground, as no drummer is alive. Both the contending
kings have fallen on the battle-field, their perfumed breasts
pierced by long lances. Alas ! what will become of their fertile
countries, in the cool rivers of which peasant girls decked with
bracelets made of lily stalks, leap and sport? [1]

Perunk-Kausikanár (A.D. 100-130), a native of Perunkunrur,
composed the Malaipadu-Kadâm, a panegyric on Nannan, son of
Nannan, chief of Chenkanma.[2] The poem describes eloquently
the grandeur of the scenery on the mountain Naviram ; the
ceaseless din on the hill sides caused by the roar of cascades falling on rocks, the shouts of the elephant trainers, the songs of
women pounding millet, the whir of sugar-mills and the sound of
drums beaten by drunken hill-men who dance merrily with their
women ; the stones with epitaphs inscribed on them set up in
memory of departed warriors ; the sign-posts planted at crossings
showing the names of the places to which the roads lead ; the
hospitality of the hill-tribes ; the rapid current of the river Cheyar
which rushes whirling and eddying down the hill ; the fort-gates
guarded by soldiers armed with swords and lances : and the
courteous reception of minstrels by the chief Nannan who
welcomes them graciously and expresses his regret for the tire-
some ascent up the hill, and waits not till they finish their songs,
but feasts them and sends them home loaded with presents.

Auvaiyar (A.D. 100-130) the most famous of Tamil poet-
esses, is even more popular than Tiru-valluvar as the work of the
latter is studied only by advanced scholars, while the poems of
Auvaiyar are read by every Tamil student, soon after learning
the Alphabet. Her two books of aphorisms entitled Attichûdi
and Konrai-venthan, written in the order of the Tamil Alphabet

---

[1] Ibid., 63. This stanza was most probably composed by an earlier poet.
[2] The tenth poem in the Pattup-paddu.

which the learned Beschi considered as "worthy of Seneca himself," [1] have been most appropriately called "the Golden Alphabet of the Tamils." [2] Being a minstrel by profession, she
acquired in her early youth considerable facility in expressing
herself in verse, and possessing naturally a literary turn of mind
and poetic feeling, she appears to have improved them by extensive learning, so much so that she was soon recognised by her
contemporaries as an accomplished poetess. She describes herself
as appearing "with a shining forehead, eyelids painted black and
wearing a jewelled girdle on her waist." [3] The best part of her
life was spent in the court of Athiyaman-Anchi, prince of
Thskadûr, who held her in great regard. She says that the halls
and towers of Athiyaman's palace echoed many a day with her
songs, which she sang to the accompaniment of a tabor. [4] Her
intimacy with Athiyaman is expressed very quaintly by her as
follows:—

"Pleasant art thou prince! to us, as the huge elephant is to
village youths, when it lies down in the river and allows them to
wash its white tusks: but ferocious art thou to thy enemies
as the same elephant is when in rut." [5] When the fruit of a
certain Nelli-tree (*Phyllanthus emblica*) which was reputed to
possess the marvellous virtue of prolonging life, was presented to
Athiyaman, he did not eat it himself: but gave it to Auvvaiyar:
and the grateful minstrel thanks him in the following words:—

"Thou Anchi! king of the Athiyar! Resistless in war: who
wearing a golden necklace and wielding the victorious sword in
thy powerful arm which is adorned with armlets, slayest thy
enemies on every battle field! may thou be eminent for ever as
the matchless God (Siva) whose throat is blue and who wears the
silvery crescent on his head! For thou hast given me the sweet
fruit of the Nelli-tree which grew on the giddy height of a lofty
mountain, knowing that it will save me from Death." [6] Athi-
yâman sent Auvvaiyar once on an embassy to Thondaiman, king

[1] Babington's Chen Tamil Grammar Introduction, p. xi.
[2] Asiatic Researches, vii, p. 350, London Edition.
[3] *Puram*, 89.
[4] Ibid., 390.
[5] Ibid., 94.
[6] Ibid., 91.

of Kanchi, most probably seeking the assistance of that king against his enemies.[1] It is not known whether the embassy was successful or not : but some time afterwards Athiyaman was killed in a battle : and the verses uttered by Auvvaiyar on the occasion are very pathetic.

"If there was little liquor, he would let us drink it : if there was much, he would also share it joyously with us, while we sang to him. Whether it was a simple meal or a grand feast, he would sit to meal with a large company of guests. Wherever bone and meat were plentiful he would place us : wherever arrows and lances were aimed he would take his stand. With his perfumed hands he would stroke my head. Alas! the lance that pierced his beloved breast, pierced at the same time the alms bowl of his minstrels, the hands of the poor whom he fed, and the tongues of the learned poets of his court. Dim are the eyes of his dependents, with weeping! Oh! where is he our dear prince? No more are there bards to sing or patrons to reward them. But many are the men who are as useless to this world as the flower of the Pahanrai which blooms on the cool banks of rivers : but is not worn by any one."[2] After the death of her patron Athiyaman-Anchi she travelled in the Tondi-Nad and some years hence returned to Thakadur, where Elini, the son of Neduman-Anchi, received her very kindly. She describes her reception as follows :—[3] "Early on a dewy morning, while the mild moon was still shining, I stood at the entrance to the palace of Elini, King of the Athiyar, and striking the drum which I carried in my hand, I sang "Long life to thee Elini! King of the Athiyar! who stormest thy enemies' forts and ravagest their fields!" Straightway he welcomed me and made me change my dirty dress and put on fine new clothes which he presented. In a golden cup he offered me strong old liquor which fired my blood to a frenzy and he feasted me right royally."

She attended the magnificent sacrifice performed by the Chola king Peru-nar-Killi, and she had the honor of addressing the three Tamil kings, Ugrapperu-Valuthy, Peru-nar-Killi and the Chera Ma-ven-ko, who were seated together on the occasion. She exhorted them to do good during all their life time, which

---

[1] Ibid., 95. [2] Ibid , 235. [3] Ibid., 392.

alone she said would save them in the future.[1] As a specimen
of the pure principles and practical philosophy she preached, I give
below a translation of the first eight lines of the Attichudi or
the Golden Alphabet :—

1. Desire to do charity.
2. Anger should be controlled.
3. Fail not to render what help lies in your power.
4. Prevent not the giving of alms.
5. Reveal not what you possess.
6. Slacken not exertion.
7. Neglect not numbers and letters.
8. Begging is shameful.

In the *Vinôda-rasa-manjari*, which is a collection of amusing
stories and anecdotes, composed by the late Virasami Chettiar,
Tamil Pandit of the Presidency College, Madras, Auvvaiyar is
frequently mentioned as a contemporary of the Chola king
Kulôttunga, who lived in the ninth or tenth century A.D., and
was the patron of the famous poets Oddaik-Kûttar, Kambar and
Pukalenti.[2] In other recent works of Tamil Pandits, she is
spoken of as having lived during the time of Sundarar the devotee of Siva, and of his friend and patron Cheraman Perumal, the
last of the Chera kings. These stories appear to be of every
recent origin and are not supported by any authority in classical
works, or in the old commentaries : and should therefore be
rejected as entirely groundless. It is clear from her poems which
are preserved in the Purananuru and Akanamuru that she
flourished during the reign of the Pandyan king Ugrap-peru-
valuti in the beginning of the second century A.D.[3] and could
not have therefore been a contemporary of the mediæval kings
Kulothunga Chola or Cheraman Perumal. But Tamil Pandits,
who love the marvellous, assert with a show of wisdom, that
Auvvaiyar lived to the extraordinary age of six or seven hundred
years, and that in her youth she was a contemporary of Ugra-
Pandya, and in her old age of Kulothunga-Chola, whose reign
commenced seven centuries later ! Two poems entitled Pantban-
antati and Asatikkovai are attributed to Auvvaiyar ; but their

---

[1] Ibid., 367.   [2] Vinoda-rasa-manjari, p. 57.   [3] Pura-nanura.

modern language betrays that they are the works of a much later poet.[1]

Idaik-kâdanâr (A.D. 100-130) was the author of the Oosimuri, a poem which is not now extant; but which is quoted in Gunasagara's commentary to the Yapp-arunk-kalam.[2] He visited the camp of the Chola king Killi-valavan, when he was besieging Karûr, the Chera capital.

Cheettalaich-châttanar (A.D. 110-140) was the son of a corn dealer of Madura. He professed Buddhism, and was eminent as a logician, theologian and poet. A stanza composed by him in praise of the Pandyan king Nan-maran is as follows:—[3]

" Thou august Valuti, whose arms are long and powerful and whose breast is resplendent with strings of precious gems! a perfect master art thou of courteous and gracious acts. Never wouldst thou tolerate what is false. To thy enemies, thou art like the burning sun, which rises above the ocean: but to thy subjects like myself, thou art like the pleasant moon."

His fame rests on his great work the Mani-mekalai, which is the earliest of the five epic poems in Tamil. It is a most finished piece of writing and contains many passages of great beauty. The style is simple and elegant; and the phrases used are well turned and full of deep meaning. He excels most in his exquisite descriptions of natural scenery. He portrays beautifully the character of the heroine Mani-mêkalai, who, though young and beautiful and the daughter of an actress, devotes herself to a religious life and becomes a Buddhist nun. She is courted by a handsome prince, the son of the reigning king, but remains faithful to her vow, and far from acting the prude, she feels for her lover like a true woman, and tries to wean his heart from the lusts of the flesh and to lead him to a holy and spiritual life. In the last four chapters of the epic, where the author describes the six schools of philosophy that were then popular, he shows himself to be a master of the logical subtleties, and metaphysical cobwebs which formed the constant theme of argument among the learned men of his time. After completing the Mani-mêkalai, he visited Karur, the capital of the Chera kingdom, and remained there for

---

[1] Vinoda-rasa manjari.   [2] Yapp-arun-kalak-karikai.   [3] Pura-na-nuru.

a long time as the guest of the king Chenk-kudduvan, and of his accomplished brother, Ilanko-adikal.

Ilanko-adikal (A.D. 110-140) was the second son of the Chera king, Athan, and grandson of the Chola king Karikal, by his daughter Sonai. In his youth he renounced the world and became a monk of the Nigrantha sect, under the following circumstances: He and his elder brother Chenk-kudduvan, were seated one day at the foot of their father's throne in the audience hall at Karur, when a seer appeared before the king Cheral Athan, and after gazing for a while at the king and his two sons, declared that the younger son had all the personal marks of becoming a great monarch. Finding that Chenk-kudduvan was enraged at this prediction, his younger brother immediately laid aside his princely dress and ornaments, and took the vows of a Nigrantha monk, to prevent all possibility of his succeeding to the throne. Thenceforth he resided in a temple outside the eastern gate of the city. Relieved of all the cares of royalty he appears to have employed his leisure in cultivating his taste for music and literature. Many years afterwards when the poet Cheettalaich-châttanâr visited the Chera court, and recited to the prince, the epic Mani-mêkalai which he had composed, the royal monk conceived the idea of writing another epic poem to commemorate the lives of Mani-mêkalai's parents, Kovilan and Kannaki. Accordingly he composed the Chilapp-athikaram, in the presence of the poet Cheettalaich-chattanar. In elegance of style, the poem approaches the Mani-mêkalai : but in the varied scenes it describes, in the wealth of information it contains regarding the different classes of society, it is far more interesting to the student and the general reader. The author displays all his knowledge of the science of music and dancing: and has embellished his work with ditties of love and play and sacred hymns, in various metres. The characters of the hero and heroine are well depicted. Kovilan, the son of a wealthy merchant, is a gay and foolish young man. He is married at an early age to an amiable and virtuous girl : but being fond of music and dance he frequents the public theatres, and falls in love with the most beautiful actress of his day : lavishes all his wealth upon her: then ashamed of his conduct he flees from his native city with his young wife to Madura, where instead of

seeking the **help of** the merchants who knew his father, he lodg
in the house of **a** shepherdess ; and going out alone to sell one
his wife's jewels, **is** accused of having stolen the jewel from t
palace, and is **killed** by one of the royal guards. Kannaki is
model wife, who loves and adores her husband although he
faithless to her. So sweet is her temper, that she never reproach
him, but studies his slightest wish and devotes herself to
service. After he had squandered all his wealth she follows hi
in his flight **to** a strange city : and when he is killed the
accused of theft, **she** appears boldly before the king of t
city and proves **that her** husband was not a thief. Then
gives way to despair ; and wandering along the road leading i
the Chera country dies broken-hearted on the fourteenth d
after her husband's death.

Arisil-kilâr (A. D. 110-140) is the author of ten stanzas
praise of the Chera king **Perum-cheral-Irum-Porai,** who captur
Thakadûr, the **capital of Atiyamân Elini. Several** of his stan
occur also in the **Thakadûr Yâthirai.**[1]

Pon-mudiyâr (**A. D. 110-140**) **a war bard who** accompanied
army of the **Chera king Perum-cheral-Irum-Porai,** when
marched against **Thakadûr. His verses are full of** martial spi
and describe vividly and graphically stirring scenes on
battle-field.[2]

Perunk-kunrur-kilar (A. D. 120-150). Ten stanzas compo
by him in praise of [3] Perum-cheral-Irum-Porai are preserved
the Patirrup-pattu.

The following list shows the names of the Tamil poe
composed between the years A. D. 50 and 150, and the num
of lines contained in each poem :—

Muppâl or Kural	...	...	...	2,660 lines.
Mani-mékalai	...	...	...	4,857 „
Chillap-adikaram	...	...	...	4,957 „
Kalith-thokai	...	...	...	4,304 „
Innâ-nârpatu	...	...	...	160 „
Perunk-kurinchi	...	...	...	261 „

[1] Tol-kappiyam, Porul-atthikaram Nachchinarkk-iniyar's commentary.
[2] Ibid.
[3] Patirrup-pattu sk.

27

Kurinchi (by Kapilar in Ainkuru-miru)

about	.	...	...	...	400 lines.
Tiru-murukârrup-padai		...	...	317	,,
Nedu-nal-vadai		...	...	...	188 ,,
Porunar-arrup-padai	...	...	...	248	,,
Perum-pân-ârup-padai		...	...	500	,,
Paddinap-pâlai		...	...	...	301 ,,
Maduraik-kânchi		...	...	...	782 ,,
Malai-padu-kadam	..	...	...	583	,,
Patirrup-patu (41—50)		...	about 150		,,
Do. (61—70)		...	about 150		,,
Do. (71—80)		...	about 150		,.
Do. (81—90)		...	about 150		,,

About 300 stanzas composed by the
poets of this period which are
found in the Pura-nânûru, Aka-
nanuru Kuruntokai and Narrinai about 4,000 ,,

Total ... 25,118 ,,

It will be seen from the above list that more than 25,000 lines of verse written by poets who flourished between the years A. D. 50 and 150 are still extant, and furnish ample material for studying the history and civilization of the ancient Tamils. Embalmed in this literature we find a faithful picture of their habits and manners and of their social and political condition, in a form which is far more enduring than if it had been engraved on brass or stone. There are several allusions in this literature to ancient Aryan works which throw considerable light on the history and religion of the Aryan races which inhabited North-ern India. The four Vedas were generally known as the " Nân Marai " or the four Secret Books, which brings out clearly the fact that the Brahmins jealously concealed all knowledge of the Vedas from the Tamils. The Brahmins were described as " the owners of the four Secret Books " and as " the learned in the six sciences " that is the six Angas[1] : viz., Kalpa, Nirukta, Chhandas, Jyotish, Siksha and Vyakarana. The ancient grammar Indra

---

[1] Kalpa (ceremonial), Nirukta (Etymology), Chhandas (metre) Jyotisha (astronomy), Siksha (phonetics) Vyakarana (grammar).

Vyakarana which is not now extant, was then studied by the
Brahmins, and proficiency in the Indra Vyakarana was considered as evidence of superior scholarship. The Tamils were
familiar with the stories of the Ramayana and Mahabharata.
They knew the Buddhist Pitakas, the Nigrantha Agamas, and
the sacred books of Markali, the founder of the Ajivaka sect.
They knew too the six schools of philosophy. It is remarkable
that there is no allusion to Pánini's Vyakarana or Patanjali's Yoga
philosophy, which were evidently unknown in Southern India,
and had not become popular in Northern India.

CHAPTER XIV.

THE SIX SYSTEMS OF PHILOSOPHY.

The following is a brief summary of the six systems of philosophy as given in the Tamil epic poem Mani-mêkalai, which I trust will be found very interesting, as it is the earliest comparative account we have of the ancient schools of Hindu philosophy; and differs in many respects from the current accounts of the six systems.[1]

" She (Mani-mêkalai) approached the professors of philosophy, eager to know the true nature of things, and going up to the Vedic philosopher requested him to explain his tenets. (He stated that) an accurate knowledge of things may be obtained by ten means: Perception, Inference, Comparison, Authority, Implication, Propriety, Rumour, Impossibility, Reversion, and Association. The authors Veda-Vyasa, Krutakôdi and Jaimini recognised ten, eight and six of these means respectively. Correct *perfection* is of five kinds. It is to know colour by the eye; sound by the ear; smell by the nose; taste by the tongue; and touch by the body. To see, hear, smell, taste and touch with feelings of pain or pleasure, with life and sense and mind in perfect health, and in light and space free from any defect, and to ascertain the place, name, class, quality and action of a thing, without the faults of prejudice, incongruity or doubt is Perception.

" *Inference* is the mental process by which we understand the nature of an object, and it is of three kinds : by co-existence; by the effect or by the cause. (Inference by) co-existence is to know the presence of an elephant on hearing its trumpeting in a forest. (Inference by) effect is to say that it has been raining on seeing floods. (Inference by) cause is to say that it will rain on seeing a dark cloud. Whether the cause and effect be past, present or future, to know the existence of a thing that is not seen by a thing that is seen, without the faults of prejudice (incongruity and doubt) is Inference.

---

[1] Mani-mêkalai, Canto xxvii.

" *Comparison* is to know a thing by similarity, for instance, to imagine that a bison is like a cow.

" *Authority* is to believe that heaven and hell exist because they are mentioned in the writings of the wise.

" *Implication* is to understand that a shepherd's village stands on the banks of the Gangai, when we are told that it is on the Gangai.

" *Propriety* is when a man mounted on an elephant asks for a thing (to know that he asks for a goad) and to give a goad and nothing else.

" *Rumour* is what people generally say : for instance to believe that an evil spirit had taken its residence on a certain tree.

" *Impossibility* is the denying of an object where it cannot possibly be.

" *Reversion* is to infer that the wicked Ravana was defeated, when we hear that Rama was victorious.

" *Association* is to know that iron changes into magnet by a peculiar alteration in its properties.

" Of fallacious mediums there are eight kinds : Prejudice, Misconception, Doubt, Decision without examination, Failure of perception, False Belief, Belief in what is felt and Imagination. *Prejudice* is to decide the nature of everything (by first impressions). *Misconception* is to suppose one thing to be another : for example, mistaking the shining shell of an oyster to be silver. *Doubt* is to be uncertain of the nature of an object ; for instance, to remain undecided whether a certain figure (seen in the dusk) is a man or the stump of a tree. *Decision without examination* is to mistake the stump fixed on the polo ground for a man. *Failure of perception* is not to know (the danger in) the approach of a ferocious tiger, although seeing it coming. *False belief* is to believe in the horn of a hare, which is imagined on hearsay. *Belief in what is felt* is for example to fancy that sitting near a fire will cure fever. *Imagination* is (for instance) to believe on the assertion of others that a man and woman are your parents.

" The different systems of philosophy are Lokâyatam, Bauddham, Sânkhyam, Naiyâyikam, Vaiseshikam and Mimânsakam :- and the authors of these systems are Brihaspati, Jina,

Kapila, Akshapâtha, Kanâda, and Jaimini respectively. Only
six of the above mediums of knowledge are recognised in the
above systems.

"She then met the Saiva-vati who holds that Isa is the
Lord (of the universe) and asked him to explain the nature of his
deity. 'He governs the two luminaries (Sun and Moon) life,
and the five elements; He unites the soul and body: and created
this world as a pastime. His form is made of rays of light.
Mighty is he to remove all sorrows by death. There is nothing
else beside him. He is our God, said he. The Brahmavati said
that the whole universe was an egg laid by a God. The earnest
believer in Vishnu said that Narayana preserves the whole world.
The Vedic Brahmin said that the Veda had the Kalpa as its
hands, the Chhandas as its legs, Jyotish as its eyes, Nirukta as
its ears, Siksha as its nose and Vyakarna as its face: and that
it is self-existent and has neither beginning nor end.

"Finding that those statements were neither true nor accepted
as such by the world, she went to the Professor of the Ajivaka
religion, and asked him to state who was his God and what
was taught by his Sacred Books. The supreme Intelligence
which is found associated with every thing and for ever, through
the boundless universe, is God. Our Book teaches of five things,
that is, the soul and the four kinds of eternal atoms. These atoms
will collect and separate, so that the soul may mix with them, and
see and feel them. The atoms are of four kinds: those of the
earth, water, fire and wind. They may collect and form mountains, trees or bodies, or they may separate and expand through
space: and what recognises these is called the soul. The atoms
of earth collect and become hard and form the ground. The
atoms of water are heavy and cool and rest on the earth, and
can be tasted. The atoms of fire are hot and ascend: and the
atoms of wind spread and move. Under special conditions they
may exhibit other phenomena. The eternal atoms never cease
to exist, nor do they newly come into existence: nor can one
atom enter another. An atom of water cannot change into an atom
of earth: nor can one atom be split into two: nor flattened out
of its shape. They may move and fall or rise. They may
collect and form a mountain, or disperse and resume their shape

as atoms. They may become very hard as diamonds, or hollow as bamboo, or appear as other objects. When they appear in large masses as the elements, they may be more or less or·equal (to each other) or appear as a whole, or three-quarters or half or quarter, and each mass will be named according to the kind of atoms which are excessive in it. If they do not possess these properties they cannot be hard as earth, or flow as water, or burn as fire, or blow as wind. Only those who have divine eyes can see a single atom. Others in their physical bodies cannot discern it, just as in the twilight men cannot perceive a single hair, but can clearly see a mass of hair. Souls are born in bodies of six different colours, viz., black, blue, green, red, yellow and white. When born in pure white bodies souls attain release and happiness. If they fail to attain release, they would again descend in the scale of births and rise up like the turning of a wheel. To gain, to lose, to meet reverses, or successes, to feel pain or pleasure, to part from associations, to be born and to die are destined when the body is conceived in the womb. Pain and pleasure may be also considered eternal atoms. It is the effect of former deeds that is felt afterwards. The book of Markali explains in this manner :

"Leaving this confusion of words she asked the Niganta (Nigranta) to state who was his God, and what was taught in his sacred books, and to exclaim correctly how things exist and are formed or dissolved. He said that his God is worshipped by Indras : and that the books revealed by him describe the following :—The wheel of Law, the axle of Law, Time, Ether, Soul, Eternal atoms, good deeds, bad deeds, the bonds created by those deeds and the way to obtain release from those bonds. Things by their own nature, or by the nature of other objects to which they are attached are temporary or everlasting. Within the short period of a Kshana (second) they may pass through the three unavoidable stages, appearance, existence and dissolution. That a margosa tree sprouts and grows is eternal : that it does not possess that property is temporary. Green gram when made into a sweetmeat with other ingredients does not lose its nature, but loses its form. The wheel of Law (Dharma) pervades everywhere and moves all things in order and for ever. In the same

way the axle of the Law retains everything (and prevents dis·
solution). Time may be divided into seconds or extend to Eons.
Ether expands and gives room for everything. The soul entering
a body will, through the five senses, taste, smell, touch, hear and
see. An atom may become a body or assume other forms. To
stop the origin of good and evil deeds, and to enjoy the effect of
past deeds, and to cut off all bonds is release (salvation)."

The professor of the *Sânkhya* system then said that the
Original Producer (*Mûla-Prakriti*) is unknowable, undisturbed
by mind, grand and all-comprising, possesses three qualities [1] and
is the source of all things. From that Being, Intelligence is born :
from it, ether : from it, air : from it, fire : from it, water : from it,
earth : from the union of these the mind is born : from the mind
self-consciousness is born : from ether sound is produced through
the ear : from air the sense of touch is produced through the skin :
from fire the sense of light through the eye : from water the sense
of taste through the mouth : from earth the sense of smell through
the nose : from the union of these appear the tongue, hands, feet,
anus and genitals : by the union of the (grosser) elements are
produced mountains, trees and other objects of this world. In
the same manner in which these objects were evolved into
existence, they will recede and disappear. Till the universal
deluge these will expand continuously throughout space. The
soul (*Purusha*) is easy to be recognised and capable of perceiving
all things, one, eternal, unchangeable and sensitive, but without
the three qualities, possesses no organ of sense and is incapable
of producing anything by itself. There are twenty-five entities,
viz., earth, water, fire, air and ether : the skin, the mouth, the
eye, the nose, and the ear : the sense of taste, light, tangibility,
sound and smell : tongue, feet, hands, anus and genitals : the
mind, intelligence, self-consciousness, the Original Producer and
the soul.

"After listening to this faultless exposition (of the Sankhya
system) she asked the *Vaiséshika* professor to explain his doctrine.
He said that there are six divisions (or categories of objects) *viz.*,
substance, quality, action, genus, individuality and *concretion*. Of

---

[1] The three qualities are (*Sattva*) goodness or purity (*Rajas*) passion or
activity, (*Tamas*) darkness or stolidity.

these, *substance* possesses quality and action and is the 'origin of all objects. It has nine divisions : earth, water, fire, air, ether, space, time, soul and mind. Of these earth has five *qualities ;* sound, tangibility, colour, savour and odour. The remaining four (water, fire, air, and ether) have each one quality less (than those possessed by its predecessor in the order in which they are named : that is to state more clearly, water has the qualities of sound, tangibility, colour and savour : fire has the qualities of sound, tangibility and colour : wind has the qualities of sound and tangibility, and ether has only one quality, sound). Collected substance has many qualities such as, sound, tangibility, colour, odour, savour, largeness, smallness, hardness, softness, goodness, meanness, form and space. *Action* is produced by substance and its qualities. The highest *genus* is truth or (being). As motion and rest are general qualities, dissolution and existence are natural to substance. *Individuality* is in atoms. *Concretion* is the intimate connection between attribute and subject."

" She then asked the *Bhútardti* to speak and he said :—Just as the intoxication of toddy is generated by adding jaggery and the flower of the Dhatakee (*Bauhinia-racemosa*) to other ingredients, so does consciousness appear when the elements mix together (and form a body). Consciousness disappears like the sound of a broken drum when the elements (which form a body) disperse. The elements which, associated with life, possess feeling, and the elements which, separated from life, possess no feeling, are born from their respective elements. This is the true doctrine : The opinions of the *Lokáyata* are the same with slight differences. Except what is perceived by the senses, all that is inferred by the mind does not exist. The world and its effect exist in the present birth. That we enjoy the effects of our deeds in a future birth is false."

Having listened to the professors of the five systems of philosophy, *viz.,* (i) The Vedic Pramânavâta or Mimânsa, (ii) the Naiyâyika which comprised the Ajivaka and Nigranta Schisms, (iii) the Sânkhya, (iv) Vaisêshika, and (v) Bhûtavâta or Lokâyata, Manimekalai was eager to learn the Baudha system and went to the venerable Buddhist monk and said "I have heard the five philosophical systems, and as none of them appear to me to be correct, I do not believe in any of them. Venerable monk, I beseech thee to teach me the truth." "I shall teach thee, listen to me attentively" replied the monk (and continued). "The sources of true knowledge according to A'dhi-Jinêndra are only two. Right *perception* and *inference*. *Perception* he has described as conscious feeling (through the senses) ; name, species, quality, action and so forth (of an object) are (known by) *infer-ence*. (In ascertaining) cause or effect and (in making a) general inference we may be wrong : but the inference of an effect as smoke from fire is correct. All other sources of knowledge are irregular inferences. There are five (parts in every inference or syllogism) *Assertion, Reason, Example, Comparison* and *Deduction*.

> ' This mountain has fire' is *Assertion*.
> ' Because it has smoke ' is *Reason*.
> ' Like the kitchen-hearth ' is *Example*.
> ' This mountain also has smoke ' is *Comparison*.
> ' As it has smoke it has fire ' is *Deduction*.

' Whatever does not possess fire cannot be accompanied by smoke' as for instance a stream (of water) is an example of the Negative of the Assertion. Enquiring into the nature of the correct Reason of an effect is as follows :—

> ' Sound is non-eternal ' is *Assertion*.
> ' Because it is made' is *Reason*.
> ' Whatever is made is non-eternal like a jar ' is *Example*.
> ' Whatever is eternal is not made like the sky ' is a *Negative Example*.

An inference without correct reason is as follows :—

> ' There is no jar in this open space' is *Assertion*.
> ' Because it is not visible' is *Reason*.
> ' Because the hare has no horn we do not see it ' is *Example*.

' Whatever exists can be seen, like the *nelly* fruit on the palm' is a *negative example*. In this manner a cause should be estab-lished. If it is asked what smoke has proved, the answer is : By the concomitance that ' where there is smoke there is fire' and the converse negative fact that ' where there is no fire there is no smoke' smoke proves (the existence of) fire. The upward and curling progress of smoke is the effect of fire ; and hence the rising black smoke proves (the cause which is) fire. If the concomitance (alone) is to prove the fact, one who saw a donkey and a harlot together at a certain place and at a certain time, should at a subsequent time, when he sees a donkey, infer also the presence of a harlot : but this is (manifestly) incorrect. (Similarly) if the converse negative fact that " where there is no fire there is also no smoke " (alone) is to prove the (above) fact (when one sees) that there is neither a dog's tail nor a fox's tail in the hind part of a donkey, he should not infer the presence of a dog's tail, when he sees the tail of a fox at another place.

" Both *Comparison* and *Deduction* are subordinate to *Example*. *Assertion*, *Reason* and *Example* may be correct or fallacious. " A correct *Assertion* is that which has a clear *subject* and a clear *predicate* distinct and well defined; as for instance (the Assertion) ' sound is eternal or non-eternal.' Here sound is the *subject*, eternity or non-eternity is the *predicate*.

" Right *Reason* is of three kinds : it may be founded on the Assertion itself ; or it may be from Analogy or from the Negative proposition. If it is from Analogy, it should be from a perfect similitude, for instance, if it is intended to assert that sound is non-eternal (the Reason by Analogy would be) ' even as non-eternal as a jar.' If it is from a Negative Proposition it is as follows : ' whatever is eternal is not made as the sky.' To be made : and to appear during a certain action, constitute a proper reason for non-eternity, according to Assertion, Analogy and the Negative Proposition.

" Right *Example* is of two kinds : it may be *Positive* or *Negative*. A *Positive Example* is (as follows) :—' Non-eternity is concomitant with Jars and the like.' A Negative Example is to show that the effect (predicate) does not exist where the cause (reason) does not exist. The above are correct premises (in argument)." [1]

Having explained the means by which a correct knowledge of the nature of things may be obtained, the Buddhist monk proceeded to expound the doctrines of Buddha as follows :— " Once upon a time when all the sentient beings (of this world) were wholly bereft of wisdom, Vâman (the beautiful) quitted

---

[1] The Mani-Mekalai explains further in detail Fallacious Assertion, Fallacious Reason and Fallacious Example.—I omit them however as their description is too technical to be interesting to the general reader. (XXIX. 143-473.)

the *Dushitalôka* (a heavenly region) and appeared (in this world), yielding to the earnest prayer of hosts of crowned immortals. He sat at the foot of the *Bôdhi* (tree) and having conquered *Mâra* (the tempter) the hero got rid of the three evils, and preached the truths of salvation, which countless Buddhas had graciously proclaimed (in past ages). *Twelve Causes* form a path (for births). They arise one out of another and disappear one after another in regular succession. They act in a cycle disappearing in the same order in which they appear; each one vanishing when the next one vanished or springing into existence when the next one appeared, and may be regarded as a continuous chain. (This chain) is in *four parts* (*Khanda*) and has *three links* (*sandhi*). It leads to *three kinds of birth*; and there are *three divisions of time* suitable to those births. Out of (this chain) spring our *defects*, *deeds* and *their results*. It ensures our *salvation* when we realise that it is ever in motion and leads to no good but ends in suffering. *Four Truths* depend on it and the *five aggregates* (*skandhas*) form its basis. It may be described by *six modes of expression*. It produces *four benefits*, through *four excellent qualities* (*of the mind*), and questions about it may be *answered in four ways*. It has neither beginning nor end. It acts continuously and never ceases. It has no creators, nor was it ever created. In it there is no idea of 'I' or 'mine' and nothing is lost or gained. It cannot be brought to a close, nor will it itself come to an end. All actions and their results, Birth and Release and all such (changes) are caused by itself.

"Ignorance, Action, Consciousness, Name and Form, The senses, Contact, Sensation, Desire, Attachment, Existence, Birth and the Result of deeds; these are the *twelve causes*. If those who are born understand (these twelve) they would attain great happiness: if they do not understand (them) they would suffer in the lower worlds.

"Not to understand those abovementioned (the twelve causes), and to act under mental illusion, forgetting the conditions of nature which are perceivable by the senses: to trust in hearsay and believe in the existence of (such imaginary objects as) a hare's horn is *Ignorance*.

"The innumerable living creatures in the three worlds are of six kinds : men, gods, good-spirits, infernal beings, beasts and ghosts. According to their good and evil deeds they are born and, from the time of their conception, they enjoy pleasure and pain in due time, and corresponding to the accumulated effect of their deeds (*Karma*).

" What are evil deeds ? listen thou fair maid who wearest choice bracelets ! Killing, theft and adultery which are the three sins of the restless body : lying, slander, abuse and vain conversation, which are the four sins of speech: covetousness, malice and scepticism, which are the three sins of the mind : These *ten* (*sins*) wise men who know the effect (of their deeds) will avoid. If they do not avoid them they would be born as beasts, demons, or inhabitants of the lower worlds, and be distracted by sorrow.

" What are good deeds ? (They are as follow): to avoid the above-mentioned ten (sins) ; to observe the rules of purity : and above all to practice charity. Those who do these good deeds will be born in the three higher forms of birth (that is) as gods, human-beings, or good spirits and enjoy pleasure according to (the measure of) their good deeds.

Consciousness is like the perception of men in sleep, and is not affected by the senses.

Name and Form are the conceptions of (one's own) life and body arising out of that consciousness.

The *six gates* (*or senses*) are the organs through which impressions are made on consciousness.

Contact is the approach of consciousness to outside object through the senses.

Sensation is the feeling created in consciousness by external objects.

Desire is the wish for more of (a particular) sensation.

Attachment is the bond created by desire. *Existence* is the life (we lead) being the sum of our deeds of consciousness drawn by attachment.

Birth is the appearance in an organised body which is the effect of former deeds.

Disease is the falling off from the natural (healthy) state and the advent of pains in the body : *Old age* is the weakness which sets in the body after long life. *Death* is the dissolution of the body, which bore a name and form, and its disappearance, like the setting sun.

"From Ignorance springs action: from action springs consciousness: from consciousness spring Name and Form: from Name and Form spring the senses: from the senses springs contact: from contact springs sensation: from sensation springs desire: from desire springs attachment: from attachment springs existence: from existence springs a continuation of births: from birth springs a train of unavoidable suffering such as old age, disease, death, grief, lamentation, dejection and despair. (In this manner) Desire acts (and reacts) in a circle ceaselessly. By the destruction of Ignorance, action is destroyed: by the destruction of action consciousness is destroyed: by the destruction of consciousness, Name and Form are destroyed: by the destruction of Name and Form, the senses are destroyed: by the destruction of the senses contact is destroyed: by the destruction of contact sensation is destroyed: by the destruction of sensation desire is destroyed: by the destruction of desire, attachment is destroyed: by the destruction of attachment existence is destroyed: by the destruction of existence Birth is destroyed: by the destruction of Birth disease, old age, death, grief, lamentation, dejection, despair and the like endless suffering will be destroyed. In this manner *salvation* (is effected).[1]

"Ignorance and action, these two being the cause of the rest, form the *first Khanda* (or section); consciousness, Name and Form, the senses, contact and sensation being the (immediate) effect of the foregoing (section) form the *second Khanda*; Desire, Attachment and existence, being the evil result of sensation form the *third Khanda*; Birth as well as disease, old age, and death all of which follow birth, form the *fourth Khanda*:

"Action and consciousness form the *first Link* (*sandhi*). Sensation and desire, faultlessly understood, form the *second Link*. From good and evil deeds (or existence) to proceed to births is the *third Link*.

"The *three kinds of birth* are as follows:—Birth with consciousness but without (external) form: Without consciousness but

---

[1] Compare Mahavagga, I, 1-2. Sacred Books of the East, Vol. XIII.

with form : with both consciousness and form : as human beings, gods, or beasts.

"The *three (divisions of) time* are :—the past which ought to be said to include (the stages of) ignorance and action : the present which may be described as including consciousness, name and form, the senses, contact, sensation, desire, attachment, existence and birth : the future which is said to include birth, disease, old age, death, grief, lamentation, dejection and despair. The *defects* are Desire, Attachment and Ignorance. Action and existence constitute our (*good and evil*) *deeds.*

" Consciousness, Name and Form, The senses, Contact, Sensation, Birth, Old-age, Disease, and Death are the natural *Result* (*of our deeds*).

"All sentient beings who suffer by the above Defects, Deeds and Results are temporary. No being has an (immortal) soul. To understand thus (and realize these truths) is *salvation.*

" Consciousness, Name and Form, the Senses, Contact, Sensation, Birth, Disease, Old-age, Death, Grief, Lamentation, Dejection and Despair are (*four*) *Distempers.* The cause of these Distempers is Ignorance, Action, Desire, Attachment and Existence.

"Birth is painful ; attachment is its cause : Release is joyful ; absence of Attachment is its cause. These are the *Four Truths.*

" Form (or organised body), Sensation, Perception, Discrimination and Consciousness are the *Five Aggregates* (Skandhas).

" The *six modes of expression* may be explained as follows :— Words denote collection, continuance, excess of a quality and division ; and they are used to express what exists, what does not exist ; a truth about what exists ; an untruth about what does not exist ; an untruth about what exists ; or a truth about what does not exist. (Words such as) body, water, country, denote a collection. The (word) Paddy which is used for the grain, sprout, stalk, etc., of rice denotes a continuance (of phenomena). (The words) cessation, appearance and growth, denote the excess of quality, (in the successive stages of an object). When several letters are spoken of as a 'word' or several days are specified as a 'month,' it denotes Division. Sensation is 'what exists.' A hare's horn is 'what does not exist.' That consciousness is associated with mind is 'a true statement about what exists.' That the mind comes into existence like a flash of lightning is 'an untrue statement about what exists.' To speak of something as an effect without knowing the cause is a 'true statement about what does not exist.' To say that a hare's horn is not seen because it does not exist, is 'a truth about what does not exist.'

"There are *four excellent faculties of the mind* which perceive (i) Agreement, (ii) Non-agreement, (iii) Non-action, and (iv) Action. To understand the connection of cause and effect in objects is to perceive *agreement*. To distinguish objects individually is to perceive *non-agreement*. To say that the mind cannot understand the primary cause which leads to effect in eternal and temporary objects is to perceive *non-action*. To say that the germ of rice springs out of the rice seed is perception of *action*.

"The four *benefits* are the knowledge that (i) the world is nothing but a concretion of objects, (ii) that attachment to them is not good, (iii) that there is no connection with a creator, (iv) that an effect springs from its immediate cause.

"Questions may be *answered in four ways*. (1) By a decided answer. (2) By answers in parts. (3) By a further question. (4) By silence.

"If it is asked 'whether an object which comes into existence will disappear or not'; the decided answer would be that 'it will disappear.' If it is asked 'whether a dead man will be born again,' it should be answered 'Has he got rid of all attachment or not (implying thereby that he will not be born again if he has no attachment and that he will be re-born if he has any attachment). If it is asked 'which is earlier, an egg or a palmyra palm?' it should be asked in reply 'which egg to which palm?' If it is asked whether an aerial flower (an imaginary thing) is old or new, no answer need be given.[1]

"There is no one competent to explain the first cause of Attachment and Release. (As far as we see) the immediate cause of all the objects above-mentioned is lust, anger and mental

---

[1] "When Malunka asked the Buddha whether the existence of the world is eternal or not eternal, he made him no reply; but the reason of this was, that it was considered by the teacher as an inquiry that tended to no profit." Malunka Sutta in Hardy's Manual of Buddhism, p. 375.

illusion. Lust should be got rid of by discerning (and realising) that (our body is) temporary, that it is suffering, is soul-less, and unclean. Feelings of love, compassion, and benevolence should be cultivated so that anger may be entirely suppressed.

"Listen earnestly (to the preaching of the doctrine), meditate upon it fervently, practise it zealously and realise its truth, so that all illusion may be thrown off. In the four ways (mentioned above) enlighten your mind."

The most popular review, at present, of the philosophical systems of India is the *Sarva-darsana-sangraha*, the author of which was the great religious reformer Mahdwacharya. It was composed in the fourteenth century, when the Buddhist and Lokâyata faiths were almost extinct in India, and hence it mentions the names of the six systems as follows:—(i) Purva Mimansa, (ii) Uttara Mimansa or Vedanta, (iii) Sankhya, (iv) Yoga, (v) Nyaya, (vi) Vaiseshika. Oriental scholars in Europe following the *Sarva-darsana-sangraha* have treated Buddhism and Lokâyatam as non-Hindu systems.[1] But it will be seen from the foregoing summary quoted from the Mani-mêkalai that the six systems of philosophy which were current in India in the early centuries of the Christian Era were the Lokâyata, Bauddha, Sankhya, Nyaya, Vaiseshika and Mimansa. These were *the original six systems of Hindu philosophy*: and the Bauddha and Lokâyata, far from being non-Hindu, formed two of the six Hindu systems. It is noteworthy however that in describing briefly the doctrines of each of the above systems, the Mani-mêkalai does not give any account of the Nyaya: but in its place it mentions the Ajivaka and Nigranta philosophies which were then evidently the representatives of the older Nyaya system. The Ajivakas and Nigrantas appear to have been very numerous during the reign of the Magadha emperor Asoka as they are mentioned in his edicts.

The student of history will be doubtless surprised to find that all the phases of philosophic thought now current in Europe have their counterpart in the ancient philosophies of the Hindus. The Lokâyata which asserts that life is a certain collocation of matter, that there is no soul nor a future existence, and that men need not care for anything but their welfare in the present life,

is identical with "the scientific creed" of the modern Materialist.
The Bauddha which teaches that "there is no one competent to
explain the First cause" and that "life is a continual suffering"
combines the Agnosticism and Pessimism of the present day.
The Sankhya which assumes a material First cause, but recognises no intelligent creator, has many points in common with
modern Atheism. The Nyaya which holds that matter and soul
and god are eternal is almost the same as recent Theism. The
Vaiseshika which does not mention a god, but believes that the
universe is made of eternal atoms, and an eternal all-pervading
soul, is very much like Naturalism allied to the atomic theory.
The Mimansa which contains very little of philosophic discussion
but is a dogmatic assertion of the authority of the Vedas, may
be compared to the philosophy of the Christian church which
believes in the Bible and claims to be the only "revealed religion."

The specimen of Hindu Logic given above, from the Mani-
mēkalai, shows that the study of Logic had received considerable
attention among the learned classes of the Hindus. It was not
however pursued as a distinct science, in the early period which
I describe, but only as a method for the correct conduct of philosophical enquiry. The Hindu syllogism of five parts is more
complete than the Aristotelian syllogism of three parts. Their
manner of stating the Major Premise avoids the use of general
propositions: for instead of stating, for example, that "all smoke
is accompanied by fire" they say "wherever there is smoke
there is fire." The argument is directly from a particular case
to another particular case, which is the most usual and natural
method of reasoning.[1] Hence there is no mention in their
system of the various modes of syllogism, the discussion of which
takes up a considerable portion of European treatises on Logic.

[1] English Logicians have quite recently adopted this view. It has been
asserted by Mill, (system of Logic, Bk. II., Chap. iii.) and partially admitted by
Mr. Fowler (Inductive Logic, pp. 13, 14) that we can argue directly from case to
case. "Professor Bain has adopted the same view of reasoning. He thinks that
Mill has extricated us from the deadlock of the syllogism and effected a total
revolution in logic. He holds that reasoning from particulars to particulars is not
only the usual, the most obvious and the most ready method, but that it is the type
of reasoning which best discloses the real process." (Deductive Logic, pp. 208,
209). "Doubtless" says Professor Jevons "this is the usual result of our
reasoning, regard being had to degrees of probability." (The Principles of
Science, p. 227).

CHAPTER XV.

RELIGION.

As usual amongst all nations ancient or modern, the philosophic doctrines of the Tamils were far apart from the popular beliefs and ceremonies. Curiosity has in all ages led intelligent men to explore the records of the past, to speculate on the future, or to dive into the mysteries of mind and matter. Whilst the learned few with an earnest mind and deep research attempted to obtain correct notions of the causes and consequences of existence, the masses whose untutored minds could not conceive nature as a whole, took a low and sensual view of life, and worshipped a multitude of gods, who were supposed to bring about all the changes in nature, and all the misfortunes which happened to the people. These divinities partook more or less of the character of the classes who invoked them. The semi-barbarous tribes, which were most addicted to war and bloodshed, had ferocious and savage deities, whose altars reeked with the blood of slaughtered animals. Communities which were a little more civilised, and had cultivated the arts of peace, worshipped milder gods, who were content with offerings of fruits, flowers and incense. More advanced societies whose cultured mind could realise abstract ideas such as, the reign of law (dharma) and the unity of nature, endeavoured to conform their lives to moral laws and addressed their prayers to the Supreme Intelligence which rules the Universe.

The aboriginal Villavar and Minavar appear to have had no gods. The Nagas who first conquered the aboriginal races, which inhabited the Tamil country, worshipped the dread goddess Kâli and sacrificed many a buffalo at her shrines. The image of Kâli was decked in a most frightful manner. Her matted hair was tied up like a crown on her head, with the shining skin of a young cobra : the curved tusk of a boar was fastened in her hair to resemble the crescent. A string of tiger's teeth served as a necklace on her shoulders. The striped skin of a tiger was wound round her waist like a garment. A strong bow bent and ready to

shoot was placed in her hand : and she was mounted on a tall
stag with branching antlers. Drums rattled and pipes squeaked
in front of her image, while fierce Nagas slaughtered buffaloes at
her altar. As the victims bled the priestess got up in a frenzy,
shivering and dancing wildly, possessed with the spirit of Kâli, and
shouted " The cattle stalls in the villages around us are full of
oxen, but the yards of the Eyinar's cottages are empty. Mild
like the peaceful villagers are the Eyinar who should live by
robbery and plunder. If you do not offer the sacrifice due to the.
goddess, who rides the stag, she would not bless your bows with
victory !" Kâli being a female deity, her votaries offered to her
balls, dolls, parrots, wild fowls and peacocks with which Tamil
women used to amuse themselves. Perfumed pastes and powders, fragrant sandal, boiled beans and grains, and oblations of
rice mixed with blood and flesh were likewise presented at her
shrines.[1] The Nagas having been largely employed as soldiers
by the Tamil kings, their goddess Kâli became in course of time
the patron deity of the warrior class. The soldiers, officers of the
army and even the kings joined in making offerings, to obtain her
favor, before undertaking any military enterprise. It is said that
some of the soldiers, in a fit of excessive loyalty, offered up their
own lives at her altar, to ensure the success of the king's armies.
Kâli was also called Aiyai in Tamil, and was believed to be the
youngest of seven sisters. She is said to have challenged Siva to
a dance, and to have torn in two pieces the powerful body of the
demon Târaka. So much was this ferocious goddess dreaded by
the people, that it is related that on one occasion when the doors
of her temple at Madura remained closed, and could not be
opened, the Pandiyan king, believing it to be a token of her displeasure, fell prostrate before her shrine, praying for her mercy,
and to appease the wrath of the goddess, granted the revenue of
two fertile villages, for the expenses for her worship.[2]

Some of the lower classes, as well as the Nagas, worshipped
also stones and springs which were believed to possess miraculous powers. For instance, it is mentioned that in the city of
Kavirip-paddinam there was a long stone set up in an open

[1] Chilapp-atikaram, xii, 22 to 39.
[2] Ibid., xx. 87-40 and xxiii. 113 to 125.

square, which was resorted to by those who were suffering from
the effects of poison, witchcraft or venomous bites.
ed round the stone reverently and worshipped it in
being restored to health. There was
reputed to possess the virtue of curing the defects of all the deaf,
dumb, dwarfs, lepers and hunchbacks, who bathe in it and walk
round it praying for its healing grace.[1]

The huntsmen and hill-tribes or *Kuravas* worshipped the
heroic god of war Muruga. This god had six faces and twelve
arms. His shrines were
or in the midst of dense
favorite weapon of the
lancer. When sacrifices
put up, and it was adorned with strings of flowers. High over
the shed was hoisted the flag of Muruga, which bore the device
of a cock. The priest tied a red thread round his wrist, as a sign
of his having vowed himself to the service of the god, and bowing
before the altar, muttered spells and prayers, and scattered flowers and fried paddy on all sides. He then slaughtered a bull, and
in its warm blood mixed boiled rice and offered it to the god,
amidst the blare of trumpets, horns, bells and drums, while the
perfumes of incense and flowers filled the place. The worshippers chanted hymns in praise of the god, and the priest went
off into an ecstasy and danced and snorted and gave out oracles
regarding the fortunes of the devotees. Many circumstances
related of this god go to show that he was not entirely an imaginary being, but a warlike king who had been deified after his
death. He is said to have been born in the sacred pond *Saravana*
near the source of the Ganges, and to have been brought up by
six nurses. He was the Commander-in-Chief of the celestial
armies when they fought with the *Asura* or demons : and he invaded Lanka to kill Soora, the *Asura* king of that island. The
Kuravas had a tradition that the god married a maiden of their
tribe.[2]

The shepherd races worshipped their national hero Krishna
and his elder brother Balaráma. Shepherd lasses amused themselves by acting in their houses plays representing the chief

---

[1] Ibid., v. 118.127.   [2] Tiru-muruk-Arrup-padai.

events of his life, such as : his childish pranks in stealing butter, and hiding the clothes of shepherd girls who were sporting in the river Yamuna : his charming play on the pipe while grazing cattle : his amour with Pinnai a shepherdess : his victory over the cunning Kansa and his embassy to Duryôdhana for the Pandavas. Krishna was popularly known as *Mâyavan* or "the dissembler" a title very appropriate to his character as portrayed in the great epic Mahâbhârata. His elder brother Balarâma was famous for his extraordinary physical strength.[1]

Among the higher classes of the Tamils the favorite deity was Siva. He is represented as a man of fair colour with tangled locks of red hair. He has three eyes, wears a tiger's skin, and armed with a battle-axe rides on a bullock. His appearance, except as regards the three eyes, corresponds exactly with that of a primitive inhabitant of the Himalayan region. The people of this region are fair in color and have red hair and ride on bullocks when travelling in the mountainous country. His abode was the snow-capped Mount Kâilas situated north of the Himalayas, near the sources of the great rivers, Ganges, Indus and Brahmaputra. His greatest feat was the destruction of Tripura or "the three castles" which were the strongholds of Asuras, who had caused much annoyance to the celestials. He married Pârvati the daughter of the king of mountains.

The Brahmins settled in the Tamil country had not yet given up the worship of the elements, and some of them still kept up in their houses the three sacred fires, as in Vedic times. They attached the greatest importance to the performance of *Yâgas* or religious sacrifices, which were performed on a magnificent scale, generally under royal patronage. Horses or cows were sacrificed with elaborate ceremonies, conducted with great secrecy, within spacious enclosures, which were strictly guarded, and the flesh of the victims was eaten by the Brahmins. Special priests learned in the Vedic rites performed the sacrifice, and the kings who defrayed the expenses and presided at the sacrifice were promised the reward of heavenly bliss after death. The Brahmins however kept the Vedas a sealed book to the masses : and consequently the worship of the elements inculcated in the Vedas

---

[1] Chilapp-atikâram, xvii.

did not find favor with the non-Aryan races. The Brahmins found it necessary therefore to adopt the gods of the alien races, to obtain influence over them. Siva and Kâli were the most popular deities of the non-Aryans, and they were first admitted into the Brahmin pantheon. Balarâma and Krishna who were the national heroes of the shepherd races were also worshipped by the Brahmins as incarnations of Vishnu. Similarly Muruga, the patron deity of the hunting tribes was adored as the son of Siva. In all the great temples served by Brahmins, in the Tamil country, images of the four gods Siva, Krishna, Balarâma and Muruga were set up.[1] Siva was however considered the greatest of the four gods, and his temples were the most stately and august of the public edifices. Kâli was held to be a form of Pârvati, the consort of Siva. Indra, the king of the celestials, Kâma, the god of love, and celestial bodies, such as *Surya* the sun and *Soma* the moon had temples dedicated to them. With a view to impress upon the minds of the people, the distinctions of caste, the Brahmins introduced also the worship of four Bhootas or gigantic idols, which represented the four castes.[2] The first was fair in colour like the moon, and was dressed like the Brahmins who keep the three sacred fires, and held in his hands the implements required for performing a Vedic sacrifice. The second, of a rosy hue, attired like a king and armed with a lance, was accompanied by drums, hair-fans, banners, and an umbrella. The third was of a golden colour and carried in his hands a plough and a pair of scales, representing the mercantile and agricultural classes. The fourth, of dark complexion, wore clothes of black colour and had with him many musical instruments indicating the class of bards, actors, drummers and other musicians. The religious service in the Brahminic temples consisted in bathing and dressing the idols, in the morning, adorning them with jewels and flowers, and offering them fruits, sweets and cooked rice, two or three times in a day, and putting the idols to sleep at night, and repeating the names and praises of the deity a certain number of times on each occasion. The dazzling pomp of the service and its touching appeal to the senses, especially in the large temples, might have affected the imagination of the

---

[1] Ibid., xiv. 7-10.   [2] Ibid., xxii. 16-102.

illiterate classes, but they were not calculated to inspire anything like a pure and rational devotion.

The chief anti-brahminical religions, which were popular among the Tamils, were the Nigranta and the Bauddha. These two religions considered the rites and ceremonies of the Vedas to be useless labor, and the exclusive privileges arrogated by the Brahmins to be empty pretensions. The Nigranta system was older than Buddhism and the Nigrantas called the Buddhists *Páshandas*, or heretics. The Nigrantas worshipped Argha whom they considered to be the Supreme Intelligence which governs the Universe. His image was generally in the form of a naked man, seated or standing under an *Asoka* tree, with a triple umbrella above him [1] They had two principal vows, not to speak an untruth, and not to kill any living creature. They trained their minds to avoid envy, greed, anger and evil speech. Their community was divided into two sections: the *srávakas* (hearers) or laymen and the religious men; and of the latter there were five classes, who were called *Pancha-para-meshtin*, namely, *Argha*, holy men; *siddha* those who had acquired supernatural powers; *Upádhyáya*, religious teachers; *Achdraya*, priests; and *Sadhu*, pious people.[2] Near their temples, and in the open squares at the crossing of public roads, they erected pulpits from which their monks preached their religion. Both men and women were allowed to enter the monastery, and take vows of celebacy. Their monks and nuns carried an alms-bowl, a hoop made of twine to suspend a water-pot, and a bundle of peacock feathers with which they could sweep off insects, without injuring them, from the places where they have to sit or lie down. They repeated a short prayer of five letters, which they called the *Pancha-mantra*.[3]

Images of Buddha had not yet come into use, but the impressions of his feet engraved on stone, and platforms built of stone representing the seat from which he preached his doctrine were objects of worship to the Buddhists. The pious Buddhist walked round them, with his right side towards them, and bowed his head in token of reverence. Standing in front of them, with joined hands, he praised the Buddha as follows: "How shall I

---

[1] Ibid , xi. 1 to 11.   [2] Ibid., x. 15 to 25.   [3] Ibid., x. 96 to 101.

praise thee! the wise, the holy and the virtuous teacher, who excelled in the strict performance of religious vows! Thou, who conquered Mâra, who subdued anger, and all evil passions: who art supreme in knowledge, and the refuge of all mankind! Have I a thousand tongues to praise thy blessed feet, on the soles of which are a thousand auspicious lines?" In the Buddhist Vihâras or monasteries, learned monks preached their sermons, seated in a place which was entirely concealed from the view of the audience.[1] One of the first virtues preached and practised by them was charity. "Those who give food give life indeed" was a common saying among them. A life of self-control and wisdom and universal charity was declared to be the highest happiness of man. Buddhist monks were very numerous in the Tamil country, as may be inferred from the statement that there were a thousand monks attached to the seven Vihâras at Kâvirip-paddinam alone. The Buddhists did not observe the distinctions of caste, and invited all ranks to assemble on a footing of equality.

One of the greatest facts of ancient Tamil society was religious toleration, the spirit of free enquiry, or the liberty of the human understanding. The monarchs themselves openly encouraged religious discussion, for, they invited teachers of every sect to the public halls, and allowed them to preach their doctrines during festivals and other occasions of public gathering. They protected impartially the temples and monasteries of all sects; and although they might have personally inclined to believe in the doctrines of a particular sect, and built and endowed places of worship for that sect, they cautiously avoided interfering with the rites and ceremonies of rival faiths. This religious liberty had a great and salutary influence upon the intellectual and moral development of the Tamils. By softening feelings and manners, Buddhism also powerfully contributed to the amelioration of the social state. The Nigrantas and Buddhists aimed at a high ideal of morality. Justice, humanity, charity to all living beings and love of truth were the virtues which they taught by precept and example. These two religions necessarily exercised a very considerable influence upon moral and intellectual order, and upon public ideas and sentiments. The pure conceptions of

---

[1] Ibid., x. 11 to 14.

morality which the Tamils had formed were the real basis of
their civilization.   That the sentiments of morality and religion
predominated in the minds of the Tamils is evident from their
ancient literature.   The authors extolled piety, charity, truthful-
ness and tenderness to life and expressed a contempt for the
perishable objects of the physical world.   Their pure and elevated
maxims were however mixed up with others of a peurile and
imaginary character, resulting from that confusion of ideas which
is natural in the early stages of civilization.   They believed in
the transmigration of souls, and were taught to suppress all desire, which was considered the cause of rebirths.   Even the best
intellects among them had not yet learned to discern the
impassable limits which divide the province of reason from
that of speculation.   They tried to understand nature and
its mysterious author, by a subtle self-analysis, instead of by
close observation and careful study of the phenomena of the
outside world: and their wise men wasted their time in
brilliant but barren reveries regarding the life after death.   So
much were they engrossed with the thoughts of a future state,
that they sadly neglected the affairs of their present state.   In
fact, they gloried in poverty and utter renunciation of the world,
as the only means of suppressing desire and securing the salvation
of their souls from the stormy ocean of re-births.   Herein lay the
seeds of national decay, which soon laid low the Tamils and all
other Hindu races, and made them an easy prey to every invading
power.

CHAPTER XVI.

CONCLUSION.

From the foregoing account of the Tamils eighteen hundred years ago, it will be seen that they were a civilised and prosperous nation settled in the extreme south of the peninsula of India. Their country was bounded on three sides by the sea and on the north by the territories of less civilised races, such as the Konkanas, Kalingas and Rattas. These races must be regarded as less civilised than the Tamils, as they had no literature of their own at this early period: and the Tamils proudly spoke of their language as "the Southern tongue" and of the Aryan as "the Northern tongue." They were known as the Tamils most probably because they had emigrated from Tamilitti (Tâmralipti) the great seaport at the mouth of the Ganges.[1] Their kings and chieftains still remembered the original Mongolian stock from which they had sprung, and called themselves Vánavar or "Celestials." They had conquered the country from the ancient Nágas, and driving them into barren and desert tracts, occupied all the fairest and most fertile portions of the sunny land. Being the conquerors of the land, and ruled by princes of their own race, they had a high opinion of themselves, and were proud of their nationality. They had grown wealthy by their agriculture, manufactures and commerce; and they enjoyed so much security of life and property in the fortified cities, that the higher classes were not afraid of displaying their wealth by their rich dress and costly jewelry. They were a gay and polite people, passionately fond of music and flowers and poetry. Their bards sang of the thrilling achievements, by field and flood, of their gallant ancestors who had won Tamilakam for them: and stimulated in them a noble desire to be loyal to their kings, to labour for the good of the poor and the helpless, and above all to love truth and righteousness and to adore their gods.

---

[1] The modern Tamluk on the Rup narain Branch of the Hoogly, 35 miles south-west of Calcutta. The Tamilittis or Tamraliptas are also mentioned as a parate nation inhabiting Lower Bengal in the Matsya, Vishnu, and other Puranas.

Sixty generations have passed since the period I describe and what mighty changes have occurred in this interval! The land has extended, rivers have changed their courses, the ancient cities have disappeared and new languages have been formed by sections of the Tamil people. The alluvial deposits which accumulated every year, during the monsoons, at the mouths of the large rivers gradually extended the land as may be seen from the map of India in which the coast line projects into the sea at the mouths of the rivers Godaveri, Kistna, Kaviri, Vaigai, and Tamraparni. In this manner, the backwater that extends from Quilon to Cochin on the Western Coast was formed subsequent to the period of which I treat, as already stated by me in my description of the Ancient Geography of Tamilakam. . On the Eastern Coast the land has extended six miles east of the site of Korkai, which was formerly a flourishing seaport. Further north near Guntoor also, the sea coast has receded several miles, and there are traces of the old coast still visible to a length of about 30 miles.

Some of the rivers have changed their courses owing to natural or artificial causes. The Palar which formerly flowed through the bed of the modern Kodu-thalai-áru has quitted its old bed near Tiruvellum, now flows in the south-easterly direction and enters the sea at a place nearly sixty miles south of its former mouth. But the old bed of the river which joins the Kodu-thalai-áru is still known as Palaiya-pál-áru or Vriddha-Kshiranadhi. There is no trace of the river Kaviri, at the site of Kavirip-paddinam, where it was once a broad and navigable river. Many centuries ago, the river breached its banks, after the construction of a dam across it near Tiru-chirap-palli, and formed a new branch now known as Kollidam. The waters of the old Kaviri, east of the dam, are now drawn off by more than a hundred channels to paddy fields stretching over an area of several thousand square miles, and the noble river shrinks to the dimensions of a small channel spanned by a bridge of a single arch before it reaches Máyáveram, ten miles west of Kavirippaddinam. On the Malabar Coast, the Kotta river which found its way to the sea through Agalap-pula, by the side of the port Thondi, now enters the sea, at a place about eight miles north of the site of Thondi, the channel near which has silted up.

The ancient capitals of the Chera, Chola and Pandyan kingdoms are now in ruins, and their very sites are forgotten. Scattered remains of massive walls incrusted with moss and lichen still attest the solid fortifications of Karur or Vanji, the chief town of the Chera King : but only the shrill cries of eagles during the day, and the dismal howls of jackals at night disturb the profound silence that now reigns in the desolate region. The wealthy and populous city of Kavirip-paddinam, which was the capital of the Chólas, lies buried under vast mounds of sand, in the stagnant pools between which may be seen a solitary stork feeding on fish or frogs. Shepherds graze their flocks on the site of old Madura where the proud Pandya had sat on his high throne surrounded by a brilliant conclave of ministers, warriors and learned poets.

The Tamils who inhabited the Western Coast and the tableland of Mysore, which were separated from the rest of the country by high mountains, differed in their speech from the main body of the Tamils, so much in course of time, that their languages became distinct dialects of Tamil, and in this manner the modern Malayalam and Canarese languages have been formed. Consequently the limits of Tamilakam have become much narrower than they were formerly. The Tamilland may now be defined as the low country east of the Ghauts between Tirupati and Cape Comorin. The Northern portion of the island of Ceylon, where the Tamils are settled for the last eight centuries, may also be now regarded as a part of the Tamilland. Even within these narrow limits, the Tamils were many a time in danger of being overwhelmed by other races, but a merciful Providence appears to have arrested every invading force before it could completely overrun the country. The Canarese, the Moguls, the Telugu Naicks, the Mahrattas, and the Mahomedan adventurers of the Dekhan successively invaded the Tamil country within the last six centuries, and threatened to destroy every vestige of the Tamils; but at last a sterner and superior race of pale-faced men dropped, as it were, from the clouds, and saved the Tamils and all other races of India from anarchy and misrule. They had sailed from a far-off land, over perilous seas, in search of new markets for their trade.

As peaceful merchants, they first obtained a footing in the country, and by their unity, energy and intelligence soon founded an empire vaster in extent than that governed by any Mogul or Magadha sovereign. Under the ægis of England, the Tamils now enjoy profound peace and present the unique spectacle of a race of people who have retained their language and civilisation almost unchanged for the last two thousand years or more.

Socially and politically however the Tamils of this day present a mournful contrast to their warlike ancestors. They are now a subject race. Their ancient royal families became extinct centuries ago. No longer the five Great Assemblies of priests, astrologers, ministers, military officers and physicians meet to advise and guide the ruling power. No more the minstrel tunes his lute at feasts and rejoicings, to sing of the matrial deeds of their forefathers. No ships of foreign nations call at their seaports for fine spun cloths, and other articles manufactured by Tamil workmen. Not only are the Tamils dead as a nation, but their industries and arts and even their old gods are dead. For, Indra and Balarâma are no longer invoked by them; Rama and Krishna have taken the place of Vishnu; and in the temples of Siva, it is the *linga* or *phallus*, and not the image of Siva that is now worshipped. The Tamils still retain however many of their old characteristics. There are more temples and more rest-houses still in their country than are to be found within the same area, in any other part of the world! temples reared with infinite patience and labour, and rest-houses built by private charity, where the poor and the rich may freely find shelter at all times and seasons. They are devoted to friends, respectful to women, charitable to the poor, fervent in piety and tireless in industry. "Wherever money is to be made, wherever a more apathetic or a more aristocratic people is willing to be pushed aside, thither" says a European Missionary who long resided among them,[1] "swarm the Tamils, the Greeks or Scotch of the east : the least superstitious and the most enterprising and persevering race of Hindus." They are still the most literate people among the native races of India. An enlightened Government has covered the land with a network of roads, railways and tele-

---

[1] Bishop Caldwell.

graphs : it has provided the best possible codes of law which are administered without distinction of caste or creed: it has opened schools and hospitals, and organised all sorts of Government Departments, some of which are unknown even in England. The Tamils should now awake from their apathy of ages, if they wish to reap the full benefit of these changes. They should realise the fact that they are now at the parting of the ways. Mistakes now made will be irretrievable, and will have far reaching effects. If, for instance, they fail to see the utter folly of retaining the caste system any longer; if they avoid all social intercourse with Europeans, being afraid of losing caste, they would surely incur the distrust and dislike of the ruling race. There can be no real sympathy then between the rulers and the ruled, and the gulf that now separates them will widen still further and lead to misunderstandings which may embarass the Government however strong, and in the end prove disastrous to the subject race.

They have too long followed the philosophy of inaction, which taught them to get rid of the sense of personality, with what deplorable results we can all see.[1] Will they now adopt the philosophy of action? Will they now strive to acquire the sense of individual life, and develop strong personalities, who will not flee to the jungle to save their souls, but will live in their midst and do their duty, to the glory of God, and the good of their fellow-creatures? If they still cherish their prejudices and superstitions, and be dreaming of a future state: if their wise men still attempt to stifle all desire, afraid of the transmigration of their souls: if they still believe that our faculties were intended not for our beneficial use, but to be repressed and rust in us unused, they would doubtless be left behind in the race of life, and eventually be only hewers of wood and drawers of water. But if they advance on the lines of western civilization, avoiding its vices: if they throw off the fetters of caste, which estrange the sympathy of one class from another and paralize the

---

[1] Bhagavad-gita II. Sankhya-yoga 71. He attains peace who giving up all desires, lives without attachment, without selfishness, without vanity. XII. Bhakti-yoga. 16. Dear unto Me is he who is pure, intelligent, unaffected, serene, giving up every undertaking and devoted to Me. XVII. Moksha-yoga. 66. Give up all action and come to Me alone for refuge. I will save thee from all evil. Do not despair !

genius and industry of the people : if they educate their women and train them to be intelligent wives and mothers: if they open technical schools and encourage scientific research : if they introduce machinery for their manufactures, remembering the fact that workmen cannot possibly compete with machinery : and if they reform their religion, giving up idolatry and sectarian prejudices and make Hinduism the true worship of a living God, they would assuredly prosper, and as part of the great Hindu nation they may rank with the foremost nations of the world. Their men of light and leading need not wait till some one sets an example: but if they quietly and steadily instil these ideas into their families and circle of relations, and carry them out in practice, as far as it is possible, without causing any violent commotion, their names would be handed down to distant generations, as the saviours of their community.

INDEX.

Aviyar 194
Avur
Ay
Ay-andiran 106
Ayar 57, 116
Ayirai ... ...
Aykudi 106
Ayntha-nâdu ...
Ayrâni ... 127
Ayyai 154
Azainia 36
Babington, Mr. ... 204
Bactria ... 1, 51
Badagara ... 17, 30
Bain, Professor ... 226
Bakarei, 17, 19, 20, 34, 37
Baladeva ... 3, 18, 26, 68, 87, 157, 194
Bâla-kumâra 96
Bala-râma, 57, 229, 230, 231, 238
Balasore ... 95
Balita 35
Bammala ... 17, 20
Bâna 85, 165
Bânâsura 127
Barace 33
Barake 33
Baris 17, 19
Barugaza ... 33 to 35
Basara-nagos ... 22, 29, 44
Bata 22
Batoi 22, 24
Bauddha 217
Bauddham 213
Bauhinia racemosa ... 217
Bay of Bengal ... 10
Bhillavar 39
Bhils ... 39
Bhogavati 39
Bhoomi-chandra, 185, 186
Bhûtas 98
Bhûta-vâti 217
Bideris 17
Bodhi ... 173, 220
Bombay 4
Bosarc 36
Brahma ... 47, 56, 113
Brahma-dharma, 170, 182
Brahma-kulam ... 18
Brahma-vâti 214
Brahmin, ... 3, 21, 52, 53, 55, 56, 57, 77, 78, 89, 97, 99, 103, 113, 116, 117, 124, 125, 132, 139, 140, 142, 143, 153, 161, 163
Brahminic ascetics, 13, 136

INDEX.

M. E. PRESS, MOUNT ROAD, MADRAS, 1904.